THE Green Bride GUIDE

Kate L. Harrison

How to Create an Earth-Friendly Wedding on Any Budget

SOURCEBOOKS CASABLANCA™
AN IMPRINT OF SOURCEBOOKS, INC.®
NAPERVILLE, ILLINOIS

Published by Sourcebooks Casablanca, an imprint of Sourcebooks, Inc.
P.O. Box 4410, Naperville, Illinois 60567-4410
(630) 961-3900
Fax: (630) 961-2168
www.sourcebooks.com

Library of Congress Cataloging-in-Publication Data

Harrison, Kate L.
   The green bride guide : how to create an earth-friendly wedding on any
budget / Kate L. Harrison.
      p. cm.
   1. Weddings—Planning. I. Title.
   HQ745.H245 2008
   395.2'2—dc22
                              2008021154

Printed and bound in Canada.
WC 10 9 8 7 6 5 4 3 2 1

To my family—old and new.

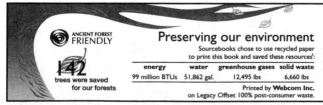

Acknowledgments

First and foremost I would like to thank all of the people who helped me through the writing process: Pam Liflander, who coached me on how to write a proposal and get an agent; my agent, Kate Epstein, who worked tirelessly to get this project off the ground; my editors Shana Drehs and Sara Appino at Sourcebooks, who did a wonderful job getting this book ready for market; and the friends and family members who gave me ideas, feedback, and spelling lessons. In particular I want to thank David Mann, who read with a fine-tipped pen and a sharp mind; my mother, Ruth, whose love of all things floral beautified both my wedding and the flower chapter; my nephew Joe Rosen, who checked all of the Web addresses; and my brother, "Webmaster" H Alex, who helped me take this book to the next level with thegreenbrideguide.com. I also want to extend a special thanks to my parents and grandparents, who made my own green wedding possible. (Dad—here is to another "good first step"! Ms. Carver would be proud.) Finally, I want to thank my husband, Barry, who believed in me and supported me from the get-go and who acquainted me with the awkward aardvark, captain of the passive-voice police. You are the best.

Table of Contents

APPENDIX

Introduction

*I*n the fall of 2006, when my husband, Barry, and I began thinking about and planning our own green wedding, we were surprised by how little information was available to assist us. I read every book and article I could find on the topic and spent hundreds of hours surfing online for green ideas, supplies, and vendors. It was an extremely frustrating and laborious process—but we were delighted with the results! To save others from having to go through the trouble, I decided to compile my efforts into this comprehensive resource—*The Green Bride Guide*.

Throughout this book I have tried to include some of the answers to the *why* of different choices—why local, why organic, why fair trade, etc.—but first, the biggest why of all:

WHY A GREEN WEDDING?

I should mention off the bat that Barry and I are both environmentalists—he's an environmental historian, and I work in environmental law and policy. However, when we announced our plan to have a green wedding, my father's first response was still, "Why would you want a green wedding—aren't weddings supposed to be *white*?"

Although the confusion about green the *color* vs. green the *concept* was cleared up quickly, my father's skepticism remained. This is the first hurdle. Although green weddings are becoming more popular, it is inevitable that some of your friends and family members will not understand what a green wedding is or why you would want to have one. So let's begin with a few reasons why one might choose to have a sustainable event.

Sidestepping the Wedding Industry. Put the emphasis on *industry* because that is what it is—a $70-billion-a-year industry. Many writers have discussed the phenomenon of being thrust onto the "wedding conveyor belt," and even well-intentioned, thoughtful couples can find themselves getting sucked in. Weddings are complicated beasts, fraught with emotions, expectations, social conventions, and etiquette, and it is all very powerful stuff. Brides feel a lot of pressure to make everyone happy and are willing to spend whatever it takes—about $30,000 these days—to make their wedding "perfect." Many couples go into debt (on average about $25,000 worth!) to pay for their weddings, so it is not surprising that ConsumerAffairs. com reported that 80 percent of couples cite money as the leading source of wedding stress. With a financial burden added to an emotionally demanding situation, it's no wonder the mythical "Bridezilla" lives on.

Part of having a green wedding is conserving resources—including money. This is not to say that a green wedding has to cost less than a comparable wedding—some cost more, and some cost less—but part of having a green wedding is thinking about who you are, what your values are, and what kind of wedding you would want if the industry were not constantly telling you what you *should* want. When planning a green wedding, you have to be prepared to take a step back and make choices based on a different set of values.

Supporting Green Business. The wedding industry has spent a lot of time and money selling a certain "look" so that you will buy its products. These products include expensive single-use bleached white dresses, disposable aisle runners, chemically treated imported flowers, toxic makeup and skin-care products, mined gem-based jewelry, individual packets of rice, little plastic picture frames with your names and the date engraved on them, and all manner of disposable flourishes and trinkets. With almost 2.5 million weddings a year in this country alone, the impact on the environment from our weddings is substantial.

Weddings offer an amazing opportunity to make a difference. In addition to saving energy, conserving resources, and decreasing pollution, imagine what a boost $70 billion a year could give to sustainable businesses. If we are going to combat the environmental problems of this century, we need to change the way businesses operate. We need to create demand. Other than a house, a wedding is generally the most expensive thing a young couple will ever "buy." By spending your wedding dollars on green goods and services, you send a signal to companies that it is time to change their ways. By simply bringing your awareness of environmental and social issues to the negotiating table with you, you can affect the impact of every purchasing decision you make and have each dollar you spend work to support your beliefs and values.

Educating Others. One of the amazing things about a wedding is that it is the only time in your life when pretty much everyone you love is in the same place at the same time. The effect of this confluence can be rather surreal, and you may spend a lot of your wedding marveling at the bizarre combinations of people mingling around the room. They come from near and far, from childhood and adulthood, from school and work, and they have all gathered to celebrate you—both the person you are and the union you and your fiancé are creating. In other words, you have a captive audience and a chance to let your eco-conscious values shine.

This does not mean you need to be preachy—you don't have to take the mic and start ranting about how we are destroying the earth when you are supposed to be saying "I do." It just means that in the same way that a wedding is an opportunity for you and your fiancé to showcase your tastes, it is also a unique chance for you to showcase your *values*. Throughout this book I offer tips on how to let your guests know about the green choices you have made and how to create a ceremony and reception that will demonstrate that you do not have to sacrifice style, comfort, or tradition to be green. By infusing your wedding with a sense of respect for the environment, you will inspire your guests and transform your wedding into an event that they will remember forever.

HOW TO USE THIS BOOK

To make this book as accessible as possible, each section is subdivided by topic (e.g., invitations) and type (e.g., paper invitations, electronic invitations, etc.). If you already know what you want to do, this structure should help you quickly and easily navigate to the sections that interest you most. Whenever possible, I have further subdivided by price, with three categories: $, $$, and $$$. These are only rough guidelines and do not signify actual values, because a $$$ dress can be thousands of dollars, where a $$$ website might only cost a few hundred. However, as almost every wedding has budget constraints, this can help you prioritize and come up with creative ideas to meet your needs.

Be aware that pinning down the "best" green choice is often tricky or impossible. For example, a honeymoon at home is green, because you do not have to drive or fly (which contributes to global warming by adding CO_2 and greenhouses gases to the air). However, many wildlife preserves and indigenous cultures rely on tourist revenue to survive—so if everyone stopped traveling, it would actually frustrate conservation efforts in many parts of the world. A similar dilemma arises when you are faced with the choice of buying something manufactured in the United States or buying something produced under "fair trade" conditions abroad. Or when you are faced with the choice between locally grown food produced with pesticides or organically grown food shipped in from out of state. There are no right answers to these dilemmas. The important thing is that you remain a conscious consumer. Which choice is right for you depends on what you value most. I have done my best to lay out the issues, and I hope the information I provide helps you come to the best answer for you.

Beware of Greenwashing

While some terms, like "organic" (in reference to food), are regulated by the government, and others, like "fair trade," are regulated by independent certifying agencies, many environmental terms like "green," "eco," "environmentally friendly," "natural," and "sustainable" are not regulated at all. This means that you have to be extra vigilant when choosing vendors—even ones that advertise themselves as green. For example, I found a balloon company that was advertising "eco-friendly balloons," which, upon investigation, were just regular rubber balloons. Although rubber does biodegrade in under a year, when released, even these balloons can harm animals by ending up tangled in their digestive tracts. The nylon strings tied to them take years to decompose. In a more egregious example, I found a baby shirt that said "100% organic" across the front but was not, in fact, made with organic cotton. The slogan was jokingly referring to the baby, but I thought the fact that the shirt was made with conventional cotton was surprising and a bit misleading.

I have worked hard to include sustainable businesses and independent certifying agencies throughout this book for you to rely on. Whenever I could, I corresponded directly with the companies and tried their products myself before recommending them. In addition to the resources gathered here, you can find reputable green products and services for all aspects of life through Green America's Green Pages (coopamerica.org) and the New Whole Earth Catalog (newwholeearthcatalog.com). I have also created *The Green Bride Guide* website (thegreenbrideguide.com), where you can find updated lists of resources and can write in and report products you think are iffy.

If you have local vendors in mind but are not sure how "green" they really are, I have also included lists of questions in the back of the book for you to ask them. You can usually tell within a few minutes of talking to a vendor whether his or her business is dedicated to being environmentally friendly or if it is "greenwashed." Do not be afraid to ask vendors tough questions. It is their job to convince *you* that they are the right choice.

The Green Bride Guide Website

The green wedding industry is just beginning to take off, and there are more eco-friendly options available every day. To supplement this book, I have launched thegreenbrideguide.com, which offers updated product information, pictures, ideas from real green weddings, and other useful links. In the Ask Kate section, you can find Q+A about green wedding planning and can contact me with any questions you have. The Quick Guide page in the About the Book section includes lists of common terms and definitions for frosting, candles, veils, and more. Throughout this book you will see the ◉ icon directing you to the website to find more information on a particular topic.

The green community is a grassroots movement—where we can all learn from and help each other. I hope that you will visit thegreenbrideguide.com and share your pictures, advice, and experience planning your green wedding with others.

A Note on Prioritizing

As Kermit the Frog would say, "It's not easy being green." Although the marketplace is changing and sustainable goods and services are becoming more available, a lot of eco-friendly products are still hard to get or are very expensive. As with planning any wedding in which budget is a consideration, you will have to make choices about which things matter most to you. While there are no right answers, try to focus on the big-ticket items. For example, using paper (instead of plasticized) stamps is a nice green touch, but it has much less impact on your wedding's overall sustainability, or "footprint," than limiting the number of people you invite, serving all locally grown organic food, or using seasonal pesticide-free flowers. This book does not prioritize for you, but as a general rule of thumb, the more expensive an item is, the more important the choice.

Don't Be Puritanical

A green wedding does not have to be an all-or-nothing proposition. Don't feel that because you cannot get biodegradable wineglasses (which don't exist as of the writing of this book) that all is lost. Depending on how early you start, your overall budget, and where you are located in the country, you may not be able to find or may not want every element of your wedding to be green. This is *okay*. A green wedding is about making sustainable choices where possible and practical and doing what you can to lessen the impact of your event. Do your best, enjoy the process, and know that every green element you choose makes a difference.

The Importance of Communicating Your Vision

This section could also be called "Thirteen Priuses, One Folding Bike, and a Stretch SUV Limo," after an unfortunate event that took place at my wedding. After my fiancé and I were featured in the *New York Times* article "How Green Was My Wedding" ("Style," Feb. 11, 2007), the cat was out of the bag that we were planning a sustainable event, and all of our friends and family members got on board with the plans. As a bridesmaid, my sister agreed to wear a dress she already owned; our neighbors offered their end-of-season blooms for the flower arrangements; our relatives planned carpools in electric cars (which is how we ended up with thirteen Priuses in the parking lot at the ceremony site); and my friend Avery decided he would bring his folding bicycle from California, so he could bike from the train station to the farm where we were staying instead of taking a cab. Everything was coming together.

Fast-forward to the day of the wedding. My new husband and I were waiting with our friends for the arrival of what was supposed to be a biodiesel shuttle, when up pulls a pimped-out (faux-leopard interior) SUV limo—pretty much the *least* environmentally friendly form of transportation you can imagine. Although it was hilarious—and made for some memorable pictures—it was not what we had envisioned, planned for, or wanted. We had been unwittingly "upgraded" by our well-intentioned but environmentally uninformed transportation company. OY. So let this be a lesson to you all: you *must* communicate your hopes, your dreams, and your vision clearly and carefully to your vendors. Instead of just asking if they can do x, y, or z, explain to them that you are planning a green wedding and why x, y, and z are important to you.

According to green event planner Danielle Venokur (dvgreen. com), if you really want to make your wedding green, you need to have one of your "people"—be it a friend, a professional coordinator, or a dedicated vendor—working behind the scenes to make sure it happens. Danielle says that despite many couples' best intentions, a lot of food and reusable items are wasted during the prep and cleanup stages of events, when vendors are trying to move quickly or wrap up and (understandably) do not want to be bothered with details like separating out the trash from the compost or repacking partially burnt candles. Choosing vendors who understand what you want and who are willing to help make it happen is essential. Ask tough questions and the (local, organic, BHT-free) cream will rise to the top.

Organization Is Key

One way to help your caterer and/or event manager make sure reusable items do not get chucked in the trash bin is to give them a list of everything that needs to be packed up at the end of the night. Because we failed to communicate clearly with our caterer, the reusable silver chargers we brought to tuck under all the guest plates vanished at the end of the night. We thought they were so *obviously* something we would want (we had reused them from my brother's wedding, and they were rather expensive) that we did not tell anyone about our desire to keep them or make plans to pick them up the next day. The same thing happened to the antique keys we used at the reception.

Unless every person cleaning up knows what you want done, it isn't going to happen the way you hope. So help them out with lists, with labeled containers, and by making sure someone is in charge of overseeing setup and cleanup activities.

Organization is also important if you have recruited friends to help out with different parts of your wedding. The best way to make sure the event flows smoothly is to designate a point person or "director" that your helpers can talk to if they have any questions. The director should have complete lists (with phone numbers) of who is doing what and should know where all the supplies are. For our wedding, with three venues and several days of events, we hired our friend Jordana, a professional theater director turned medical student, to play this role. She was amazing, and I literally do not think we could have pulled our wedding off without her. If you take nothing else from this book, remember to find yourself a Jordana.

Consider a Co-op

I don't know who thought of the wedding co-op first, but it was immortalized in the *Offbeat Bride* by Ariel Meadow Stallings, and I love the idea. In a wedding co-op, like-minded brides pool their resources to buy generic items that can be reused at each of their weddings. Participating in a wedding co-op (no matter how informal) decreases your costs and your ecological footprint in one fell swoop. It is probably easiest to do a co-op if you are getting married the same year as a number of your friends, but with the Internet, you can establish or join one in

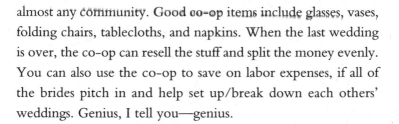

almost any community. Good co-op items include glasses, vases, folding chairs, tablecloths, and napkins. When the last wedding is over, the co-op can resell the stuff and split the money evenly. You can also use the co-op to save on labor expenses, if all of the brides pitch in and help set up/break down each others' weddings. Genius, I tell you—genius.

Green for All

Finally, I want to note the original title of this book was *The Green Wedding Guide*. Despite the name change, my goal is to provide a comprehensive resource for couples looking to plan a green wedding. Many men, including my husband, are actively involved in the wedding-planning process these days (which is great!). Also, I honor and respect same-sex couples looking to consecrate their love with a green wedding. For the purpose of this book I use the words *bride, fiancé,* and *husband*—I hope you will substitute the terms appropriate for your gender and situation.

CHAPTER 1

Rules of Engagements

$\mathcal{E}$very wedding starts with an engagement—whether it is a formal affair on bended knee or a casual conversation about wanting to spend the rest of your lives together. Although each couple's story is different, the choices they face are the same. How and when will we tell people? Will either or both of us wear engagement rings? Will we have pre-parties (engagement, shower, bachelor and bachelorette, etc.)? Do we want to have a formal wedding, or should we elope?

According to the Wedding Report, a company that compiles wedding statistics and market research for the wedding industry, the average length of engagement in the United States is seventeen months. This can be a magical but also stressful time. People will constantly be asking you about the planning—where will the wedding be? What will you wear? What will you serve? What color napkins do you want? The number of decisions you have to make is staggering. If you want to talk about anything other than your wedding during your engagement, it is important to lay down firm boundaries with friends, family, and yourselves about discussing and working on the wedding. Your wedding, a celebration that may be just one evening long, can consume your life for over a year. I have seen it happen, and it is not pretty. To relieve some of the pre-wedding pressure, and to give ourselves time to think about what we really wanted, my husband and I put a moratorium on all wedding discussion for the first three months after we were engaged. It gave us a chance to adjust to our new status and to create a united vision before getting down to business. I highly recommend this strategy.

Now to the planning. This chapter is about the engagement period—whether it be ten days or ten months. In addition to providing a timeline to help you stay on track and keep you from being overwhelmed, this chapter will walk you through the primary choices of the engagement itself and give you green options at every turn.

RINGS

Between the engagement ring and the wedding rings, average American couples spend over $7,000—a total of $16 billion a year nationwide. If you already have an engagement ring, use the resources in this section to think about green wedding ring options. For those of you who have not received or picked out a ring yet, there are many different types of green engagement and wedding rings that will make your jaw drop.[*]

Clear-Conscience Diamonds

Blood Diamond, the 2006 movie staring Leonardo DiCaprio, helped raise awareness about the problem of "conflict diamonds"—diamonds mined in unstable regions of Africa that are used to finance civil war and widespread brutality. The human rights group Amnesty International (amnesty.org) estimates that the sale of blood diamonds has already contributed to the death of 3.7 million people in Angola, Sierra Leone, and the Democratic Republic of Congo. Today, diamonds mined in rebel-controlled areas are fueling conflicts in Côte d'Ivoire and Liberia. However, the tragedy of diamond mining does not end

---

[*] See the Eco-Products section of thegreenbrideguide.com for pictures of sustainable wedding and engagement rings from more eco-conscious designers.

there. Diamond mines are also notorious for the environmental damage they inflict, including soil erosion, flooding, and water pollution. So what's a bride to do?

Diamonds are beautiful, and thanks to the ingenious "A Diamond Is Forever" advertising campaign launched by DeBeers in the 1940s, they are still extremely popular. In fact, three out of four brides still receive diamond engagement rings. Diamonds are, after all, "a girl's best friend." The good news is that there are now a number of "green" diamond options available that an eco-conscious bride can wear with pride.

$ Heirloom Diamonds

If diamonds are forever, why buy a new one? One of the easiest and most meaningful "green" things you can do in your wedding is use a family diamond or gemstone for your engagement ring. If you or your fiancé are lucky enough to have a family ring with a setting you love, you can have it resized in just a few days. If you have an heirloom piece that is not your style, any good local jeweler should be able to reset the stones in the style of your choice. When shopping for jewelers, ask if they can melt down and reuse the gold or silver setting to create your new ring. If you cannot find someone locally who can reuse the ring's materials, recycled jewelry designers, like Greenkarat (greenkarat.com), allow you to send in raw metals, which can be melted down to create your ring or exchanged for store credit.

$$ Antique Rings

Diamonds that predate 1880 were harvested before the advent of large-scale (more environmentally destructive) mining operations. When you buy a pre-1880 ring, you are not only recycling, but you can rest assured that the diamond's extraction did not contribute to widespread mining pollution. Search online auction sites like eBay or places like the Antique Jewelry

Exchange (antiquejewelryexch.com) that specialize in Victorian and antique jewelry. Antique usually means older than a hundred years, so make sure to check the exact date.

$$ Synthetic and Cultured Diamonds

Synthetic, or simulated, diamonds, which were once considered a faux pas, are all the rage now that stars such as Angelina Jolie and Gwyneth Paltrow refuse to wear real diamonds. Synthetic diamonds look like real diamonds to the untrained eye but have different compositions. Buying a faux diamond guarantees your ring did not come at the expense of others or the environment. It will also save you money.

There are a few different kinds of simulated diamonds available on the market today, including cubic zirconium (CZ), moissanite, flanit, and yttrium zirconium oxide ($YZRO_2$). CZ is the most popular and least expensive diamond simulant. Companies like Green Earth Jewelry (greenearthjewelry.com) now offer CZ diamonds in recycled silver and gold settings for the ultimate in green fashion. Moissanite is a silicon carbide that was discovered as part of a meteorite in Arizona in 1893 and is now manufactured by Charles and Colvard (moissanite.com). It costs about one-tenth as much per carat as mined diamonds but more than CZ (see fromthesky.com).

In addition to synthetic diamonds (which are not diamonds), there are man-made, or cultured, diamonds, which are structurally identical to mined diamonds but are produced in a laboratory. These diamonds are actually more "perfect" than natural diamonds, which is how jewelers can tell they are man-made. Cultured diamonds are particularly nice because you can get colors that are rare in nature, like yellow and red. See Gemesis (gemesis.com) or Apollo Diamond (apollodiamond. com) for more information about cultured diamonds and a list of retailers.

$$$ Canadian Diamonds

After many funny "hypothetical discussions," Barry knew that I did not want to wear a conflict diamond, but he wanted to pop the question with a classic diamond ring. The solution—a certified Canadian diamond bought from a local jeweler. Diamonds that are mined, cut, and polished in the Northwest Territories of Canada are subject to strict environmental and working condition regulations. You can learn more about Government Certified Canadian Diamonds, or "Polar Bear" diamonds, at Canadian Arctic Diamond (canadianarcticdiamond.com). A number of American jewelers now offer certified Canadian diamonds. If there is not a local artisan you want to use, you can design your own ring using conflict-free Canadian diamonds set in recycled precious metals at Brilliant Earth (brilliantearth.com) or buy a pre-made ring in reclaimed yellow gold, white gold, or platinum.

CONTROVERSY IN THE ARCTIC

The diamond industry has been working hard to address consumer concerns about "conflict diamonds." To this end, the Canadian government has created a certification system that ensures that its diamonds are harvested under strict environmental and labor standards and are mined, cut, and polished in the Northwest Territories. However, some companies, like Greenkarat, a leading eco-jeweler, do not use Canadian diamonds or any other diamonds harvested in recent history. They argue that even in Canada mining destroys environmentally sensitive ecosystems, disrupts the cultural and social lives of native people, and displaces wildlife. Instead, they advocate for recycling pre-owned vintage and heirloom diamonds and recasting them in recycled metals to create a modern look.

Diamond Alternatives

Although now ubiquitous, diamond rings were not always the default engagement-ring choice. In Victorian times, it was common for engagement rings to be made with the bride and groom's birthstones, to spell out "regards" or "dearest" in gemstones, or to open up to reveal a channel where the betrothed could store a piece of her suitor's hair (can you imagine?!). Still, in many parts of Europe, couples use plain gold bands or rings with colored stones to signify betrothal, and there are many other green options available for those willing to think outside the (diamond-ring) box.

$ The Inside Joke

If you want to signify your engagement with a material gift but do not want to buy into the ring phenomenon, it is perfectly okay (and extremely cute) to give or receive something meaningful to both of you. One of my friends was proposed to with a duct tape ring, because she and her boyfriend had an ongoing joke about duct tape and its magical properties. Another couple I heard about had a quarter they would pass back and forth, hiding it in unexpected places as a way to say they were thinking of each other. When it came time to pop the question, the quarter turned up in a classic ring box. If there is something that is meaningful to you, nothing makes a cuter story than incorporating that item into your engagement. Just because the industry is pushing you to have both an engagement ring and a wedding ring does not mean you need to have either (or both).

$ Tattoos

I always thought it was "biker chic" to get matching tattoos with your partner, but tattoo rings are a "green" alternative that seems to be making a comeback. In fact, Justin Ruben, the organizational director of MoveOn.org (a Web-based political education and action group), and his wife, Autumn, got tattoo engagement rings in 2007. Perhaps it's the symbolic "for better or worse" pain of getting them or their practical indelibility—you can't take your tattoo off and chuck it across the room when you are angry—that makes tattoo rings a popular green option.

$ Natural Treasures

If you want a ring but are interested in a creative non-diamond alternative, consider buying or having a ring made with moonstone, tiger's eye, pearl, river stone, or a piece of beautiful sea glass. See the artist Rebecca Zelis's work (rebeccazelis.com) for an example of what can be done with opal, glass, and stone. Almost anything can become the focal point of a truly unique piece of jewelry.

$$ Wood

For eco-conscious couples, wood engagement rings or wedding bands are exceptionally lovely. Touch Wood Rings (touchwoodrings.com), a company that uses fallen trees and scrap woods, and Simply Wood Rings (simplywoodrings.com) both carry luminous, handcrafted rings that can be inlaid with turquoise or mother-of-pearl. When I decided, in the name of parity, to purchase an engagement ring for my husband, I found him a wood and silver band from another company—Wood-Rings (wood-rings.com)—which partners with American Forests (americanforests.org) and plants a tree for each ring it sells. It is so unique, I sometimes suspect he likes it more than his wedding band.

TWO-IN-ONE

If you find a band you love or get a ring with inlaid stones, consider letting your engagement ring do double duty as a wedding band and save thousands of dollars. If you later decide that you want a second ring, you can always get one as an anniversary present. In the meantime, you can feel good knowing that you have decreased your environmental footprint and can use the money for your honeymoon or as a down payment on your first house.

$$$ Gemstones

Although many of the traditional gemstones, such as rubies and emeralds, are harvested under similar circumstances as diamonds—and thus suffer the same social and environmental problems—there are a number of sustainable alternatives. True Blue sapphires offered by Brilliant Earth (brilliantearth.com) are one popular option. They come from family-owned mines in Australia and Malawi that pride themselves on being "ethically sourced" and following "strict labor, trade, and environmental protocols." Another good source of "fair trade" gemstones, including garnets, tourmaline, and rubies, is Columbia Gem House (columbiagemhouse.com), and you can buy pre-made jewelry from its subsidiary, Trigem Designs (trigemdesigns.com).

Gold, Silver, and Other Mined Metals

Metals are mined from the earth, and mining is a dirty business. Oxfam America and Earthworks maintain nodirtygold.org, a website that details the myriad of environmental, social, economic, and human health impacts of the gold mining industry. Some of the perils include soil, water, and air pollution; deforestation; human rights violations; worker injuries (15,000 mining fatalities each year); and the displacement and marginalization of local communities. The "No Dirty Gold" campaign estimates that the gold used to create one ring produces *twenty tons* of mining waste. According to the Environmental Protection Agency, other metal mining can result in similar consequences. Political pressure and consumer awareness has forced a number of companies to reform their ways, and you can find a list of retailers who have pledged to follow the "golden rules" of sustainable sourcing on nodirtygold.org. There are also companies like Cred Jewellery (credjewellery.com), that specialize in custom fair trade and ethically produced gold, silver, and platinum jewelry.

However, the best way to buy "green" gold or silver is to buy antique rings (which is a form of recycling and decreases the demand for newly mined materials) or to buy rings made from recycled and reclaimed metals. See the heirloom diamond section above for more information.

ANNOUNCEMENTS

Soon after you're engaged, you'll want to spread the good news. There are many different ways to do that these days. For a full list of ideas and options see Chapter Five.

PARTIES

The wonderful thing about a wedding is that it offers so many opportunities to celebrate. In addition to the actual wedding, you can have an engagement party, bridal showers, bachelor and bachelorette parties, bridesmaid luncheons, and more. There is a lot of etiquette involved for each of these events, including who should host, what happens during the event, and what guests are expected to bring. A lot of the planning for pre-wedding camaraderie will be out of your hands, but you can delicately discuss your preferences with those in charge or give them a copy of this book. A lot of the advice and resources offered in the following chapters can also be applied to pre-wedding celebrations. However, there are a few general principles to make any event more sustainable that you should keep in mind.

Stay Close to Home

As I will discuss in Chapter Two, the farther you travel, the more fuel you burn and the more greenhouse gases you release into the environment. Instead of flying all your friends to Vegas for a weekend, try to stick with activities within striking distance. It will be less expensive, more convenient, and better for the environment.

Support Green Businesses

If you want to go out and about, use the resources in Chapter Two to find green hotels and restaurants. Today you can even find green bars, like Elixir in San Francisco (elixirsf.com), where owner H. Joseph Ehrmann designs organic cocktails and hosts special green events.

Consider a Green Theme

For my wedding shower, my mother hosted a "green" event—green in the sense of the color as well as the environment. The food was green (seasonal melon salad, organic spinach wraps, and avocado chips); the drinks were green (mint mojitos); the clothing was green; and the gifts were green. We sang "green-themed" songs and went swimming in the green seawater off the dock near our house. It was a lot of fun and very, well, green.

While you may want to skip the whole monochrome thing, when planning a pre-wedding get-together, consider having a nature-themed event or activity. Instead of cheesy games, take everyone on a hike, plant trees, go fruit picking, or spend a day sipping wines at an organic vineyard. If you want to do the whole toilet-paper-dress routine, and it certainly can be "a hoot" as my grandmother would say, ask your host to buy recycled toilet tissue instead of rolls made from virgin (heehee) wood. Request, or provide, locally sourced organic food or regional specialties. Top off your party with green gifts. In addition to the ideas offered in Chapter Twelve consider asking your guests to bring something specific—an ornament for your Christmas tree, a square for a quilt, or a homemade baked good and a printed recipe. You can also throw a charity-themed event and ask all guests to donate to a specific cause in your honor instead of bringing gifts.

More Activity-Based Ideas

The days when the girls had male strippers and the boys flew to Vegas are over. Modern bachelor and bachelorette parties are about quality time with the ladies and gents. Save the flyer miles, reduce the waste, and choose a local adventure. Encourage your friends to plan a luxurious day at the spa or get tickets to a concert and bring a festive picnic to enjoy on the lawn. Pack the men off on a sailing or fishing trip, or do what my brother-in-law did and rent a cabin in the woods where the men folk and their dogs can hang out and bond for a few days. Co-ed parties are the new rage, too, so don't feel like you have to go your separate ways. You can plan a ski or scuba trip, a bowling party, miniature golf, or a horseback ride through changing autumnal forests. The goal is to bring your friends and family together to celebrate and to get to know each other better before the wedding. So skip the plastic veils and petit fours and make your pre-wedding celebrations meaningful and memorable for you.

PLANNING TIMELINE

Most bridal magazines offer a several-page checklist of things to do before the wedding. The truth is that a lot of the items are there to fuel the multibillion-dollar wedding industry. For example, you do not need to start getting regular manicures and pedicures for six months leading up to your wedding. You may want to get one (or give yourself one) just after you don your new ring because so many people will be looking at your hands. You may also want one right before the big day to make sure your nails look beautiful in that close up ring shot. However, all of those sessions in between have the whiff of nail-polish industry propaganda.

Don't get me wrong, if you are looking for an excuse to be pampered, you can shamelessly milk the wedding for all kinds of relaxing treatments—just don't feel like you *have* to. A $30 treatment once a week for six months is more than $700. If your budget is tight, you might want to skip it. My point is that there will be a lot of "experts" telling you what you should be doing. It is not just about manicures; it is about everything. As you go through this book, and as you get closer to your wedding, always remember that your wedding is about you and your beloved. You are the ones who will be standing up there, and these days, statistically, you will be the ones paying for it, too.

The following is a rough timeline to keep you on track, but it will obviously differ depending on how long your engagement is and what kind of wedding you are planning.

As soon as you can
- *Announce your engagement*
- *Take a few weeks to enjoy the novelty of engagement*
- *Meet with your families and discuss the budget*
- *Start creating a vision*

Twelve to fourteen months
- *Begin researching venues*
- *Hire a wedding planner (if you want one)*
- *Think about the guest list*
- *Look at venues*

Nine to twelve months
- *Make a wedding website*
- *Start your gift registry*
- *Finalize the guest list*
- *Choose attendants*
- *Pick a date*
- *Book venue(s), caterer, and officiant*
- *Ask officiant about his/her schedule for meeting before the wedding*

Six to nine months
- *Book musicians, photographer, florist, etc.*
- *Start dress shopping*
- *Discuss attire with bridal party*
- *Make all rental arrangements*
- *Meet with the caterer*
- *Send save-the-dates*
- *Think about invitations*
- *Start reserving blocks of rooms at nearby hotels*
- *Mull on your honeymoon (update all travel documents)*
- *Round out your registry*

Three to six months
- *Make/order invitations*
- *Obtain a dress and all accessories*
- *Get fitted and book final fitting*
- *Make honeymoon reservations (check visa requirements)*
- *Make/buy any non-perishable favors*
- *Plan rehearsal time and place and make reservations for dinner*
- *Shop for a tuxedo*
- *Shop for wedding rings*
- *Meet with florist*
- *Order wedding cake(s) (if applicable)*

- *Make/buy gifts for wedding party*
- *Make sure your accessories and undergarments are in order*
- *Get invitations ready to go out*
- *Update website with all transportation info, etc.*
- *Make a rain plan—reserve tent, heaters, etc.*
- *Mail invitations if you plan to skip save-the-dates*

One to two months

- *Mail invitations*
- *Get marriage license*
- *Get any necessary permits*
- *Figure out day-of transportation*
- *Meet with officiant*
- *Work on your vows and the ceremony*
- *Get all ritual objects lined up*
- *Pick ceremony and reception music and tell musicians/DJ*
- *If using an iPod, make play lists, test speakers, and burn backups*
- *Pick up wedding rings*
- *Get hair and makeup supplies and do a trial run*
- *Create programs or events schedule (if applicable)*
- *Put together welcome baskets (if applicable)*
- *Schedule final fitting*
- *Appoint a director (if you do not have a planner)*

Two weeks before

- *Make seating chart*
- *Give final head count to caterer and venues*
- *Give picture lists to photographer(s)*
- *Make detailed lists of activities and objects for vendors*
- *Ask friends to take on specific roles and send them lists*
- *Break in your shoes (if new)*
- *Write toasts*

One week before

◄ *Make perishable favors*

◄ *Pick up dress and tuxedo*

◄ *Put tips in labeled envelopes/organize final payments*

◄ *Pack for wedding and honeymoon*

◄ *Check in with all vendors for any last minute changes*

One day before

◄ *Drop off welcome baskets and information packets*

◄ *Give yourself a manicure/go to a salon*

◄ *Rehearse and enjoy dinner (eat something)*

◄ *Check in with all friends about their duties*

◄ *Sleep!*

Each of these elements can have multiple steps, and it can be overwhelming. I suggest that in addition to following this list, you get a book like the *Busy Bride's Essential Wedding Checklists* (Sourcebooks, 2005) to help ease your mind.

HIRING A PLANNER

There are many reasons to hire an event planner. A wedding planner can save you time and hassle, can negotiate reduced-rate contracts for you, and can act as the "day-of" director for your event—coordinating vendors and smoothing the behind-the-scenes logistical issues that are sure to arise. Choose your planner carefully. If you are committed to having a green wedding, it is essential that your wedding planner understand, be on board, and be excited about the idea. Your planner is going to be your champion—your representative and your liaison—so it is worth spending the time and money to find a good match.

There are now a number of event planners who specialize in sustainable affairs. In San Francisco, Vibrant Events (vibrant events.net) plans green parties using only local and organic vendors. Some companies, like Great Performances (great performances.com) and dvGreen (dvgreen.com) in New York, offer top-to-bottom wedding planning services. Great Performances provides its own organic catering, and in addition to planning all of the traditional aspects of a wedding, Danielle Venokur of dvGreen personally arranges for and oversees the composting and recycling for her events, even if it means renting a composter or taking the scraps to a facility herself. If this were a MasterCard commercial, the tagline for these services would be "priceless." Use tools like the online green-wedding gateway Portovert (portovert.com) to find green wedding planners and other green vendors in your area.

CHAPTER 2

Location, Location, Location

Location is the first and hardest choice you face when planning a wedding. It is also one of the most important. In addition to providing the physical backdrop for your event, the choice of location can limit how many people you have, the date and season of the affair, and the style of the reception. A wedding on a mountaintop in Vermont in the fall is going to be strikingly different from one on a beach in California in the summer or one at a fancy hotel in the winter. Once you have settled into your engagement, you and your fiancé should discuss your "vision" in general terms. Do you have a place that is particularly meaningful to you? Where are your families from? Where did you first meet? Try to be as free and imaginative as possible—there will be plenty of time for compromise and technical dealings soon enough. Once you have narrowed it down to a few of your favorite ideas, start investigating them more seriously.

Because the average couple spends about 40 percent of their budget on the reception, choosing an eco-friendly location can have a huge impact on the environmental footprint of your wedding. There are many different types of green wedding venues, so don't be daunted if you do not consider yourself the "outdoorsy" type. This chapter is designed to help you find a green location to suit your needs, whatever they may be. So sit back, relax, and start thinking about your perfect day.

CREATING A SUSTAINABLE VISION

An essential part of creating a green wedding is finding a location that meets all your needs while minimizing your impact on the earth. Before you begin, ask yourself the following questions and consider the effects of each choice.

How Many People Should We Invite?

The size of your wedding is the most influential factor affecting both the cost and the sustainability of your wedding. Generally speaking, the smaller the wedding, the less expensive it will be and the less environmental impact it will have. A fifty-person wedding at $100 a head is $5,000. A two-hundred-person wedding at the same location is $20,000 and has roughly four times the environmental impact. Couples often face a lot of pressure from their parents, their friends, and even co-workers to have a large, all-inclusive affair. Perhaps this is why the average wedding in the United States has almost 170 guests!

It is important to establish clear lines early, and you may want to tell people who ask about the guest list that you are "probably going to have a small family affair." That way, if you decide to expand it, they will be delighted, and if you end up keeping it small, they will not be disappointed. The numbers game depends on several factors, including what your budget is and who is footing the bill. Having a clear vision of what you want your wedding to look like early on can help you hold your ground as the negotiations unfold.

Do We Want an Indoor or Outdoor Wedding?

There is no inherent advantage or disadvantage, environmentally speaking, to having an indoor or outdoor wedding. A green wedding can take place in a garden, on a mountaintop, in a museum, or in a traditional place of worship. It just comes down to a question of aesthetic taste and availability. If you want to have an outdoor wedding, you will need to think about rentals and the possibility of inclement weather. For indoor weddings, the choice of venue can limit your choice of vendors.

What Season Should We Choose?

As with the indoor/outdoor question, there is no right season in which to have your wedding. However, if you want to make your wedding more sustainable, the seasons will affect what type of food you serve, what kind of flowers you use, and other aesthetic choices as well. For example, in the spring you might have a garden wedding, serve lamb, and give out seed favors. In the summer, a beach-themed wedding with sea glass and shell decorations and a BBQ with local corn and s'mores for dessert might be fun. Fall is harvest season. You might have your wedding in a vineyard or overlooking a forest with changing leaves. You can write guests' names on miniature pumpkins, serve hot apple cider and pie, and use branches to create a colorful woodland feel. Winter is a season for snuggling in. You can rent a historic mansion with a huge fireplace, decorate with evergreens and Christmas lights, arrive in a horse-drawn sleigh, have ice sculptures, and serve hot soup and cocoa with cardamom or peppermint.

Playing up the season makes sense from an environmental standpoint, and it can save you money. It is much less expensive to buy foods and flowers that grow locally in season—when they do not need to be shipped in from South America.

When discussing seasons, it is worth noting that most venues have different peak and off-peak season rates. According to *Bride*'s magazine, you can save 10-20 percent in most parts of the country by having your wedding between November 1 and April 30. For tropical locations, avoid the winter months and holidays. If you make plans even one week off the peak season, you will have more choices of sites and vendors. Every season can be the backdrop for a wonderful and memorable wedding, so think about what kind of theme or environment you want to have and go from there.

Which Day of the Week?

As with peak seasons, there are also peak days. Saturday is the most popular, because it allows friends and family to come in on Friday evening, stay for the wedding and for a brunch the next morning, and still make it home before work on Monday. Friday night and Sunday morning are close seconds. Having your wedding on a Friday night is almost always less expensive than having it on the weekend, and Sunday afternoons are cheaper than Saturdays. A midweek wedding will give you the most flexibility but may limit who can come if you want to have a lot of out-of-town guests. The upside is that those who do fly in will save money on airfare and hotel rooms, no matter where you go.

What Time of Day?

The time of day you choose to have your wedding can also influence which location is most appropriate. Morning and afternoon weddings often cost less and use fewer resources because people eat less at a luncheon than at a dinner, and you can use natural daylight. The general rule of thumb is the earlier in the day the better—who doesn't love a lavish brunch, after all?

One Venue or More?

It is fairly common practice these days for weddings to utilize a series of different venues. Even one-day weddings can have two or three stops: the ceremony at the botanical garden, the reception on a boat, dessert and dancing back at the yacht club, etc. Instead of having your wedding and reception in different locations, try to find one venue that can accommodate all of your needs. In addition to being more convenient for your guests, having your wedding at one venue simplifies the planning process, decreases the overall cost of your wedding (fewer site fees, transportation costs, etc.), and is usually better for the environment.

Which Part of the Country?

When choosing your wedding location, think about who will come and try to pick a destination that is close to the majority of your guests. If you have a big family, consider having the ceremony in the town you grew up in. If mostly friends and colleagues will attend, the place you currently live may be the best choice. Picking a location that is convenient for the bulk of your guests will increase your attendance rate and decrease the overall travel required to attend your event—thus decreasing the carbon footprint of your wedding.

If half of your relatives live on one coast and half on the other, forgo choosing a venue in Colorado (a choice that will force *everyone* to travel) just because it splits the difference. Instead, see what green venue options are available close to your home, where the planning will be easier. When you have a local wedding, not only do you have more control, but you will also be able to rely on friends and family who live in the area to help you execute your big day. As an added bonus, all of the money you spend will go to support local businesses, and if you choose green vendors, it will bolster sustainable business practices in your area.

What about a Holiday?

There are advantages and disadvantages to having your wedding over a holiday. The disadvantage is that guests may already have plans, and depending on which holiday it is, it may be harder for them to travel. The advantages are that most people have federal holidays off, and a three day weekend will allow your guests an extra day to travel and/or party with you. Another advantage is that many venues will already be "decked out" for the holiday—which can save you money on decorations.[●]

Do You Want a Destination Wedding?

According to the Wedding Report, 250,000 (or 10 percent of all brides), choose to have destination weddings. While these weddings may feel more exotic, there are several disadvantages to choosing a location far from home. First, *all* of your guest will have to travel, increasing your guests' expenses as well as the amount of pollution generated by getting everyone there. Second, fewer of your friends and family members will be able to attend. Then there are the disadvantages in terms of planning, which can be frustrating and time-consuming when done from afar.

If you still have your heart set on having a destination wedding, first see what eco-retreat options are available locally. You don't have to fly to the Caribbean to give your guests a memorable and relaxing vacation. Use the resources in this chapter to find spas, vineyards, and eco-lodges in the United States. If you would still prefer to go abroad, research your destination carefully, and try to use sites and vendors working to be more environmentally friendly. See Chapter Thirteen for more ideas.

[●] For holiday-themed wedding ideas, see the Ask Kate section of thegreenbrideguide. com.

What about a Traveling Wedding Show?

This is one of the most brilliant ideas I have seen yet. Obliterate the carbon footprint of your wedding and keep the party going at the same time with a traveling wedding show. Instead of having friends and family fly to you—you fly to them. Book yourselves on tour and have different receptions in different states. You can kick off your adventure with a wedding and reception in your parents' hometown (make sure to tape it—so you can show the wedding video at the other parties!). Next stop, your spouse's parents' house—then on to your college town, etc. You can bring pictures, wear your wedding attire, and can even have mini-versions of the same cake made over and over. Give sponsoring friends and family members copies of this book, and ask them to throw you their own version of a green wedding. You may be surprised and delighted by the diversity of parties that unfold.

Other Considerations

In addition to the questions above, you and your partner should brainstorm about other considerations that might affect your location choice. Do you want your wedding to have a certain theme? Do you want your wedding to coincide with a large event—like a parade or state fair? Should your wedding be sophisticated or laid back? The answers to these questions can be just as important in helping you pick a location as the issues raised above. If neither of you has strong feelings about the location one way or another, use this book as a starting point. Consider all of the suggestions offered in this chapter and in Chapter Thirteen, and see which ideas resonate with you.

WEDDINGS IN THE UNITED STATES

The types of green venues available will depend on which place you select. For example, in a large city, you will have better luck finding an organic restaurant but will have a harder time finding a large, natural wildlife area or an eco-lodge. Although this chapter offers a number of ideas for green venues, there is no way for me to provide a comprehensive directory for every place in the United States. You will have to do some investigating on your own for your particular area. The chamber of commerce, yellow pages, and online search engines are all invaluable planning resources.

$ Natural Surroundings

John Muir, the great preservationist and founder of the Sierra Club, often likened his experiences in the California mountains to being in church. Having a ceremony outside, surrounded by the beauty of the world on your wedding day, can be an amazing experience—and picking a beautiful setting significantly decreases the need for additional embellishment. A few popular options include beaches, forests, lakefronts, deserts, and meadows. My husband and I were lucky enough to have our ceremony on a hilltop overlooking the Hudson Valley on a picture-perfect day in October, and it was unforgettable. But planning a wedding outside is a risky prospect. If you choose a natural location, it is absolutely essential that you have a rain plan. You should also do your best to anticipate and take care of your guests' needs ahead of time (see the section on guest comfort in Chapter Seven for more information and ideas). Having your reception outside can also pose additional logistical problems. You may need to rent a tent, lighting, tables, chairs, linens, port-a-potties, and space heaters and may also need to get a special permit to use a natural space. Be sure to look into rentals early and to check the rules of the area as far in advance as possible.

A NOTE ON ECOLOGICALLY SENSITIVE AREAS

If you and your partner are very outdoorsy, you may dream of having your wedding at the foot of that amazing waterfall you hiked to last year or on a pristine cliff overlooking the ocean. While weddings of this genre are doable (some couples even hire helicopters to bring them to especially secluded natural areas), they are often more disruptive to the natural flora and fauna than having a wedding in a more conventional location. Some ecological areas, like sand dunes, wetlands, and coral reefs, can be destroyed by relatively minor foot traffic. Before you make the final decision, consider choosing a more readily accessible location for your vows—there are many places where you can find an exquisite view without having a significant negative impact on the surroundings. If you still want to go adventuring, see the tips in Chapter Thirteen on minimal-impact travel.

$ Raw Spaces

Raw spaces are similar to natural surroundings in that they require you to bring in (and to take away) everything you will need to host your wedding. Commonly used raw spaces include ballrooms, yoga or dance studios, exhibition spaces, gymnasiums, and warehouses. Although events in raw spaces take more work to plan, using a raw space gives you room to be extremely creative. Because you have to arrange for everything from the tables to the cake, it also allows you to choose all of your vendors, making it easier to ensure that every element of your wedding is as green as you want it to be.

$$ Sculpted Landscapes

Landscaped areas like vineyards, orchards, botanical gardens, arboretums, historical estates, city parks, and zoos can offer the beauty of nature with fewer logistical issues. Vineyards, for example, often have wedding packages with local wine, good food, and a beautiful vista. Most parks are set up for visitors, with bathrooms, parking, and signs to scenic areas. Choosing a well-traveled natural venue can save you a lot of headaches when it comes to dealing with the details and still allow you to enjoy the beauty of the natural world. Most of these venues can be found online or through the local chamber of commerce. To find a local garden or farm, search Local Harvest (localharvest. org) or the Organic Trade Association (ota.com).

$$ Green Restaurants

Green restaurants are restaurants that serve organic and local food and use environmentally sound products and practices. It could be fun to host an event at one of the famous green restaurants, such as Chez Panisse in Berkeley or Restaurant Nora in Washington, D.C., but there are now green restaurants popping up in every major city and many places in between. The Green Restaurant Association (dinegreen.com) has a limited but useful online directory of certified green restaurants, museums, resorts, and even fast-food outlets. The Chef Collaborative is a network of restaurants and wholesalers dedicated to using locally grown, sustainable ingredients. Its website, guide.chefscollaborative.org, is a wonderful resource that allows you to search by name, location, and type. Having your wedding or rehearsal dinner at a green restaurant ensures that your guests will have a fresh, delicious, and sustainable meal.

$$ Quaint Places

Weddings are extremely romantic affairs, and if you are the romantic type, you may want to select an appropriately picturesque location like a covered bridge, the platform of a historic train or trolley station, the lawn outside a historic mansion or castle, a lighthouse, or the living room of a cozy, family-owned bed-and-breakfast (see Chapter Thirteen for more information on how to locate a green B&B). Most privately owned venues of this sort can be rented at an hourly rate or may be free if guests stay overnight.

$$$ Museums and Public Venues

Being green is not just about being environmentally conscious but about supporting education and cultural awareness in the larger sense. Along these lines, there are many wonderful public venues that lend themselves to interesting and exotic events. For example, consider having your wedding in a natural history or science museum, an aquarium, an art gallery, or even the public library. Choosing one of these settings can take a lot of the work out of wedding planning—providing decor and often entertainment as well. Many venues have lists of preferred vendors that are well acquainted with the space and know the setup and breakdown procedures. If you want to use some of these vendors for convenience but are concerned that they are not green, use the sustainability worksheets in the back of this book to see if they can make a few green adjustments to their usual routine.

$$ Festivals and Events

A great way to save money on entertainment is to have your wedding coincide with a large festival or event. Who needs a band when you can all rock out at a concert or dance the night away at a street festival? Give your guests an experience they will never forget by taking them to the Minnesota State Fair, the circus, a rodeo, or even Burning Man. If you are a sports fan, rent a box at a ball game or have a bowling party. Many sporting venues will allow you to bring in a caterer for fancier events, but be sure to ask ahead of time. Depending on which venue you choose, you may have to spend money on your guests' admission, but if you keep the guest list short, you can save in the long run.

$$$ Green Hotels and Resorts

If you want to have a wedding indoors and host your grand affair at a hotel or resort in the United States, consider a hotel that is working hard to decrease its environmental footprint. The best way to find one is through certifying agencies and associations that require their members to live up to specified eco-friendly standards. The Leadership in Energy and Environmental Design (LEED) certification program sets out strict environmentally-friendly construction and design standards for new buildings. A number of resorts, like California's Gaia Hotel in Napa Valley (gaianapavalleyhotel.com), are now LEED certified.

There are also organizations that focus on hotel hospitality practices (their recycling policies, what kind of soaps they use, etc.). Green Seal (greenseal.org) is a third-party certifier of this type with hotels in nine states and the District of Columbia. The Green Hotels Association (greenhotels.com) is another good resource, offering contact information for hundreds of properties across the country trying to decrease their impact on the environment. With a little searching, you can find cool luxury hotels like the Sheraton Rittenhouse Square in Philadelphia, where you recline on 100 percent recycled furniture and sleep on organic mattresses. If you want to see how a hotel measures up, use the sustainability worksheet at the end of this book.

DESTINATION WEDDINGS

Destination weddings are often referred to as "weddingmoons," because, in effect, you are taking your entire party on your honeymoon with you. If you are close with your family and want to have a relatively small wedding, the prospect of a wedding/group vacation combo may be very appealing. As mentioned earlier, a small wedding abroad can be better for the environment than a lavish affair back home.

The hardest thing about a destination wedding is making plans from afar. Because your guests will have to ask for time off from work, buy tickets, and make reservations, the earlier you can nail down the details, the better. (Don't forget to check the marriage requirements of the country you plan to visit!) Chapter Thirteen offers a list of eco-destination options. This section focuses on getting you the help you need to make a wedding-moon happen.

On-site Wedding Coordinator

When considering different venues, make sure to ask about their bridal services. It helps to have an on-site coordinator, and ideally, your location has a staff person dedicated to this job. If not, you can hire a local wedding planner to make arrangements for you. Either way, you should ask questions about green options early—preferably before you make your first payment. Even if the place you want to go is not inherently eco-friendly, a good wedding coordinator should be able to help you find and negotiate several green options. You can use the sustainability worksheets in the back of this book as a guide.

Green Travel Agents

As the green wedding market has grown, a new industry of green wedding providers has grown along with it. If you want to plan an eco-conscious destination wedding but don't have the time to do a lot of research, search online for a green travel agent. Most ecotourism agencies will be able to help you. Additionally, there are now agents who actually specialize in green weddingmoons, like Go Green Destination Weddings (gogreendestinationweddings.

com), which helps couples book weddings at certified green resorts in the Caribbean and Mexico.

Site Visit

Although it may be expensive or hard to schedule, it is important to go to the location at least once before the wedding to meet with the coordinator and to make sure everything is in order. Things may not always be as they appear on the Internet. Try to pick a date two to three months out at the latest. Ask your on-site coordinator to schedule meetings for you with caterers and other vendors. People are more likely to help you out if they have a face to go with the name, and if you want to ask for special favors (like the substitution of organic flour for the regular flour in the wedding cake), it is best to do this in person—assuming your coordinator has not been able to work these details out for you already. Remember that you are going to be paying these people a lot of money, so it is not unreasonable for them to accommodate practical requests. You can also use the opportunity to talk about your organic vision, to ensure you do not arrive to a room of Mylar balloon arches or to fruit bowls resting on ice cubes that have been dyed green a la Saint Patrick's Day (it has happened).

CHAPTER 3

Here Comes the Eco-chic Bride

As the old saying goes, marriage is about two people, but a wedding is about the bride. When the bride walks down the aisle, all eyes are on her, and women spend months planning and preparing for that special moment. The good news is you don't have to sacrifice style or beauty these days to be green. When the eco-savvy bride walks down the aisle, her dress is stunning; her hair is perfectly coifed; and her skin has a radiant glow. The only difference between her and a regular bride is that creating her fabulous look had less impact on human health and the environment.

This chapter outlines some of the best options for eco-chic attire, hair, and makeup that will make you look stunning and stylish on your wedding day. Whether you plan to wear a simple organic cotton frock with sandals or a designer gown with diamond chandelier earrings, this chapter will help you find a green version of everything you need.

GOWNS

Whether A-line, mermaid, or ball gown, the wedding dress is a focal point of most weddings. Because it is so important, many brides search long and hard to find the perfect dress: one that is flattering, stylish, and falls within the budget. The green bride is no exception.

Most wedding gowns in the Unites States today retail for somewhere between $800 and $1,800, although it is easy to spend more. Because of the train and layers, many wedding dresses use yards and yards of white fabric (most bleached with toxic chemicals). They are often produced in sweatshop environments and are imported from overseas, which requires gallons of fuel and contributes to global warming. At the end of the day, it is a lot of money and a lot of waste for something you only wear once. If you know where to look, however, you can find many green alternatives. Whether wearing a hemp dress, a vintage dress, or a brand-new couture gown, every bride can look magnificent on her wedding day without sacrificing her values.

Previously Worn Gowns

The must-have-a-new-dress rule is one of the least-green wedding phenomena to develop in recent years. Up until about forty years ago, it was standard for women to wear their mother's or a close family member's dress on their wedding day. However, in the 1960s, women began to toss aside the traditional dresses offered by their families in favor of flowing hippie wedding gowns—and a new tradition was born. Perhaps it is ironic that the same generation that inspired Earth Day came up with this very un-environmentally sound practice. So why abide by this silly new tradition? When some brides are now buying not one but *two* wedding dresses so they can make a second "dramatic" entrance, it's time to consider a new twist on the old tradition.

$ Granny's Gown

When I announced my engagement, I was surprised and delighted by how many friends and relatives came forward offering me their wedding dress. What could be more sustainable or more sentimental than a recycled wedding gown? Especially now that designers are mimicking vintage looks, really think twice before passing over your mom's, your aunt's, or even your grandmother's wedding dress. A little hemming or letting out, a reworking of the bust line, adding a layer of brocade, beadwork, or lace, and other easy changes can make an old dress a beautiful and unique addition to your wedding day. You could also think about how an heirloom gown might be altered for another occasion, even if you do not want to wear it down the aisle. For example, it is now fashionable to wear your mom's dress to your rehearsal dinner.

VERSATILE ALTERNATIVE

If you cannot find a dress that was previously worn, consider buying a dress that you can wear again. See if you can find a dress with a detachable train or one that can be hemmed below the knee and still look good. This will allow you to reinvent your gown after the wedding into something you can enjoy again and again. This works particularly well if you want to wear a non-white dress. The wedding runways are filled these days with blue, red, and champagne gowns—so why not find something a bit unique? If you buy a white dress, you can have it dyed another color after the wedding. You can also recycle your gown by having it recast as a smaller version of itself or turned into a baby blanket (ideal for use at a christening, bris, or other such occasion).

$$ Secondhand Gowns

Cruise thrift, vintage, and consignment shops for used bridal gowns. Most dresses, even if bought new, need alteration, so don't be afraid to buy one that is too big or has straps you don't like. Once you have the gown, any good tailor can change the train or neckline, take in the skirt, remove crinoline, and customize your dress to your taste in many other simple and elegant ways. Think about what style you are going for and buy a dress in that genre that can be tailored to your body.

For online vintage finds, check out Vintage Vixen Clothing Company (vintagevixen.com), which has unworn vintage gowns starting at $300. Vintage Gown (Vintagegown.com) carries a large selection of wedding dresses from the mid-1900s, and Save the Dress (savethedress.com) is like eBay for designer wedding dresses, where prices range all over the map. Finally, for an amazing selection of current designer gowns under $250, go to preownedweddingdresses.com.

If a vintage wedding gown is not for you, consider buying a vintage rehearsal dinner dress or "Sunday brunch" outfit. Vintageous Vintage Clothing (vintageous.com) has a great collection of adorable dresses from the 1950s, 1960s, and 1970s perfect for these occasions.

TAILORING TIPS

If you are considering a previously worn gown, make sure the dress you fall in love with is not badly stained. It may be impossible to remove the stain without discoloring the gown, so if it is stained, check with a seamstress first to make sure that the stained area can be cut away without affecting the look, style, or drape of the dress. This can add about $200 to the cost of alteration. Similarly, if you fall in love with a dress that is too small, a good tailor may be able to let it out to fit, as long as there is enough material in the seam. Before you buy the dress, ask if you can leave a deposit and take it to a tailor for a consultation.

$$ Rent a Gown

Renting a bridal gown is becoming increasingly popular and is a great way to save money while getting to wear a truly exquisite dress. You can often get gowns worth thousands of dollars for a few hundred, and many stores rent accessory packages as well. Alterations are often included in the rental price, sparing another expense. Renting is also a great option for your attendants, who may never wear their dresses again and would rather not spend the money buying a gown they didn't pick. Look in the yellow pages or online to find a rental location near you.

$$$ Designer Dresses for a Cause

There are a number of organizations popping up that sell previously worn, high-end designer or sample gowns to raise money for charity. This is a great option if you want to buy a modern designer-label dress. Some organizations, like Brides Against Breast Cancer (makingmemories.org), have a traveling trunk show, while others, like the Bridal Garden in New York (bridalgarden.org), have retail stores. Even if you buy a new dress, you can often find designers who donate a portion of their profits to charities. Buying a dress that supports a worthy cause is a simple and direct way to add "something more" to your "something old, something new, something borrowed, something blue."

$$$ Vintage Couture

Vintage couture dresses can be *amazing*, with intricate beadwork and unparalleled craftsmanship. If you have a large budget to work with and long for a wedding dress with unique style, you should really consider old designer dresses. The Frock (thefrock. com) is a great example of a high-end, used-dress shop with jaw-dropping selections, but there are many others.

JUST MY VINTAGE SIZE?

If you fall in love with a vintage dress you find online, make sure to buy based on *measurements* as opposed to size. As the years have gone by, the numbers have gone down, and you will probably need a significantly "bigger" dress than you think. This is especially true of designer dresses, which tend to run small anyway. For example, a size 12 dress from 1940 will be approximately a size 8 today. Even modern wedding dresses run one to two sizes smaller than you normally wear. When making your selection, remember that it is easier to take a dress in than to let it out.

Buy a Gown Made from a Sustainable Material

Unlike petroleum-based synthetic fibers, such as nylon, polyester, and acrylic, there are many fabrics available today made from renewable resources. Most high-end dresses are made from cotton, linen, or silk, all of which can be produced in a sustainable way, and many designers, like Vera Wang, now carry green dresses in their lines. Before you buy just any old dress, consider the following eco-friendly alternatives.[*]

$ Hemp Heaven

Hemp is a sturdy fiber made from a renewable resource (the cannabis plant), which is naturally pest-resistant—meaning it can easily be grown without pesticides. It thrives in a variety of climates and yields three times more fiber than cotton. So why is this miracle plant essentially absent from the American wardrobe? The 1937 Marijuana Tax Act banned its cultivation on American soil. Although hemp production was briefly reinstated during World War II, hemp was exiled again when it became falsely associated with marijuana (which is actually a different species). Conspiracy theories blame the cotton and synthetic fiber industries for hemp's continued stigmatization. That said, the use of hemp fiber is on the rise, thanks to our eco-conscious Canadian and European neighbors.

---

[*] Many up-and-coming designers now offer gowns made from sustainable fabrics. For more ideas, see the Eco-Products section of thegreenbrideguide.com.

Although the word *hemp* often conjures images of thick, brown twine, hemp can actually be spun into a fine, silklike fabric. If you are looking for a simple dress made from all-natural materials, check out the options at Rawganique (rawganique. com). Threadhead Creations (threadheadcreations.com) also has a few inexpensive hemp dresses for a more classic look, as does Utopian Living (utopianliving.com). For more elaborate hemp dresses, Conscious Clothing (getconscious.com) has luscious gowns made from hemp-silk.

$$ Organic Cotton

Although synthetic gowns may cost less, they are made from non-sustainable resources (and tend to make you sweat). While it is good to buy a dress made from a natural fiber like cotton, this too can come at a cost to the earth if the cotton is not grown in a sustainable way. Shockingly, 10 percent of the world's pesticides are used to grow non-organic cotton—an average of 5.8 pounds of pesticides per acre! If you are thinking about a cotton gown, consider ordering one from an organic cotton dressmaker, like Wholly Jo (wholly-jo.co.uk).

$$ Other Natural Fibers

The world of natural fibers is becoming increasingly sophis-ticated. Today, you can find beautiful material made from Tencel (a wood pulp cellulose fiber from tree farms), bamboo, and even pineapple (called piña). Piña wedding dresses are particularly popular in Latin American cultures and are often made with colored accents to liven up the day.

$$$ Eco-couture

It took a while to catch on, but models are now strutting eco-friendly designs down the Paris runways. High-end dresses made from organic cotton, "peace" silk (where the worms are not killed to extract the silk), and other alternative fabrics, like bamboo and modal, are turning up all over the place. A great place to find eco-couture gowns is Conscious Clothing (getconscious.com), which has sexy and unique styles that start around $1,800. A British company with fabulous peace silk dresses is Gaia House (gaiahouse.uk.com), and Deborah Lindquist (deborahlindquist.com) uses hemp-silk and recycled saris to make exquisite, one-of-a-kind pieces.

Custom-Made

Nothing is more unique than a handmade dress. Whether you sew it yourself or have a friend or professional sew it for you, in an age of machine-made clothing, a handmade dress is a true luxury. The best part about a custom dress is that you have complete control and can pick the style, fabric, and design, down to the last detail. Making or having a dress made is also a great option if you have expensive taste and a limited budget, or if you are having trouble finding a green version of a particular style. Bring a picture of your favorite couture dress, sari, kimono, or other wedding wear with you to a good dressmaker and have something similar made for a fraction of the price.

Find a Good Pattern

If you want to make your own dress, you need to find a good pattern. Although there are thousands of ways designers make wedding dresses unique, almost all wedding dresses are based on one of six primary shapes (A-line, ball gown, basque waist, empire, mermaid, and sheath). The best thing to do is to go into a good bridal store and figure out which of the designs looks best on your figure. Once you decide which style you want, look online for a pattern that suits your style and taste. Folk Wear (folkwear.com) carries vintage bridal-dress patterns. Denver Fabrics (denverfabrics.com) also has a large collection of modern wedding-dress patterns for very reasonable prices. Generally, patterns cost about $10.

Pick a Fabric

Once you have decided on a cut and style, it is time to pick a fabric. The book *Bridal Gowns: How to Make the Dress of Your Dreams* by Susan Andriks has a list of recommended fabrics for different styles. As previously discussed, it is best to shy away from synthetic fibers and to use natural materials whenever possible. A great site that sells a wide variety of natural fabrics is Pick Hemp (pickhemp.com). Hemp Traders (hemptraders.com) also has an excellent selection. Peace silk can be purchased by the yard from Aurora Silk (aurorasilk.com). For embellishment, consider buying glass beads, cotton ribbon, or handmade lace.

Sew, Sew, Sew

If you are a good seamstress or have one in the family, consider making the wedding dress yourself. Otherwise you can hire a dressmaker to sew the dress for you. Party Pop (partypop.com) offers a state-by-state list of vendors who specialize in custom wedding-dress creation. The cost of custom tailoring varies dramatically based on the intricacy of the dress and the skill of the dressmaker, and you generally get what you pay for.

Before commissioning a dress, ask to see a portfolio of the dressmaker's work and get a reference or two. You should also ask for a price quote in writing and an estimated timetable for production. To be safe, ask the dressmaker to make you something else first to make sure that you like his or her work and that you work well together. When it comes time to make the actual dress, try to have it completed as early as possible to leave room for contingency plans and last-minute changes.

After the Wedding

Unless you have purchased a "versatile alternative" above, when the wedding is over, you will find yourself the owner of a very expensive white dress. I suppose you could wear it to a

Halloween party or plan a wedding-dress tea with your friends, but most brides leave their dresses hanging in their closets, untouched for decades. Unfortunately, without proper cleaning and preservation, that dress you plan to save for your children might be yellow and moth-eaten—and what a terrible waste that would be! If you choose to preserve your dress, use a green dry cleaner and store it carefully. If you are willing to part with your dress—consider donating it to a worthy cause.

$ Donate Your Dress

Before you plunk down another couple hundred dollars to clean, press, and plastic-wrap your gown for hypothetical offspring, consider donating it to a worthy cause, where it will be appreciated much sooner and will also make a difference. I donated my gown to Brides Against Breast Cancer (makingmemories.org), and although it was hard, I am glad I did it.

The Bridal Garden (bridalgarden.org) in New York uses the proceeds from the sale of donated gowns to raise money for Sheltering Arms, an organization dedicated to bettering the lives of children. The I Do Foundation (idofoundation.org/resources/dresses/) will give 20 percent of the sale price of your gown to the charity of your choice. They use the remaining 80 percent to further their mission of encouraging charitable giving at weddings.

$$ Green Dry Cleaning

Almost all formal wear requires dry cleaning in order to be worn again. Despite its name, dry cleaning is not really a dry process. It involves the use of liquid volatile organic compounds (VOCs), or chemical solvents called "perc." These chemicals are extremely hazardous. Exposure to perc can cause an array of ugly symptoms including nausea, headaches, and skin rashes. Long-term exposure has also been linked to liver and kidney damage. Perc exposure is not only a problem for the people working in dry-cleaning establishments, but the chemicals also cling to dry-cleaned clothing and can contaminate your home. According to one report by the Coalition for Clean Air, 85 percent of the more than 35,000 dry cleaners in the United States still use these toxic substances, so it is important to specifically seek out greener alternatives.

There are currently two types of green dry cleaning available: professional Wet Cleaning and Liquid Carbon Dioxide Cleaning. Wet Cleaning uses soaps and conditioners instead of solvent chemicals. Liquid Carbon Dioxide Cleaning uses pressurized liquid CO_2 in place of perc. According to Green America, a national nonprofit consumer organization, the CO_2 used in Liquid Carbon Dioxide Cleaning is recaptured from other manufacturing processes, so the dry cleaning is carbon neutral. Because the term "green dry cleaning" is not yet regulated, make sure to ask which technique is being employed, to weed out false advertising. You can download Green America's dry cleaning quick-reference brochure for more information on different types of dry cleaning, available at coopamerica.org/pdf/greendrycleaning.pdf. GreenEarth Cleaning (greenearthcleaning.com) allows you to search for green cleaners in your state. You can also skip the dry cleaning entirely by carefully washing "dry clean only" clothing, like silk, wool, and rayon, by hand. For detailed instructions on how to wash these fabrics at home, visit care2.com/greenliving/wet-clean-wool-silk-and-rayon.html.

SHOES

Once you have found or made your perfect dress, it is time to find the shoes to match. With the exception of color (usually white), there is no such thing as a classic bridal shoe. It is important to find shoes that are comfortable—this is your wedding day, after all, and you will be on your feet for many, many hours. Most bridal shops carry an array of overpriced, poorly made shoes that are tempting only because buying a pair with the dress means one less thing to worry about. But shoes that are made of leather require hazardous chemicals to process. Synthetic shoes can be just as environmentally damaging and are often shipped from overseas. So before you reach for those new faux-diamond strappy sandals, consider some of the following eco-chic alternatives.

Something Old

If you need "something old" for your wedding anyway, it might as well be your shoes. Using a pair of shoes that you or someone else already owns is a form of recycling and keeps toxic chemicals and transportation exhaust out of the environment. Instead of buying new shoes you will probably never wear again, consider these pre-worn options.

$ Closet Case

If you think back, can you remember a single pair of shoes worn by a bride? Many wedding dresses are so long that you barely see the shoes at all, and shoes are often cast off when the dancing begins, anyway. Thus, almost any white heel or strappy sandal will do. See if you have something that might work.

SOLE COMFORT

As the saying goes—if the shoe fits, (you are more likely to) wear it. Do you have a pair of shoes that would work well but are not quite as comfortable as you would like? Or does a friend have a pair half a size too big for you? One easy way to make shoes fit perfectly is to buy foot cushions and shoe liners. Dainty Footings (daintyfootings. com) sells a Beautiful Bride set that includes ball-of-foot cushions and heel liners. Kiwi (kiwismilingfeet.com) has a fabulous line of clear gel products that are smooth on one side and sticky on the other for easy insertion. I am fond of the strappy strips—which help hold slingbacks in place without chafing. Finally, for a shoe that fits but makes your legs tired, try a weight-shifting heel-high insert from Insolia (insolia.com).

$ Something Borrowed

If you have any friends that are your size, ask if they have shoes you can borrow. If you are particularly lucky, they will have gotten married first and will have stylish wedding shoes hanging around in their closet. This option saves you money and, according to superstition, brings your friend good luck!

$$ eBay

There is a huge selection of once-worn wedding shoes on eBay for next to nothing. You can narrow your search by size, style, heel height, and color (ivory, cream, white, etc.). Make sure the seller has a good rating, and find out what the return policy is in case the shoes are not comfortable or do not arrive in good condition. For more tips on how to use eBay successfully, see the Q+A in the Ask Kate section of thegreenbrideguide.com.

Something New

If you can't locate a pair of pre-owned shoes to suit your needs, there are many ways you can reduce the impact of your purchase. Before you hit the department stores, consider the following alternatives.

$ Generic Shoes

If you are going to buy shoes, try to find ones that are generic enough that you could wear them again. For example, simple ballet flats are very popular right now, are comfortable, and will not distract from your wedding gown in any way. Dance shoes are another popular option, because they are designed to be comfortable and to last a long time.

$$ Dual-Purpose Shoes

If you like to dance, consider investing in a good pair of ballroom dancing shoes. These shoes are well made and are designed specifically to keep your feet comfortable while still providing a few extra inches of height. This is a great alternative to the modern trend, where brides buy two pairs of shoes—heels for the aisle and flats for dancing.

$$ Eco-fiber Shoes

Well-made leather shoes last a long time, but the process of making leather, known as tanning, releases a number of highly toxic chemicals into our rivers and streams. Instead of buying leather shoes, consider some of the many eco-friendly alternative fabrics already discussed in this chapter. For example, hemp is extremely durable and is now being used to make breathable, lightweight shoes and sandals. For a casual summer wedding, check out the 100 percent hemp shoes at EcoDragon (ecodragon.com).

$$ Made in America

In addition to displaying American pride and supporting American manufacturing jobs, buying products "made in the USA" benefits the environment. Products made here do not have to be shipped from overseas, which means fewer fuel miles and less impact on global warming. Environmental standards are stricter in the United States than in many other countries, so the actual manufacturing of "made in the USA" products often causes less damage to the environment. There are many stylish American-made shoes available at every department store. Some companies, like Shoes USA (shoesusa.com), allow you to choose the material, color, and design of the shoe, and all of the money goes to American workers.

$$ Native American Sources

Buying shoes and accessories from Native American tribes helps support some of the poorest and most depressed regions of the country. Native American leather sandals and moccasins are well made and can help you create an elegant ensemble.

$$$ Peace Silk Shoes

If money is no object or shoes are your priority, you should really consider peace silk heels. One store with high-end silk pumps is the Natural Store (thenaturalstore.co.uk). It proves you don't need to sacrifice one iota of fashion to be green.

VEILS

When I went to buy a veil, my mouth literally fell open: $180 for *this*?! "This" was a foot-long piece of tulle on a plain, brown hair comb. It was truly shocking—especially because, unlike shoes or wedding jewelry, you can't buy a veil that you'll wear again. So before you dish out your hard-earned money on an overpriced disposable veil, consider some of the following alternatives.[*]

Something Old, Something Borrowed

As with shoes, a wedding veil is a great item to borrow or buy used. This is especially true if you are looking for a classic tulle veil. Tulle is petroleum-based, meaning it comes from a non-renewable resource and does not biodegrade for hundreds of years. If you can't find a veil to borrow, or if you want a more intricate style, buy a used or vintage veil. It recycles materials that have already been processed, so you don't create any new pollution! What could be greener?

---

[*] For a list and description of veil styles, see the Quick Guide page in the About the Book section of thegreenbrideguide.com.

$ Borrow a Veil

The first step is to ask your friends and family if they have a veil you can borrow. If you have a style in mind, you may be able (with permission) to alter a borrowed veil to suit your taste, especially if you can get your hands on one of the longer versions and are interested in going shorter. Some fabrics can just be cut, and others will need a hemline. You can add lace or a ribbon that matches your dress along the edge to create a romantic ensemble.

$$ Find a Once-Worn Veil

eBay is a wonderful place to find used veils of every shape and style. You can often find them for just a few dollars, which will allow you to experiment a bit more, and no one will mind when you make alterations. After the ceremony, you can relist your veil on eBay so that it may be reused again.

$$$ Rent a Veil

Most people are not aware of it, but in addition to dress rentals, you can also rent a veil. This is a great option, especially if you are interested in wearing an elaborate silk or lace veil, which can be extremely expensive and requires a lot of time and material to make. Rental costs vary depending on the quality of the veil but are generally about 30 percent of the retail price. Look for stores that do bridal-dress rentals in your area.

$$$ Handmade Lace

For an elegant, classic look, consider a handmade lace veil. Although more costly than a piece of tulle, a lace veil is something you can keep in the family forever. You can turn it into a canopy for a child's bed or keep it for future weddings. An heirloom-quality piece is an investment. Prices vary dramatically, but one good site is Designs by Kristen (designsbykristen. com). You can also find used or vintage lace veils online.

The Crafty Bride

If you have any inclination toward gluing or sewing, you can make a veil from sustainable materials for the same price or less than the price of a new veil. Veils are not rocket science—especially the simple, one-layer kind. Almost every city has a wedding or garment district where you can find all the materials and advice you desire, and there are a number of books available on the subject. Your veil can match your wedding dress or complement it, and customizing the headpiece gives you total flexibility to accommodate your taste and hairstyle. You can buy fabric samples for pennies, and it is a great way to get inspiration. Think about what would look best with your dress and leave enough time for mistakes.

$ Revamped Veil

You can buy a used veil on eBay and add a new trim, flowers, lace, or beads to transform something plain into something spectacular and unique.

$$ Alternative Fabrics

When you begin shopping for veil fabric, remember to choose natural materials (e.g., silk, organza, or bamboo) instead of a petroleum-based synthetic fabric (e.g., nylon tulle) whenever possible. Silk Road Fabrics (srfabrics.com) has a nice selection, including some that are already embroidered. See if you can find recycled material or odd lots that would otherwise go to waste. If you need to use a synthetic fabric, try to find an old veil that has been damaged and can be recast so that you are recycling products that would otherwise be discarded.

Glamorous Embellishments

Not every bride wants to wear a veil on her wedding day. Whether you are going for an earthier feel or just don't like the way veils look, there are many other glamorous green options out there.

$ Nontraditional Veils

Instead of a traditional veil, consider using a beautiful scarf that you could wear again. If you want to maintain the "veil feel," there are many charming lace headscarves or table covers that can be converted into a beautiful veil (and no one needs to know). As soon as you remove the word "bridal" from the seller's vocabulary, prices come down significantly. For a great example of lace "headscarves," see Headcoverings by Devorah (headcoverings-by-devorah.com), which specializes in religious head coverings. You can find what looks just like a lace veil without the clip for less than $30. If you buy something made of lace, you can always reuse it as a decoration around the house.

$ Real Flowers

For petite women like me (I am only five foot two), it's easy to look like you are drowning in a veil. My mother, who had clear pro-veil leanings, took it all back when she saw how well small, white begonia blooms worked with my dress. After all, nothing says natural beauty like real flowers! You can use anything from roses to sprigs of berries. A few well-placed stems in your locks can celebrate the season, highlight the theme of your wedding, or simply match your bouquet. Flowers can easily be woven into an updo and secured with plain bobby pins. You can also ask your florist to put flowers on a headband or comb. See Chapter Six for more information on how to choose local, in-season flora that will make your guests drool.

$ Pearl or Crystal Hairpins

It has become very fashionable to place several small crystal or pearl hair pins around a cluster of pinned up curls. While these are not sustainable unless purchased secondhand, you are more likely to reuse them than a veil. Try to pick pins that are versatile and go with other clothes in your wardrobe.

$ Headbands, Ribbons, and Feathers

Headbands are making a comeback as the 1970s styles reemerge. The great thing about headbands is they can be made of almost anything—from flowers wired together to a lush band of white peace silk. They are fun and elegant at the same time. They also keep your hair out of your eyes, allowing you to show off those rosy cheekbones. Bridal magazines are now coupling headbands and fancy ribbons with all sorts of exotic feather creations. A single peacock feather connotes the flapper era, while a stylish, snowy white feather clip makes a sheer empire-waist dress downright dreamy. You can make your own headpieces using feathers, clips, antique brooches, and ribbon.

$$ Antique Clips and Combs

A lot of vintage stores have beautiful combs and clips waiting to be rediscovered. Antique silver, enamel, or diamond hair ornaments can be magnificent and can be reused for future galas. If there are none available in your family to borrow, these are great items to find on eBay or in vintage shops online. For a selection of antique hair combs for less than you might imagine, go to Michelle's Vintage Jewelry (michellesvintagejewelry.com). Antique stores are also a good source of ornamental hair sticks.

$$ Hats

Elaborate hats are now showing up in bridal magazines across the country. Depending on the style of your dress, a white or even lushly colored hat can be the perfect accent for your look. Big, small, feathered, veiled—there are so many styles to choose from!

$$ Gloves

Okay, so they don't technically go on your head, but a long, luxurious pair of gloves has the same elegant effect as donning a veil. Let the glamour of the past provide a romantic flare to your ensemble with vintage velvet, satin, lace, or leather elbow-length gloves. There are many pairs available online. Since old leather can crack if it has not been taken care of properly, if you can't try them on before you buy, make sure your purchase comes with a money-back guarantee.

$$$ Vintage Fur

While I am offering up non-head-oriented veil alternatives, I must make a pitch for vintage fur accents. While there are a number of ethical issues associated with buying new fur, buying a vintage fur (or faux fur) coat, stole, or muff, or using one already part of a family collection, adds an elegant touch to a fall or winter wedding without harming animals or the environment. One good source of vintage fur pieces online is Vintage Designer Clothing (vintagedesignerclothing.com). Most Salvation Army stores also have a decent vintage fur selection.

$$$ Antique Tiaras

For women who want a vintage tiara to be the crowning glory of their outfit, Head Piece Heaven (headpieceheaven.com) is a great site for high-end antique crystal and rhinestone tiaras.

DONATE YOUR HAIR

Many brides grow their locks out for their wedding, and almost as many chop them off soon after the big day. When you are ready for a bold, modern cut (a la "the Posh"), have your hairdresser start with a straight cut of ten to twelve inches. Then donate your locks to a program that makes wigs for children with cancer. The two primary organizations are Wigs for Kids (wigsforkids.org) and Locks of Love (locksoflove.org), which only require 10 inches.

JEWELRY

Unlike wedding dresses and veils, which you may be able to refashion or donate but generally only wear once, if you buy carefully you can wear your earth-friendly wedding accessories again and again. Nothing pulls an outfit together like the right jewelry, and brides spend almost as much time accessorizing as they do shopping for a dress. Unfortunately, mining precious stones and metals causes a lot of damage to the earth. This does not mean that you should abandon the thought of wearing jewelry on your wedding day, but if you are thinking about buying something for your wedding, consider choosing an eco-friendly alternative.

Recycled Jewelry

Whether you already have something beautiful in the family or buy something made from recycled metals and gemstones, there are many ways to don eco-friendly accessories on your wedding day.

$ The Family Jewels

If you are lucky enough to come from a family that has a beautiful necklace or bracelet that might look nice with your dress, consider using the piece as your "something old" or "something borrowed." In addition to the sentimental statement you will make, wearing something from your family can bring you great comfort during the ceremony. If it is an inherited piece, it is a nice way to honor a family member who cannot be with you to celebrate.

$ Vintage Costume Jewelry

This is the type of thing eBay was made for. You can find hundreds of high-end costume jewelry pieces from all decades for under $10—often including shipping! See the Quick Guide page in the About the Book section of thegreenbrideguide.com for eBay shopping tips.

$$ Recycled Silver

Instead of buying something made from new silver, a number of companies melt down vintage silver to form contemporary creations. One company that offers high quality pendants crafted from melted Austrian coins is One World Projects (oneworld-projects.com). They also have a number of tagua nut pendants, which are made from sustainably harvested Ecuadorian nuts that look and feel like ivory.

$$ Reclaimed and Recycled Diamonds, Gemstones, and Precious Metals

If you are thinking about incorporating some colorful stones in your wedding-day ensemble, consider a jeweler who uses recycled gems and metals. When you buy jewelry that has recycled stones and metals, you prevent tons of mining pollution. Earthwise Jewelry (leberjeweler.com) has a number of standard as well as custom design options. You can also ask a local jeweler to refashion an inherited piece to your liking. My cousin turned diamond studs she inherited into a beautiful wedding ring, and Barry tuned a piece of a bracelet his grandmother gave him into a lovely pendant for our anniversary. Although it requires some energy, recasting family jewels saves money, saves the environment, and adds sentimental value as well.

$$ Jewelry Rental

Ultra-posh brides who want luxury at a fair price can rent high-end wedding jewelry for a fraction of its retail value. One store, Doyle and Doyle in New York (doyledoyle.com), is famous for the over-the-top glamour of its estate jewelry, rental necklaces, earrings, bracelets, and brooches. Ask your local tuxedo rental shop for jewelry rental options in your area.

$$ Antique Jewelry

In addition to local antique and consignment shops, look online for reasonably priced antique jewelry. The Antique Jewelry Mall (antiquejewelrymall.com) has a nice selection of art deco filigree pendants, along with antique rings, bracelets, and other treasures all in the $100 to $500 range.

$$$ Recycled Gold

Gold is easy to melt down and recast, and a number of jewelers now use recycled gold in their products. GreenKarat (greenkarat.com) is probably the best-known source of recycled gold jewelry available online. In addition to artisan wedding rings, GreenKarat makes some beautiful wedding necklaces and earrings.

$$$ Estate Jewelry

Let the riches of the past sparkle on your special day! Consider buying one of the thousands of vintage silver, diamond, gold, and other gem-encrusted wedding jewelry sets available online. One place that has a lot of options is faycullen.com. Another great option is antiquejewelryforsale.com, where exquisite estate diamond earrings run from $2,000 to $20,000. The Victorian necklaces and brooches at Lang Antiques (langantiques.com) are also remarkable.

Beautifully Unique

Not every wedding calls for diamonds and pearls. In an era of casual elegance where garden, beach, and farm weddings are becoming increasingly popular, you can think outside the box for jewelry as well. There are a lot of beautiful, one-of-a-kind necklaces and earrings out there that may match your dress and event better than traditional jewels and are better for the earth as well.

$ Nature's Bounty

Consider wearing something a bit less traditional—like a necklace made from beautiful glass, seashells, or nuts, especially for a semicasual or beach wedding. One great source for non-traditional necklaces is the Natural Store (thenaturalstore. co.uk/). The Green with Envy store (store.greenwithenvygifts. com/jewelry.html) carries lovely earrings made from vintage buttons, among other treasures, and VerdeRocks (gwen-davis. com/verde/) has many unique pieces made from shells, bamboo, and other botanical gems from around the globe.

$$ Pretty Paper

Believe it or not, paper can be turned into beautiful and delicate jewelry creations. Colorful paper can be rolled to form beads or made into pendants. Although not completely without environmental impact, the damage is minimal compared to mining and processing precious metals and gems. One of my favorite sources for artisan paper jewelry is Etsy (etsy.com). You can also get paper beads from suppliers (beadforlife.org), but these are easy to make yourself, if you are so inclined, and there are many how-to books and websites available.

$$$ True Blue Sapphires

True Blue sapphires are from Australia and are mined under strict environmental standards. Sapphires cost less than diamonds and can add a touch of color to your ensemble. One source of True Blue sapphire jewelry is Brilliant Earth (brilliantearth.com).

Jewelry with a Conscience

If you have your heart set on new, traditional jewelry, you can ensure that a percentage of the price goes to charity and that the workers who mined the material were treated with dignity by choosing one of the following options.

$ Fair Trade Products

Fair trade is an international movement that promotes fair labor and trade policies. Fair trade certified manufacturers pay their workers a living wage and often have to meet higher environmental and working condition standards as well. A lot of organizations now provide handcrafted fair trade jewelry, the proceeds of which go to support women and children in developing countries and other worthy causes. One source of inexpensive yet beautiful jewelry is World of Good (worldofgood.com). Novica (novica.com), a company affiliated with National Geographic that supports artists around the world, offers thousands of individually crafted earrings and necklaces, many with silver and pearls that would be perfect for a wedding. Lucina Jewelry (lucinajewelry. com) has a small, intriguing selection of pieces that might work well for a casual wedding or rehearsal dinner.

$$ Jewelry for a Cause

If you are looking to buy traditional wedding jewelry, like pearls, consider purchasing them through a clearinghouse fair trade site like Greater Good (greatergood.com). This site links to a number of cause sites, such as TheHungerSite.com, TheBreastCancerSite.com, and TheRainforestSite.com. It allows you to browse jewelry collections from a number of different vendors. A percentage of every sale goes to support the charity of your choice.

HAIR AND MAKEUP

The eco-conscious bride does not need to forgo makeup or the perfect hairdo in order to be green. However, before you sign over your face and hair to the salon stylist, educate yourself about product alternatives. If you want it all professionally done, find a salon that uses some of the eco-lines mentioned below. Search for "green," "organic," or "eco" salons in your area. You can also buy your own products and bring them with you, a strategy that has the added advantage of allowing you to continue to look eco-fabulous after your wedding day.

Nontoxic Alternatives

They may make us look good, but many hair and makeup products contain small quantities of toxic ingredients. For example, benzene, a common nail polish ingredient, disrupts hormones, and parabens, which are found in soaps and shampoos, can cause birth defects. In 2002, a report released by the Environmental Working Group (ewg.org), a nonprofit environmental research organization, found that of seventy-two top name-brand beauty products, fifty-two tested positive for phthalates—a family of chemicals linked to birth defects and liver, kidney, and lung damage in animals. In addition to known toxins, many products contain chemicals that have never been tested, because the FDA does not require cosmetic testing, and the industry's review panel only tests about 10 percent of what they use. While the amount of these chemicals you are exposed to in your daily routine will probably not harm you, the cumulative effect of these products when washed down the drain and put in the landfill is significant.

As you primp and prep for your green wedding, consider the following green options. In addition to the companies mentioned below, you can also research the chemical makeup and toxicity of many popular products online with the Environmental Working Group's Cosmetic Safety Database, Skin Deep (cosmeticsdatabase.com).

Nontoxic Scents

Did you ever notice that most perfumes do not have to include a list of ingredients? It's a good thing for them, because most perfumes contain phthalates, the harms of which were described earlier. Instead of using a conventional perfume, consider applying deliciously scented, all natural essential oils. One company, Florapathics (florapathics.com), has eighty-four different organic essential oils—from allspice to ylang-ylang. For more traditional perfume made with all organic ingredients, try Rich Hippie (rich-hippie.com) or Pacifica perfumes (pacifica-candles.com), which are particularly divine. For something truly elegant, Aftelier (aftelier.com) offers delicious-smelling solid perfumes in refillable sterling silver compacts.

Soaps

Most soaps on the market today are petroleum-based products that contain chemical softeners and colorants. In addition to the potential hazards of long-term chemical exposure, these products can irritate your skin and contribute to eczema and dermatitis. Natural soaps clean your skin without stripping its moisture. There are so many wonderful natural soaps available in stores, online, and at farmers' markets that it is worth shopping around for one that you love. My favorite is the Bisous de Provence Wild Rose Triple Milled Soap that has some exfoliating grit, available at Trader Joe's and online (frenchbathproducts.com). For hands, use a biodegradable soap like the fragrant bar soaps available from Pacifica (pacificacandles.com) or the liquid hand soaps from Nature's Gate (natures-gate.com).

Hair Products

Many well-known companies have produced chemical-free hair-care products. My personal favorites are the thick and creamy lavender shampoo and conditioner by Avalon Organics (avalonorganics.com). If you will be traveling for your wedding, EO (eoproducts.com) makes a set of organic travel-sized toiletries, including shampoo, conditioner, bar soap, and body lotion. For natural hairspray and gel, Kokopelli's Green Market (kokogm.com) offers a number of different eco-products. Do not be afraid to bring your own products to a hair salon. Just because someone else is doing your coif does not mean you have to use whatever is offered. And who knows, maybe when they see how fabulous you look, they will switch to greener lines.

Hair Dye

It is estimated that more than fifty million American women regularly dye their hair, and statistics from the *Journal of the National Cancer Institute* and the *International Journal of Cancer* show that women who use permanent dyes are more likely to develop diseases like non-Hodgkin's lymphoma and bladder cancer. It is hard to find a permanent dye without some known allergens, such as ammonia, peroxide, p-Phenylenediamine (PPD), and diaminobenzene, so it is best to avoid permanent dye altogether if you can. If you need long-lasting color, some dyes are better than others. Ecocolors (ecocolors.net) uses a soy and flax base and flower essences instead of chemical scents, and Naturcolor (naturcolor.com) reduces waste by allowing you to mix only what you need so you can save the rest for later.

Henna, which is made from powdered leaves of the henna plant (*Lawsonia inermis)* is a semipermanent, all-natural dye and is a great alternative. You can find henna dyes ranging from red to dark brown in most grocery stores and online. Because it covers your existing hair and does not contain any harsh chemicals, it cannot make your hair lighter, but it can enrich the color and is great for covering gray. Make sure the henna you buy is all natural—be especially careful to avoid purchasing "black henna."

HARSH HENNA

In addition to using henna to dye hair, some brides use henna to create elaborate (nonpermanent) tattoos on their hands and feet in preparation for the marriage ceremony. While natural red henna is derived from a non-toxic plant, "black henna" is actually made from p-Phenylenediamine (PPD), which can cause severe allergic reactions including blistering, itching, and permanent scarring. According to *Contact Dermatitis* by Jung et al., black henna reportedly produces an allergic reaction in 3 to 15 percent of people. If you want to use henna, make sure it is 100 percent natural, and do a test run well before the big day.

Moisturizers and Sunscreen

Nothing cures chapped winter hands like shea butter, which is made from a nut from the karate tree in West Africa. This thick, vitamin-rich cream is also renowned for hiding stretch marks, curing eczema, and reducing the appearance of scars. Nature's Shea Butter (naturessheabutter.com) offers 100 percent natural and organic versions in a wide range of scents. Their shea-based moisturizer is particularly smooth and silky.

You should also protect your skin with a daily sunscreen year-round. Juice Beauty (juicebeauty.com) makes an age-defying green apple–scented sunscreen and tinted moisturizer, and Badger (badgerbalm.com) offers a delicious cocoa-scented sunscreen in SPF 15 and SPF 30. If you forget to put it on, Badger also makes a nice-smelling after-sun body balm with cocoa butter and shea butter.

Shaving and Deodorizing

Disposable razors are (surprise, surprise) destined for the waste stream—and according to the EPA, over two billion disposable razors end up in landfills every year. Instead of choosing a disposable razor, use a good non-disposable razor, or buy a recycled/recyclable razor. Preserve (recycline.com) offers a disposable razor made from recycled plastic. When the blade is dull, you just pop it off and recycle the handle. Instead of using shaving cream, you can shave with a regular bar soap (just make sure it does not have chunks of flowers or oats in it), or use a natural shave cream, like the mint-and-calendula-scented version by Toms of Maine (tomsofmaine.com). For women's deodorant, Natures Gate's products have mild natural scents (natures-gate.com), as do Jason Natural Cosmetics's organic deodorant sticks and roll-ons (jason-natural.com). Jason's Tea Tree Deodorant Stick has a fresh, woody scent. There are lots of organic men's products as well. Aubrey Organics (aubrey-organics.com) offers a 100 percent natural Men's Stock line, including my husband's favorite, North Woods Aftershave, and Herbal Pine Deodorant.

Face and Eye Makeup

If you do not usually wear a lot of makeup, the worst thing you can do is let the salon give you a "wedding mask." You want to look like yourself on your wedding day and don't want to scare the children! To make sure you get the look you want, and to prevent tears, always do a test run at least six weeks in advance. Some makeup artists use all natural products already, but this is another great place to bring your own. For a light, all-natural foundation, try Aubrey Organics, or use tinted moisturizer from Lavera (lavera.com). Aveda (aveda.com) is a popular line, which offers organic, plant-based makeup. Some of their products even come in recycled metal compacts. For eye shadow, mascara, blush, and other cosmetics try Dr. Hauschka's holistic (organic and biodynamic) skin-care products (drhauschka.com). They also sell daily skin-care sets to make your skin silky smooth and all-natural makeup brushes.

It has become fairly common for brides who have trouble wearing contacts to get Lasik surgery before their weddings so they do not have to wear glasses down the aisle. If you choose to do this, remember to donate your old glasses (and/or nonprescription sunglasses) to an organization like New Eyes for the Needy (neweyesfortheneedy.org). It has collection centers at LensCrafters, Lions Club, and Goodwill Industries. You can also mail glasses in a padded envelope to:

New Eyes for the Needy
549 Millburn Avenue
P.O. Box 332
Short Hills, NJ 07078.

Lip Care

For soft lips, always avoid petroleum jelly, which is made from non-renewable oil and actually dries out your skin. Instead, try natural products like Ecco Bella (eccobella.com) FlowerColor lipsticks for refreshing eco-chic moisture. Another popular choice is Cargo's PlantLove botanical lipstick (available at sephora.com). They come in corn-based plastic tubes and plantable seed-paper boxes, so nothing is wasted. For a beach wedding, Juice Beauty (juicebeauty.com) sells mineral-tinted fruit-flavored lip balms with SPF 15.

Teeth

Tom's of Maine (tomsofmaine.com) toothpaste is very popular and comes in a variety of flavors, from the traditional spearmint to the more exotic cinnamon (my favorite) and anise. The tubes are recyclable and are packaged in recycled-cardboard boxes. Tom's also carries natural mouthwash and dental floss. If you want to whiten your smile, instead of chemically bleaching your teeth try a natural whitening toothpaste, like the PowerSmile line from Jason Natural Cosmetics.

Nail Care

Try to avoid conventional nail enamel. Instead, use either natural oil or a water-based nail polish, like Acquarella (acquarella polish.com). Honeybee Gardens (honeybeegardens.com) has a pretty pink nail polish that would work well as the base for a French manicure or by itself to add a little shine. They also offer a natural nail polish remover, which you can apply with an organic cotton ball or makeup round from Organic Essentials (organicessentials.com).

LEAPING BUNNIES

Although not as prevalent today as twenty years ago, a number of cosmetic companies continue to test their products on animals. I will not go into the details of animal cosmetic testing, which are pretty horrifying (for more information visit PETA.org or caring-consumer.com). The good news is that many companies have taken a pledge against animal testing. An extensive list of these companies is available at idausa.org/facts/crueltyfree.html. You can also search for products with a leaping bunny symbol at any grocery store.

Personal Products

Bleached tampons often contain irritants like aluminum, boron, alcohols, and acids, which can increase the risk of endometriosis—abnormal tissue growth that can impair fertility. As I will describe in Chapter Five, cotton bleaching is also toxic to the air, soil, and water. For unbleached pads and tampons, try brands like Seventh Generation (seventh-generation.com) or Natracare (natracare.com). For an even greener take on disposable personal-care products, you can buy washable menstrual pads from Many Moons (manymoonsalter natives.com), where reusable pads come in leopard print as well as traditional white. Do not forget that no matter how they are made, you should never flush sanitary products down the toilet. Most septic systems cannot handle them, and they often end up polluting rivers, streams, and beaches.

CHAPTER 4

Greening the Groom and Bridal Party

This chapter provides a number of creative ways to dress the groom and bridal party in stylish eco-chic attire. For the groom and groomsmen, you'll find new twists on old traditions, like renting tuxedos or buying suits that can be worn again and using an eco-friendly dry cleaner to clean the garments after the ceremony. There are also alternative options, such as having ties or jackets made from bamboo fabric or wearing a European-made hemp linen suit.

Many of the ideas presented for brides in Chapter Three also apply to bridesmaids. This chapter adds a few more dress resources and highlights ways to tie the bridal party together without requiring them to wear the same dress. By using one of the suggested alternatives, brides can have a coordinated affair while decreasing their impact on the earth and helping their friends and family save money.

MEN'S HABERDASHERY

Although a lot of wedding attention goes to the bride, grooms want to look dashing, too. Some grooms will want to wear the same thing as the groomsmen and just have a larger boutonniere. Others will want to stand out with a flashier tuxedo or a different-colored suit. However, since the differences in menswear are subtler than that of the bride and her maids, the green options in this section can be easily applied to all of the men in the bridal party.[*]

In many ways, it is easier for men to be green than it is for women, because (1) it is socially acceptable and easy to rent a tuxedo, and (2) unlike a wedding dress or classic bridesmaid dress, any suit or tuxedo can be worn again without people thinking the man is "a bit off." Whether your groom and groomsmen borrow, rent, or buy their wedding garb, there are many ways for them to be more environmentally sound.

Previously Worn Suits and Tuxedos

In addition to the traditional rental options, encourage your groom and groomsmen to explore the following possibilities.

$ Closet Comfort

Most men own at least one good dark suit. Save your groom and groomsmen the hassle and expense of buying or renting something new, and let them wear a suit they already own. For a more casual wedding, consider khakis and a polo shirt or wool pants and a white button-up shirt. Your pictures will come out better if you choose simple colors and styles, and you can always create a cohesive look by giving them matching pocket squares, ties, or boutonnieres.

$ That's What Friends Are For

If you have a friend or family member with a build similar to your fiancé's and a good wardrobe, see if you can get a loan for the big day. Make sure to have the garment cleaned and pressed before you return it. If the suit really isn't dirty, ask the dry cleaner to spot clean and press the garment to minimize the environmental impact. See the Green Dry Cleaning section

---

[*] For a list and description of men's accessory options see the Quick Guide page in the About the Book section at thegreenbrideguide.com.

in Chapter Three for more information about environmentally sound dry cleaning options.

$$ Rent a Suit, Tuxedo, or Kilt

The most popular green choice for men is to wear a rented ensemble. The only downside is the dry cleaning, which can be bad for the environment. However, even if you use a regular dry cleaner instead of a green dry cleaner, the environmental impact of renting is minimal when compared to buying something new. You can rent a tuxedo for as little as $50, and there are often specials for the groom if the other members of a bridal party rent from the same vendor. Most tuxedo rental shops also rent suits and accessories. Because tuxedo rentals are so common, it is usually easy to find a local vendor to work with. Check the yellow pages for listings and prices. The Internet is also a good tool for specialty rentals, like kilts. For a description of different jacket styles see the Quick Guide page at thegreenbrideguide.com.

$$ Secondhand Stores

You can often find nice suits and tuxedos at consignment, antique, and thrift stores that can be tailored to fit for approximately the same cost as renting. This is a particularly good option if your man is looking for a vintage style, unique fabric, or offbeat color. In addition to local stores, there are many online vintage and used-clothing outfitters. The Rusty Zipper (rustyzipper.com) has a great selection of men's suits and tuxedos from the 1960s and 1970s. American Vintage Classics (americanvintageclassics.com) also offers suits and tuxedos for under $200, including some very cool tuxedo shirts. Vintage Swank (vintageswank.com) offers stylish, more expensive tuxedos and MyOwnTuxedo (myowntuxedo.com) is a good source for contemporary looks.

$$$ Deadstock

Never-worn vintage clothing is known as "deadstock." Deadstock is generally less expensive than new clothing and is often in pristine condition. Dress That Man (dressthatman.com) is a fun source of deadstock with some wild things, like 1970s sports jackets, as well as some very classic looks.

Alternative Materials

If your fiancé wants to wear a new suit or tuxedo on your wedding day, encourage him to buy one made from a sustainable material. From light summer linen to thick natural tweed, there is a green alternative for every season.

$ Inexpensive Hemp

Fashionable hemp options are also available for men. Although some hemp suits are considerably more expensive (see "Eco-couture Hemp" later in this chapter), a few companies, like Sandstone Designs in Hemp (sandstonehemp.com), offer inexpensive, summer-weight hemp-cotton suits. For reasonably priced hemp sport coats, try Downbound (downbound.com).

$$ Custom Creations

Another option is to have a suit made from washable natural fabric, like cotton, linen, wool, hemp, or even silk. Patterns for suits are available at The Sewing Place (thesewingplace. com), as well as from Harper House (longago.com) and FolkWear (folkwear.com). A talented seamstress or tailor can make a pattern using a picture from a magazine and the man's measurements—but leave enough time for alterations. For good sources of fabric, check the National Green Pages, put out by Green America (coopamerica.org/pubs/greenpages/). You can also get natural-blend fabrics from Dharma Trading (dharma-trading.com) or Fabric Indulgence and Art Supply (fabricandart.

com), which sells hemp and organically-grown cotton clothes in a number of elegant colors.

$$$ Eco-couture Hemp

For men who appreciate high-end fashion, there are now earth-friendly designer hemp suits. The pioneering company mentioned in the previous chapter, Rawganique (rawganique. com), offers stylish hemp suits in a variety of colors. HempWorld (hempclothing.com) is another good source of elegant, dark, all-natural suits.

$$$ Eco-couture Tweed

For a winter wedding, nothing beats a warm three-piece wool suit. One company, Greenfibres (greenfibres.com), uses European organic wool from Highland sheep to make debonair jackets and waistcoats.

ACCESSORIES

Whether your men wear suits or tuxedos, they can round out their eco-conscious outfits with earth-friendly shirts, ties, shoes, cufflinks, and other accessories. For a description of common accessory styles, see the Quick Guide page at thegreenbrideguide.com.

$ Pre-owned

Some accessories, like ties, vests, and even shoes, are great to buy used. When my husband was looking for silk ties, I found "lots"—or collections—of designer ties on eBay for a dollar a piece. You can buy a "lot" of ties and let your fiancé pick his favorites. Then he can turn around and resell the rest. Gently used tuxedo shoes are another great buy and can easily be resold after the wedding at cost—which means you only pay for the shipping. Buying and selling once-worn attire like this can be even less expensive than renting, and offers you a large selection of high-end designer options.

$ Recycled Materials

For accessories like cufflinks and shirt studs, consider buying sets made from recycled materials. There are many options out there that can add a little bit of fun and creativity to the wedding without detracting from the overall elegance. For example, a quick search on etsy.com for "recycled cufflinks" yields ones made from Scrabble tiles, wine corks, and even expired transit tokens. See Chapter Nine for more ideas and resources.

$ Natural and Organic Fibers

Natural fibers like organic cotton, hemp, and tencel are soft, breathable, and environmentally sound. There are already many outfitters offering 100 percent organic cotton polos, dress shirts, and ties. You can use a general search engine like Bizrate, or buy from specialty stores, like Boll Organic (bollorganic.com). Hemp Clothing (hempclothing.com) is a great source of plain but inexpensive hemp ties.

$$ Luxury Blends

For more luxurious sustainable fabrics, look for organic silk blends and high-thread-count organic cotton. One great company for hemp-silk shirts is Grass Roots Natural Goods (grassrootsnaturalgoods.com), which has reasonably priced lightweight dress shirts. Pure Luxury Atelier (pureluxuryatelier. com) offers organic silk shirts made with tagua nut buttons that look like ivory. Tãne (taneonline.com) specializes in elegant, eco-friendly executive dress wear. For each purchase made, they plant a tree.

$$$ American-Made

You may be surprised to learn that today, 98 **percent** of American footwear is imported. As discussed in the last chapter, when you buy clothing made in the United States, you support American families and keep your dollars out of sweatshops. Buying American goods also ensures they were produced under U.S. environmental standards, which is especially important when dealing with notoriously "dirty" or chemically intensive products like leather shoes. For American-made shirts, try No Sweat apparel (nosweatapparel.com) or the All American Clothing Co. (allamericanclothing.com). For shoes, Johnston and Murphy (johnstonmurphy.com), SAS Shoemakers (sasshoes.com) and Allen-Edmonds (allenedmonds.com) all have high-quality dress shoes. Allen-Edmonds even pays return shipping when its shoes wear out, and you want them "recrafted."

$$$ Custom Creations

If you're not fond of the premade options or have a specific color or fabric in mind, you can have shirts, ties, and pocket squares custom-made. PM Organics (pmorganics.com) has a wide selection of organic fabrics sold by weight, with green options for every season. Green Sage (greensage.com/fabricstr.html) offers subtly patterned organic cotton fabrics in earth tones that are worth looking at as well. For bolder patterns, try Indika Organics (indikaorganics.com). You can find tencel (Lyocell) fabric, which is a soft fabric made from wood pulp cellulose, at Silk Road Fabrics. Finally, for comfortable and attractive tencel-hemp blends, check out Sweetgrass Natural Fibers (sweetgrassfibers.com).

BRIDESMAID DRESSES

Most bridesmaid dresses cost over $200. Then there are the additional costs of alteration, matching shoes, and jewelry. Despite brides' best intentions, most bridesmaid dresses are never worn again, either because they don't fit well; they are not the bridesmaid's taste; or they look, well, very bridesmaidy. Perhaps it is for these reasons that the practice of having perfectly matched bridesmaids is falling out of fashion. Today there are many ways to create a unified look for your bridal party that won't hurt anyone's wallet or the environment.

Instead of asking your maids to buy new dresses, let them wear something they already own in a generic color, like black or navy, or encourage them to buy a dress that has been worn before. Either option will save them a lot of money and will reduce the waste generated from producing and shipping all those new dresses. It is my experience that bridesmaids who are allowed to wear something unique feel more comfortable, are more likely to dance, and definitely harbor less resentment toward the bride. If you have your heart set on having matching maids, consider dressing them in a dress made from a natural or recycled material, which they can recycle after the wedding by selling or donating it to a worthy cause.

$ Dig in the Closet

When it came time to choose bridesmaid dresses, my fiancé and I went down to the local fabric store and put together a collection of samples of our favorite autumnal colors. I cut these strips into small squares and glued them onto cards to make pocket-sized color palettes. I sent a card to each member of the wedding party with a note asking that they wear a solid colored dress in an autumnal hue matching the card.◉ Everyone chose something different, and despite my fears about clashing, they really looked beautiful when standing together. This idea works well even if you want just one color. You can allow everyone to wear a unique shade of blue or ask for a unified black. Email a picture from a wedding site or send a crayon or a swatch of cloth. There are many ways to create a matching wedding party

---

◉ To see a picture of the card and the resulting look visit the Real Green Weddings page at thegreenbrideguide.com.

without requiring your friends and family to buy a specific dress, ensuring everyone looks great and increasing the chance those gowns will be worn again.

$ Take a Trip to the "Salv"

A huge number of bridesmaid dresses find their way to the Salvation Army and other used clothing stores. If your maids live in the area, take a field trip to the closest thrift store, and see if you can find dresses that work well together. Chances are you can put together a very pretty collection of similar or harmoniously hued dresses in no time. Afterward, anyone who does not love her dress can donate it back to the Salvation Army or sell it online, saving all but the cost of alteration.

$$ Rent a Gown

As with wedding gowns, there are now places where you can have your maids rent matching dresses. Look in your local yellow pages or online for stores like Rent A Bridal Gown (rentabridalgown.com) or L&L Rental (llrental.com).

$$$ Natural Materials

There are beautiful, colorful, quality dresses now manufactured with hemp, bamboo, organic cotton, and "fair wage" silk. Olivia Luca (olivialuca.com) offers classic bridesmaid dresses fashioned from these materials for a small premium, and Earth Speaks (earthspeaks.com) has a small selection of organic cotton dresses.

$$$ Made in the USA

One of the many problems with traditional bridesmaid dresses is the sweatshop conditions in which they are manufactured. By encouraging your maids to buy dresses designed and manufactured in the United States under fair wage conditions from companies such as Aria Dress (ariadress.com), you send a message to the dress industry that you will not support exploitative labor practices. If every bride made this choice, it would have a profound effect on the industry.

Donating Bridesmaid Dresses

No matter what type of dresses your bridesmaids wear, they can donate them to a worthy cause after the wedding. The Cinderella Project (cinderellaproject.net) collects gowns and suits and gives them to Los Angeles high-school students who are unable to afford formal wear for occasions such as prom and graduation. The Glass Slipper Project (glassslipperproject.org), based in Chicago, has a similar mission.

UNIFYING ELEMENTS

One trick that looks beautiful in photographs is to use a unifying item to tie dresses of different styles or colors together. Depending on the theme and season of your wedding, this can be anything from a pashmina to a parasol. The following are a few sustainable suggestions, but use your imagination to come up with other interesting and appropriate items.

$ Shawls, Scarves, and Kinte Cloths

A few years ago, my husband and I attended a friend's wedding in Vermont. To celebrate the groom's Ghanaian heritage, the bride had all of her maids incorporate a colorful kinte clothe into their ensemble. One wore it as a skirt, another as a headband, a third as a shawl. She used the same pattern to have ties made for the men, and the result was a beautifully coordinated party. You can buy a sustainable fabric by the yard and have something made for each member of the party, or just send your attendants the fabric and allow them to get creative. Either way, you will not be disappointed with the results! For premade fair trade wool and silk shawls from Nepal, look at Sunrise Pashmina (sunrise-pashmina.com). For animal-friendly, PETA-approved peace silk scarves, browse PETA's online catalog (petacatalog.org). For a lush hemp-silk blend wrap, Hemp Elegance (hempelegance. com) has a colorful selection.

$$ Eye Candy

Pull maids outfits together with a splash of the unexpected. Instead of giving your maids a traditional bouquet, have them carry something more exotic, like a peacock feather or a carved-tin lantern. See the Non-Flower Alternatives section of Chapter Six for a list of ideas.

$$$ Jewelry

Use the sustainable jewelry suggestions in Chapters Three and Nine to find your maids elegant matching necklaces or chandelier earrings. These items can double as thank-you gifts and can be given out at the rehearsal dinner with a personalized note.

CHILDREN

Because children grow so quickly, the chances of them being able to wear a fancy dress or miniature suit again are slim. For this reason, parents might resent shelling out $200 to have their child participate in your big day. The truth is, kids are adorable—no matter what they wear. Watching a small herd of children trying to make its way down the aisle can be a highlight of any wedding. If you want to include children, consider the following options for dressing them more sustainably.

$ Sunday Best

Especially if they come from a religious family, most children have a formal outfit they wear to church or synagogue—a "Sunday best." For little boys, this is probably a generic suit and tie. For little girls, it's usually a frilly or satiny dress. If you don't need the kids to look like carbon copies of each other, just ask them to come dressed for the occasion. They will be show-stopping adorable no matter what they wear.

$$ eBay

Tell your friends and relatives about the joys of eBay and consignment shops. Because kids' clothing turnover is so fast, many items are available that have been worn once or have not been worn at all. You can find posh three-piece suits and white communion dresses online for less than $20. As with bridesmaids, you can have the kids wear simple colors like white or black, or ask them to wear outfits in the palette of your choice.

$$ Tie Them Together

If you decide to have all the little girls wear plain white frocks and the little boys wear dark suits or khakis and a polo shirt, you can add zest to their outfits with a unifying element. For example, you can tie matching ribbons or scarves around little girls' waists or give them each a matching coronet of flowers. For little boys, add a small pocket square of color to their suits or pin richly colored boutonnieres to their lapels.

$$$ Made to Fit

If you want to have matching outfits, search for companies using sustainable fabrics like organic cotton, linen, wool, peace silk, or hemp. You can also have matching outfits made from the fabric of your choice. Just ask the kids' parents for their measurements and make sure to send them the final product a few weeks before the big day so they can make sure no further tailoring is needed.

CHAPTER 5

Say It Green with Save-the-Dates, Invitations, and Wedding Websites

The save-the-date, wedding invitation, and wedding website are the new trinity of pre-wedding correspondence. While serving slightly different functions, they all convey key information and help set the tone for your event. This chapter will walk you through creative, cost-efficient ways to create beautiful, memorable, and sustainable save-the-dates, invitations, and wedding websites. Along the way, we'll review some of the best shops, companies, and online do-it-yourself boutiques available in the marketplace today.

The rules of pre-wedding communications have changed significantly since the advent of the Internet. Depending on the size and formality of your wedding, options that were once considered only appropriate for save-the-dates (like postcards) are now perfectly acceptable for invitations. Therefore, instead of breaking this chapter up by type of communiqué, I have divided it by the method of correspondence: virtual, tangible goods, paper, and paper alternatives.

THE BASICS

Timeline

Although you can certainly buck the trend if you want, the general timeline for wedding correspondence is as follows.

As soon as you are engaged—Make phone calls, announce it on your blog, or send out a card. It's time to let your friends and family know the good news!

Six to eight months before the wedding—Send out a save-the-date. If you plan to have a shorter engagement, a save-the-date is not necessary.

Four to five months before the wedding—Make or order your invitations. Be sure to get a few extras for last-minute additions and parental archives!

Six to eight weeks before the wedding—Send out your invitations. You can send them earlier if you are planning a short engagement or if you expect to have a lot of out-of-town guests who will need time to make travel arrangements.

Three to four weeks before the wedding—The day after your RSVP deadline, you can start making phone calls to those guests who have not replied. It is good to have your RSVP deadline a week or two before you final catering deadline so you have time to track everyone down.

Less Is More

If you walk into any paper store that sells wedding invitations, you will quickly be introduced to the "wedding wardrobe." Wardrobe is an appropriate name, because most invitations are dressed in layer upon layer of unnecessary paper. Opening an invitation that features envelopes inside envelopes with layers of vellum, bows, and tissue in between feels more like participating in an archeological dig than having a glamorous experience.

Instead of an oversized, elaborate, multienveloped extravaganza, find or create a small, elegant alternative—or forgo paper entirely! By simplifying your invitation, you will save money and paper, and often end up with a more unique, more memorable design. If you are having a small wedding, ask your family to spread the word or call your guests directly. If you plan to have a short engagement (less than six months), skip save-the-dates, and send the invitations out a month ahead of schedule. For longer engagements, consider the fact that save-the-date cards are not traditional—perhaps a virtual card will do? Before you spend the time and money creating the magnets, postcards, and triple-layer invitations the wedding industry is touting these days, consider some of the green options in this chapter.

Problems with Paper

Despite the rise in Internet technology, the average American still uses 700 pounds of paper each year. To fill our annual paper demands requires over 12,000 square miles of forest. Most of the wood we use comes from virgin forests. Wood from tree farms can also be problematic, because monocultures replace natural habitat and reduce biodiversity by as much as 95 percent. Paper processing is also an extremely toxic business. In order to make paper pulp bright white, pulp mills bleach paper with chlorine, which produces extremely hazardous organochlorine compounds, including dioxins. Exposure to these chemicals can cause cancer and birth defects. One EPA study found dioxins to be three hundred thousand times more carcinogenic than DDT (the pesticide banned in the United States in 1972). These toxic chemicals not only affect the health of paper-mill workers but also are released into the environment through the paper-mill wastewater, where they poison wildlife and contaminate the water, air, and soil. The bottom line is that the process for making the "white wedding" bright white does significant environmental damage and threatens human health, so consider some of the following green alternatives.

VIRTUAL CORRESPONDENCE

If green is the new black, then virtual is the new paper. The Internet generation has come of age and so have new ways of announcing, planning, and celebrating weddings. Internet technology allows you to be creative, costs less than paper, and has the least impact on the environment. In the next few years, the virtual options will certainly continue to expand, but there are already a number of fun and creative ways to share your good news and broadcast the details of your event.

$ Ring in the Good News

The telephone, one of the most old-fashioned forms of virtual communication, is still a wonderful device for spreading good news. To announce your engagement, you can also send text messages, but nothing beats the intimacy of a personal phone call. If you plan on having a small wedding, it is entirely appropriate to forgo sending invitations and convey all of the invitation information your guests will need over the phone. Not only will this save you time and money, but it also offers a nice chance to catch up with everyone who will be at your wedding and build excitement for the big day.

CALLING ALL ENVIRONMENTALISTS

When you make those special calls, the money you spend on cell phone service can now go to help the environment. Earth Tones (earthtones.com) is a communications company that donates 100 percent of its profits to environmental organizations like

Environment America, the National Environmental Law Center, and the Toxics Action Center. They offer monthly cell phone plans with no minimum contract, and free cell phone recycling for their customers. For those of us who are locked into cell contracts, they also offer residential phone and Internet services.

$ Blog

If you are Internet savvy, a blog is a great way to announce your engagement to friends. If you have never blogged before, blogger.com can help you get a wedding blog up and running in minutes. Blogger is free and easy to use and has a number of excellent web page templates. Although I am sure the software out there will continue to get better in the next few years, Web 2.0 is a popular program for creating wedding blogs. Blogs are also a great way to organize pre-wedding parties, get feedback on your wedding ideas from your bridesmaids, and keep your friends and family updated on your planning. A quick search online will give you lots of ideas for how to maximize a wedding blog.

$ Email

Want to tell everyone about your engagement at the same time and save yourself the trouble of telling the story over and over? Send out an electronic announcement with a picture of the two of you and your story. You can post the contents of the email on your website or blog as well to make sure everyone gets to see it. Be sure you have a few days free afterward, though—because the phone calls and emails will start pouring in as soon as you hit "send."

Email also works well for save-the-dates. You can attach a link to your website or can use email as you would a paper invitation. One woman I know spent many hours creating one perfect hand-drawn invitation. She scanned it in and sent the

JPEG to almost everyone on her invite list. For the few older relatives without an Internet connection, she printed out copies of her drawing on her home printer and mailed them.

$$ E-cards and Survey Programs

Instead of sending a save-the-date postcard or paper invitation, try an e-card. Some e-card services have modest subscription fees, but you can also find e-cards that you can send for free. You can use a basic site, like Blue Mountain (bluemountain. com), for a classic card look, or use a program like Evite (evite. com) to create an interactive invitation with a built-in RSVP. You can also use a tool like SurveyMonkey (surveymonkey. com) to create an elaborate RSVP where guests can sign up for activities, share carpool information, and choose which meal they would like. Having a virtual RSVP will guarantee no one's reply card gets lost in the mail and allows you to ask for more detailed information.

A word of advice from our wedding—take your survey on a test-drive with a middle-aged relative to make sure the instructions are as clear as you think they are. We got a number of phone calls before we smoothed out all of the wrinkles. Even if your survey is perfect, you will probably need to call a few elderly relatives and delinquent friends to get a final head count. It is also worth noting that some web programs, like Evite, display the responses on the main web page and do not allow you to edit or remove them. You may not want your college drinking buddy's response up there for Mom to read, so think about paying for a service that gives you more control.

$$ Wedding Websites

Many couples these days have some form of wedding website, because they are easy to set up and are extremely convenient for conveying detailed information about travel and hotel options. With a website, you can offer many more alternatives than you would otherwise be able to, save a lot of paper, and make last-minute changes. For the few guests who are not Internet savvy, you can cover your bases by including a note on your invitation that says something like, "For more details, visit our website at ourwebsite.com, or please call (123) 456-7890."

There are many excellent, reasonably priced companies out there ready to help you set up and host your wedding web page. These companies have elegant, easy-to-use templates so that even the most inexperienced Internet user can create a beautiful and highly functional website. As a novice, I used Wedding Window (weddingwindow.com) and in minutes made a site with pictures, MapQuest directions (mapquest.com), links to local hotels, and a comprehensive schedule of events. If you want to have an easy-to-remember web address, these companies are equipped to help you buy and link to the domain of your choice. They really can't be beat. If you are a bit more sophisticated and do not need the page templates, there are companies that will host your web page for free. Just google "free wedding websites," and you will find many companies ready to help you create the perfect information portal.☺

$$$ Webcasting

With the advent of numerous do-it-yourself digital video-editing programs, it is becoming easier for couples to make their own videos. This year we received an adorable save-the-date video of a family dog wearing various billboards with the wedding information. Webcasting is a clever and memorable way to get guests' attention if you have a flare for the dramatic. You can upload videos to YouTube and email them around, or you can use a pricier and more elaborate

---

☺ For a list of ten things to include on your wedding website, visit the Quick Guide page in the About the Book section of thegreenbrideguide.com.

option of a packaged webcasting service. Sites like ourwedding cast.com offer e-engagement announcement packages that allow you to create a slideshow set to your favorite music to play alongside your engagement story. After the wedding, you can use the webcast services to upload your wedding video footage and share it with friends and family members who could not make it to your big day.

TANGIBLE CORRESPONDENCE

Instead of sending a postcard or paper-based announcement or invitation, send your guests something they will remember and enjoy. There are now many clever tangible—and even edible—products out there to help you spread your message with a splash.

$ Magnets

Although perhaps not the most sustainable option, a tasteful save-the-date magnet that features a cute picture of the two of you is always fun and will be used to hold up shopping lists on your friends' fridges for many years. If you plan to have a website, do the cursory setup (buy the web address and have a "coming soon" message, at a minimum) before you make the magnets, so you can print the wedding website along with your picture. You can have magnets professionally made from any number of online companies or can buy magnet paper for your printer and make them at home. For our wedding, I used the program Comic Life to add cartoon lettering and was able to print six magnets to a page. If you make them small enough, you can fit your magnets in thank-you card envelopes instead of the regular 4-by-6-inch size.

$$ Seed Packets and Paper

A fun way to announce a wedding in spring is with a personalized packet of organic seeds, like the ones available from Earthly Goods (earthlygoods.com). You can get preprinted and custom-made invitations on "grow-a-note" plantable seed-imbued paper at Green Field Paper Company (greenfieldpaper.com) or can make your own seed paper (see the Make Your Own Paper section later in this chapter for more information).

RAINY DAY BLUES

Take basic precautions to keep the sky from raining on your proverbial parade. When sending out packages or paper invitations, check the weather forecast to avoid rainy days. This is especially important if you plan to put your mail in a public mailbox instead of taking it to the post office, because it may sit in the box for several hours. Even if your letters and packages do not get wet directly, dampness can damage seeds, ruin chocolate, and cause ink to run.

$$ Edibles

A fun idea for a save-the-date or as a way to broadcast your wedding website is to send your guests a personalized cookie or chocolate bar. This is especially nice if you announce your plans around Valentine's Day, Easter, or Halloween, as your treats can do double duty. There are companies that will make personalized organic treats with your name and date in frosting, like Beautiful Sweets (beautifulsweets.com), which offers absolutely addictive vanilla and chocolate cookies in the shape of wedding dresses and cakes. You can also buy organic treats in bulk, put them in natural cellophane bags (which are derived from plants), and add a homemade label printed on recycled paper.

$$$ Boxed Invitations

As with all things wedding, invitations are becoming increasingly elaborate. An emerging trend is for couples to send three-dimensional boxed invitations instead of the traditional two-dimensional paper versions. There are many different kinds of boxed invitations already available, and if you are compelled to go down this route, there are a number of ways to be more sustainable. First, make sure the box itself is either made from recycled material or is something decorative that can be used again. Second, avoid disposable trinkets and bobbles, like plastic starfish, small tin rings, sequins, and rhinestones. Instead, opt for long-lasting, useful, or edible items that fit the theme of your event. For our boxed invitation, Barry and I included a magnifying glass along with personalized chocolate and organic tea.[○] Finally, use recycled or natural packing materials, like wood-scrap excelsior and non-plasticized stamps, so that all parts of the invitation can be reused, recycled, or composted. Boxed invitations can be outrageously expensive—as much as $40 per box—and they cost even more to ship. You can save money and ensure that the components are environmentally sound by buying pieces separately and constructing your treasure boxes at home.

PAPER CORRESPONDENCE

The most traditional and still most common form of invitation is the paper invitation. Even with a rise in electronic save-the-dates and online RSVP services, paper invitations are holding their ground. If you want to send a paper invitation or print paper reply cards, there are a number of ways you can achieve the classic look using sustainable products. Whether you want to create something at home or buy the most elaborate store-bought variety, there is a green option available.[○][○]

[○] For pictures see the Real Green Weddings section at thegreenbrideguide.com.
[○][○] For a list and definitions of printing terms and processes, see the Quick Guide page at thegreenbrideguide.com.

$ Double Duty

A great way to save money and paper at the same time is to have your cards serve multiple functions. For example, you can send out Valentine's Day or Halloween save-the-dates or put your thank-you note on the back of a holiday card. For traditional invitations, choose a paper and printing technique that allows you to print on both sides so that you can include maps, directions, or other useful information on the back.

THE SKINNY ON POST-CONSUMER WASTE PAPER

Not all recycled papers are the same. There are two main types of recycled paper: pre-consumer waste paper (aka regular recycled paper) and post-consumer waste paper (PCW). Most paper that says it is "recycled" is made from pre-consumer waste unless otherwise indicated. Pre-consumer waste is leftover paper from the manufacturing process. For example, when envelope patterns are cut from large sheets, the leftover sheets can be turned back into pulp and made into more paper. Although it just seems like good business practice, this is technically recycling, and the new paper is labeled "recycled." By contrast, post-consumer waste paper is made from paper that has reached its "end use," like paper that ends up in your recycling bin and is reclaimed. For obvious reasons, PCW recycled paper is preferable, so when shopping for paper, try to find stock that is made with as much PCW paper as possible.

$ Small Is Beautiful

As discussed earlier in the chapter, less can be more when you are talking about paper correspondence. If you are inclined toward paper reply cards with mini envelopes, consider opting instead for prestamped reply postcards, which is the new vogue in Europe.

You can have postcards made with your invitation design on the front or use personalized reply postcards from Of the Earth (custompaper.com). You can also make reply cards with your home printer and a good pair of scissors or a paper cutter. Just make sure the dimensions of each card do not exceed 6 x 4.25 inches, or you will have to include extra postage. Postcards on thick stock can be very chic when you add letterpressing or embellish with soy-based inks. Postcard invitations work particularly well for setting the mood for a destination wedding or a wedding set in a national park or historic building.

$$ Recycled Paper

According to Do Something (dosomething.org), an organization that educates youth about the benefits of conservation, for every ton of paper that is recycled, we save 17 trees, 380 gallons of oil, 4,000 kilowatt hours of electricity, 7,000 gallons of water, and 60 pounds of air pollution from being released into the environment. We also save 3 cubic yards of landfill space. If you want to print traditional wedding invitations and response cards, consider using one of the many businesses now offering printing on 100 percent PCW paper. You can also buy home-assembly invitation kits from companies like Twisted Limb Paper (twistedlimbpaper.com), or you can buy recycled paper and print invitations yourself.

Finish your cards off with recycled envelopes. You can find plain recycled-paper envelopes in many shapes and sizes at Treecycle (treecycle.com) and fancier recycled and handmade paper envelopes at Of the Earth (custompaper.com). For a funkier look or for a destination wedding, Good Humans (goodhumans.com) offers cool envelopes made from recycled subway maps. If you don't need your thank-you cards to match

---

To learn about common printing techniques see the Quick Guide page at thegreenbrideguide.com.

your invitations, Verde Paperie (verdepaperie.com) offers a nice selection of recycled-paper greeting cards and stationery sets.

$$ Make Your Own Paper

If you like crafts, consider printing your invitations on handmade paper. You can buy a papermaking kit, instructional video, and a number of useful papermaking books from Arnold Grummer's (arnoldgrummer.com), a family-owned and operated business based in Wisconsin. According to Kim Schiedermayer, Arnold Grummer's daughter, the thing to remember when you make your own paper is that what goes in is basically what comes out. If you want white invitations, use recycled envelopes and printer paper. You can add petals, confetti, and even thin ribbon to create beautiful, one-of-a-kind pieces. You can even make your own plantable seed paper by adding organic seeds to the mix.

$$ Print at Home

There are a number of advantages to printing your save-the-date and invitations at home: (1) it offers you complete control over the layout, paper type, size, etc.; (2) it usually saves you money; and (3) it is almost always better for the environment, because most professional print jobs use non-recyclable printing plates and toxic cleaning solvents. There are many programs out there to help you create beautiful, one-of-a-kind invitations. You can use a generic graphics program like Photoshop, Quark, or InDesign, or a specialized invitation program, like the wedding software available from Mountain Cow (mountaincow.com). There are rumors that soy-based ink cartridges will be available soon—so keep your eyes open. When you print at home, your imagination is the only limit!

$$$ Original Artwork

It's nice to make your invitation or save-the-date something that can be enjoyed for many years to come. In addition to the ideas listed under "Tangible Correspondence" and "Double Duty," you can also make a two-dimensional card your friends and family will want to frame and keep. If you are an artist, consider printing your invitation on the back of small prints of your work. Each invitation does not have to be an original piece, either. For our wedding, I watercolored a scene of the old New York Harbor taken from a map cartouche, and my fiancé scanned it into the computer. We then printed the images on watercolor paper from our home computer. I was very pleased with the result.[*] If you like this idea and are not artistically inclined, you can always commission a piece or use clip art images, like the intricate drawings available from Dover Press (doverpublications.com).

ENCOURAGE RECYCLING

If you use paper that can be recycled (e.g., not glossy, foil, plasticized, or vellum), encourage guests to recycle their invitations, programs, and wedding information packets by including a small note or recycling symbol at the bottom corner of the page or on the back. If you use paper with seeds embedded in it, make sure to direct guests' attention to the fact that the invitation can be planted.

Tree-Free Paper Alternatives

Paper made from wood pulp became popular in the 1840s; before that, paper was usually made from fiber crops like papyrus, bamboo, flax (linen), and hemp. As concerns about industrial papermaking have grown, so has the popularity of "tree-free" paper. Today there are many beautiful and interesting paper alternatives, which can be manufactured without the use of harsh chemicals.

---

[*] You can see a picture of our invitation in the Real Green Weddings section at thegreenbrideguide.com.

$ Leaves, Shells, and Unexpected Sources

Papers made from traditional materials like banana leaves, corn stalks, and bamboo are now readily available online from websites like Creative Papers Online (handmade-paper.us) and Langdell Paper (langdellpaper.com). You can find many beautiful colors and textures to help you create a truly organic look. For the more adventurous, you can even find paper made from dirt or elephant dung in every color, available at Rainbow Gifts-USA (rainbowgifts-usa.com).

$$ Recycled Cotton

There are many paper products on the market that are actually made from cotton, including vellum and "rag" paper. Large invitation companies, like Oblation Papers and Press (oblation papers.com), now offer classic letterpress invitations on recycled-cotton paper, a much greener choice.

$$$ Fabric

When I was looking for a non-traditional invitation for my wedding, I came across an invitation silk-screened on white fabric and sent to guests rolled up in an ornamental scroll. If you are crafty, you can buy organic cotton and a chemical-free screen-printing kit, like the one available from EZScreenPrint (ezscreenprint.com), and make cloth invitations at home. If you would prefer a paper invitation but like the idea of using cloth, you can send your invites in a beautiful, reusable cloth envelope.

Additional Considerations

In addition to using recycled or tree-free natural papers, there are other things you can do to make you invitations even more sustainable.

$ Stamps

The most environmentally sound way to stamp invitations is probably to print the postage directly onto the envelope with a prepaid-postage machine. The problem is that the time-stamped ink mark is not very romantic. Many couples are now opting for personalized stamps (with their picture or the family dog), "Love" stamps, or special-edition "wedding" stamps available at the post office. The problem with these is that they are printed on plastic and are sold on non-recyclable plastic backing. For a truly green option that looks cool and will save you money, buy unused, or "mint," stamps on eBay. Decorating the front of your invitations with a handful of small-increment vintage stamps in this way creates a beautiful, exotic effect.

Vintage stamps are usually sold in "lots" and are often offered at a fraction of their face value. A two-cent stamp from 1930 is worth two cents today, so you don't have to worry about adjusting for inflation—just count out the postage you need and stick it on. Non-plasticized postage is better for the environment, and you can use a glue stick or a concoction of flour and water to adhere worn-out stamps. If you want the convenience of plasticized stamps, consider buying stamps for a cause, like the breast cancer stamps.

$$ Botanical Embellishments

I have received several invitations in the last few years containing faux or plasticized botanical elements. If you want to include flowers or ferns on your invitation, there are two ways to be more sustainable. You can buy paper already imbued with leaves, seeds, and petals, or you can add a small botanical embellishment, like the dried and pressed flowers available at Preserved Gardens (preservedgardens.com), to a regular invitation. Simply use a little white glue or a glue stick to attach the flowers. When buying dried flowers from retailers be sure to ask if they sell organic or pesticide-free varieties. It is also easy to pick and press your own flowers using a premade press or paper towels and a heavy book.

$$$ Inks

It's not just paper selection that impacts the environmental footprint of your invitation—it's the ink you choose as well. Most inks are petroleum based, which means they are made from non-renewable resources and are usually shipped from overseas. The good news is that the number of companies using green alternatives is on the rise. For an example of preprinted letterpress invitations using soy ink, see Mariella Designs (mariella designs.com). If you want to print your own design, ask around to find printers in your area that use soy or vegetable inks, or consider a company that works nationally, like GreenerPrinter (greenerprinter.com), that prints with soy inks on 100 percent PCW paper and has worked with companies like Whole Foods and Equal Exchange. Watch for soy-ink cartridges for your home printer, which are currently in development, and always recycle cartridges when they run out of ink or toner.

RECYCLE YOUR INK CARTRIDGES

Ink cartridges take hundreds of years to decompose in landfills and can easily be recycled. You can find drop off points at computer and office supply stores, and companies like Hewlett Packard offer free postage-paid envelopes for you to return old cartridges from home. Some companies, like FreeRecycling.com and the eCycle Group (ecyclegroup.com), will even pay you to collect certain types of cartridges for them. There are also a number of programs, like the Staples Recycle for Education program (staplesrecyclefored.com), that reward schools for collecting empty ink or toner cartridges. These programs are great, because they raise awareness about the benefits of recycling while providing much-needed funding for school programming and improvements.

CHAPTER 6

Gathering the Green Flowers

Open any bridal magazine, and you will quickly discover that along with finding the perfect wedding dress, finding the right flowers is a top concern for many brides. From the bridal bouquet to floral arrangements in the restrooms, the average couple spends over $2,000 on flowers. "What could be more naturally beautiful or *green* than a floral arrangement?" you might ask. Well, unfortunately, there are lots of problems with conventionally grown flowers.

First there are the environmental concerns. About 60 percent of the flowers available in the United States are imported, and because flowers are not eaten, the government does not regulate the levels of pesticide residue on imported blooms. Customs agents are, however, concerned about invasive pest species, so there is an incentive for growers to heavily spray their flower crops with pesticides and fungicides before shipping. According to the Pesticide Action Network North America (panna.org), most growers rely on methyl bromide, which is a chemical that depletes the ozone layer. With each watering, pesticide residues are washed into rivers and streams, polluting the aquatic habitat and contaminating drinking-water supplies, both in the country where they are grown and again here, when florists rinse the flowers before arranging them.

In addition to environmental degradation, conventional flower production threatens the health of flower-farm workers. According to the *New York Times*, 60 percent of flower-farm workers—the majority of whom are women in South America— suffer adverse health effects from their jobs, including headaches, nausea, blurred vision, and higher rates of miscarriage. This is not surprising, when you learn that flowers are the most pesticide-intensive crop in the world. Clearly, a rose is not always rose.

The good news for an eco-conscious bride is that there are many ways to create gorgeous and sustainable floral arrangements. This chapter offers ideas for both the ceremony and reception, but you should feel free to mix and match according to your taste and vision. If you plan to use a florist, use the sustainability worksheet at the back of this book to help you find a vendor whose values and work ethic will reflect your own.

THE DIRT ON FLOWERS

Organic Flowers

Organic flowers are grown as nature intended—without the use of chemical pesticides, fungicides, or petroleum-based fertilizers. By purchasing organic flowers you not only support a better way of farming, you keep those chemicals from polluting air, water, and wildlife, as well as from poisoning farm workers and their families. There are many places to find organic flowers, including local food co-ops, produce stands, nurseries, farmers markets, and health-food stores.

You can also buy (or have your florist buy) organic flowers online from one of the companies certified by Veriflora (veri-flora.com). For example, Organic Style (organicstyle.com) has a wonderful selection of premade bouquets with organic roses, irises, and calla lilies. California Organic Flowers (california organicflowers.com) is a good source for colorful blooms like anemones, narcissus, peonies, sunflowers, and dahlias. It also offers fall essentials, like broom corn, pumpkin peppers, and chrysanthemums. Its flowers are available on a seasonal basis (another hallmark of sustainability), so be sure to check the flower calendar on the website before ordering.

Local/Seasonal Flowers

When you buy flowers that were grown locally, you are supporting local business as well as eliminating the environmental impact of having to pack and ship flowers thousands of miles. Seasonal flowers are flowers that can be grown outside without the shelter of energy sucking greenhouses. To find flower farms in your area, ask your local chamber of commerce, or search for "flowers" by zip code in the database at Local Harvest (localharvest.org).

Forcing Bulbs

In addition to growing your own flowers from seed in your garden, with a little pre-planning you can grow flowers "off season" by forcing bulbs. Forcing is really a form of tricking a bulb into thinking that it is spring. The easiest way to do this is to buy bulbs in the fall and plant them according to the package directions directly into the pots you want to use. Water them and stick them somewhere cold—ideally between 35 and 45 degrees—for eight to twelve weeks. A cool cellar, an outdoor shed or garage, or an unheated pantry usually does the trick. Most bulbs can also be stored in paper bags in a freezer. Move the pots to well-lit windowsills about four weeks before the big day. Keep the soil moist until the bulbs produce flowers.

With this technique, you can have beautiful homegrown spring flowers such as narcissus, lilies, miniature iris, tulips, and daffodils at a winter wedding. These live plants also make delightful centerpieces. You can add live ivy, available during the late fall in most parts of the country, to the pots around the base of the plants for a more natural effect. It is worth noting that some bulbs do not need to be cooled and can therefore be grown more quickly. For more information on forcing, I recommend buying one of the many good books on the topic, such as *Forcing, Etc.: The Indoor Gardener's Guide to Bringing Bulbs, Branches & Houseplants into Bloom,* by Katherine Whiteside. If you want to give forcing a try but are worried about the timing or results, you can always have an order with the florist "on hold" as a backup plan.

Simplicity

Sometimes simple arrangements are the most elegant and most memorable. I still recall the flowers at a friend's wedding a few years ago. They had six or seven glass vases of varying shapes and height, each holding a few sprigs of different species of pale green flowers. It was spare, modernist, and extremely beautiful. The new trend of carrying a single calla lily down the aisle is another example of an elegant minimalist aesthetic.

You can also switch things up with bountiful flowers in some parts of the wedding and streamlined flowers in others. For our wedding in October, we used elaborate bouquets of colorful seasonal blooms, including hydrangea, dahlias, poke weed, and other common garden-variety flowers, in antique silver teapots for the rehearsal dinner. For the reception, my husband made table fountains using glass vases, battery-operated pumps, and river stones. We surrounded them with simple marsh grasses.⊚ In addition to creating visual interest, you can save a lot

---

⊚ For pictures of the bouquets and table arrangements from our wedding, see the Real Green Weddings section at thegreenbrideguide.com.

of money by paring down the floral extravagance. The imaginative use of sustainably grown and harvested flowers can bring out the very best the florist has to offer.

FINDING A FLORIST

Unless you are having a very small wedding, it is advisable to have a professional florist in charge of ordering and arranging the flowers for you. The easiest way to ensure your flowers are sustainably sourced is to find a florist who already has a relationship with local farms or wildflower merchants. However, any good florist should be able to accommodate your request for seasonal, organically grown flowers, and you can always buy the flowers yourself and hire someone just to make the arrangements. Use the sustainability worksheet in the back of this book to compare florists and to get them thinking about green options. You should also look at thegreenbrideguide.com's Quick Guide page in the About the Book section for a list of ten things to include in your florist contract.

Asking florists to show you something similar to what they will make for you is a good way to be sure you will be happy with what you get. However, nature is not always cooperative in producing the precise shade or color of a specific flower. If you must have white flowers, pick varieties that only grow in white. Similarly, if scent is important to you, make sure to have the florist include herbs or spicy plant materials, such as flowering sage, scented clover, jasmine, and lavender, in the arrangements. Organic flowers make a big difference for scent, because many of the non-organic plants have been bred for looks and transportability instead of smell. Many florists now spray flower scents onto the plants—adding yet another layer of unregulated chemicals to the mix.

Other Florist Materials

It is a common practice for florists to use non-biodegradable or petroleum-based materials, like wire and nylon ribbon, to hold cut flowers together. Instead of wiring your bouquet, ask you florist to use biodegradable ribbon, like the kind available from Paporganics (paporganics.com) or Cream City Ribbon (creamcityribbon.com). You can also use cotton butcher's twine, raffia, hemp, leaves, or even feathers. If you want to keep things simple, you can hold flowers in a basket or carry a single unbound stem. For corsages, ask your florist to use reusable posy holders instead of florist tape.

CEREMONY FLOWERS

Flowers are a wonderful way to create a glamorous and romantic ambiance for your ceremony and a unified look for your bridal party. There are two ways to use this section to make your flowers "green." You can read through it and see which ideas grab you, or you can spend some time browsing through magazines, bridal-flower books, and flower collections on websites like The Knot (theknot.com), and then come back and find the green version of what you like best. Either way, there are many different eco-conscious choices available and a green option to match any style.

Bouquets

It is very common for brides and bridesmaids to carry bouquets of flowers (non-floral alternatives are discussed later in this chapter). The following are green options for any bouquet style.

$ Single Stems

According to the Wedding Report, couples spend almost $500 on the bride's and bridesmaids' bouquets for their wedding. You can cut your cost to a fraction of that and save resources by having everyone in your party carry a single perfect stem. Calla lilies are the most popular single-stem flower, but you can also use irises, roses, tulips, birds-of-paradise, or any other flower with large-enough petals to be seen from a few rows back.

$ Wildflowers

Wildflower populations are very delicate. Unlike cultivated plants, wildflowers must compete with grasses, trees, and other species for sun, water, and soil nutrients. Although nothing seems greener than walking into a field of wildflowers and harvesting them the day before your wedding, you can actually do quite a bit of damage by disrupting their established niches and seeding patterns. Instead of harvesting your flowers from the wild, grow regional species yourself from seed, harvest from your own or a friend's garden, or buy them from a local grower. To find out which seed mix is appropriate for your geographic region, see the American Meadows website (americanmeadows. com). Classic wildflowers in nearly all American gardens include wild carrot (aka Queen Anne's Lace) and yarrow (often white or yellow), both of which look nice in wedding bouquets.

KEEPING BLOOMS FRESH

If you want to include flowers from your garden, cut them the day before the wedding and place them in water in the fridge, covered loosely with a plastic bag. Be sure to take all the fruit out of the fridge first because fruit releases ethylene, a ripener that will make the flowers wilt. You can transport flowers to your wedding site in coolers with ice and water. I heard about one couple who took a honeymoon in Hawaii before the wedding and brought all of the flowers for their wedding back in a cooler on the plane!

$$ Dried Flowers

Incorporating dried flowers into your bouquet can be extremely beautiful and will allow you to collect flowers months or even years in advance. The general rule is that the faster flowers dry and the darker the environment they dry in, the better their color will be, so you should place fresh-cut flowers or branches upside down in a warm, dry, well-ventilated place, like an attic. Once they are dried, put the flowers in a sealed paper bag or box so that they keep their fresh look and do not collect dust. There are hundreds of species that dry well and excellent books on how to dry and how to arrange dried flowers available on Amazon. You can also get a wonderful selection of pre-dried, pesticide-free flowers from Dried Flowers Direct (driedflowersdirect.com).

$$$ Classic Bouquets

It is traditional for the bride to carry a large bouquet and the bridesmaids to carry smaller bouquets. Bouquets come in many different styles (see the Quick Guide page at thegreenbrideguide. com) and can be made up of virtually any combination of flowers. Use the sourcing suggestions above to find organic, local, and seasonal options. For a winter wedding, consider carrying a cluster of evergreen branches—which can be an extremely elegant seasonal alternative. Fresh aromatic herbs, like rosemary and sage, can stand alone as a boutonniere or add a beautiful look and fragrance to any bouquet. You can also buy premade "charity bouquets" from Organic Style (organicstyle.com) which support charities like the National Wildlife Federation (nwf.org), Women for Women (womenforwomen.org), and Amnesty International (amnesty.org).

$$$ Silk Flowers

Silk is green in the sense that it is a natural substance that is biodegradable. However, many silk flowers are actually petroleum-based, and because silk comes from worms, the traditional harvesting process is pretty gruesome. Realistic silk flowers can also be very expensive, so you may want to think twice before buying faux flowers. That said, silk flowers (or dried flowers) can work well in summer, where high temperatures can wilt conventional wedding flowers, like roses, very quickly. The nice thing about silk flowers is that you can bring them home and use them to decorate after the ceremony, and even if you have a "black thumb," they will still look great on your twenty-fifth wedding anniversary. Watch out for "toss" bouquets made from faux flowers (a common practice, because they are lighter), which tend to be cheaply made and quickly thrown away.

NON-FLOWER ALTERNATIVES

In addition to traditional floral arrangements, there are a number of items you and your bridal party can carry down the aisle alone or incorporate into bouquets to create a beautiful and intriguing effect.

$ Feathers

Instead of flowers, consider having your bridesmaids carry long luxurious ostrich or peacock feathers. Ostrich feathers are a lovely, natural, biodegradable touch for a white wedding but are not appropriate for vegetarians, because they are a by-product of the ostrich-meat industry. However, according to the staff at Deer Hill Ranch in California (deerhillranch.org), which runs humane-farming education programs for at-risk youth, peacocks shed their feathers naturally after mating season, so even vegans can enjoy their beauty!

$ Bells

For our wedding, we had the little girls carry baskets of petals from our extra dahlias and the little boys carry bells.[◉] It was really nice to have them herald us down the aisle. If you decide

[◉] See pictures in the Real Green Weddings section at thegreenbrideguide.com.

to incorporate bells into your wedding—especially if you want kids to carry them—make sure there is an adult posted near the end of the aisle to collect them. You do not want your vows to have to compete with the ringing.

$$ Parasols or Fans

Who wouldn't want to carry an elegant parasol or fan down the aisle? Pamela's Parasols (pamelasparasols.com), which has been featured in *Martha Stewart Weddings* and *Modern Bride*, offers fabulous bamboo umbrellas in sixteen colors. They also sell unadorned parasols and bamboo fans, which can be personalized with water-based paints. These are perfect for a spring or summer wedding, adding a touch of romantic whimsy. They also make nice keepsakes for your attendants after the wedding.

$$$ Lanterns

Lanterns are the perfect bridesmaid accessory for a dusky wedding or a wedding under the forest canopy. You can now find intricate handheld lanterns made from recycled tin, iron, and glass. Lanterns are also good items to find from fair trade catalogs or antique dealers, and because they have become rather popular, you can often find sets of lightly used Moroccan tin lanterns on eBay for a steal.

Aisle Style

As you will see in Chapter Eight, there are many different ways you can beautify your ceremony. In addition to creating a sense of place with your layout and decor, you can use flowers, plants, and wood-based items to really bring your ceremony to life.

$ Tiki Torches and Palm Fronds

For a beach wedding, it is fun to use bamboo tiki torches and palm fronds to play up the tropical theme. You can get matching

---

You can find a large selection of parasols and fans in the Eco-Products section of thegreenbrideguide.com.

bamboo table torches to carry the look into the reception. If open flames are not permitted, there are solar tiki torches available from Amazon and from Solar Home (solarhome.org). If you don't have a place to reuse tiki torches and would prefer to rent them, check out the American Rental Association (ararental.org).

$ Buckets of Cut Flowers or Herbs

To spruce up your aisle, hang or place buckets of cut flowers or herbs at the end of each row. You can get a flower-cone pattern online and make your own cones. Add a piece of natural ribbon or hemp string to hang them off the end of the pews or on the last chair. If you fill them with aromatic herbs like lavender and rosemary, it will make the entire place smell delicious.

MONEY-SAVING TIP

Instead of putting a floral arrangement at the end of every row or pew, place them on alternate rows. You will get the same effect for half the cost.

$$ Trees and Branches

In addition to topiaries, you can often rent, or buy and resell, small trees from a local nursery. For a winter wedding, you can also get a wonderful effect by placing branches from dormant flowering trees (like cherry, apple, peach, forsythia, flowering quince, redbud, red hawthorn, and dogwood) in warm water for a few days before the ceremony—which will make the leaves and flowers bloom. Use the branches around the pole for your canopy, or place them in tall vases along the aisle to create a winter paradise.

$$ Wreaths

Wreaths are particularly nice for fall and winter weddings and can be used to decorate the ends of pews or the main doors to the church. You can find organic evergreen wreaths at Organic Style (organicstyle.com), lavender wreaths from HoodRiver Lavender (lavenderfarms.net), and colorful dried-flower wreaths that support homeless and low-income women from Woman's Organic Flower Enterprise (homelessgardenproject.org).[*]

$$$ Topiaries

The word *topiary* comes from the Latin word *topiarius,* or ornamental gardener. Topiary is the art of sculpting trees and shrubs a la Edward Scissorhands. But not all topiaries are of dinosaurs and deer—most wedding topiaries look more like perfect trees and can be constructed out of cut flowers. They are often used to create an entrance to the aisle, to frame the ceremony, or at the doors to a church or synagogue. You can usually rent topiaries from florists, garden stores, or landscapers. Look in the phonebook under plants, interior design, leasing, and maintenance.

RECEPTION FLOWERS

According to the Wedding Report, the average couple spends about 65 percent of the flower budget ($1,300) on flowers for the reception. There are many creative ways to save money and to decrease your impact on the environment when planning the decor for your reception. In addition to the suggestions for cut flowers above, you can use live plants; recycled, natural, or reusable containers; and a host of sustainable non-floral alternatives.

See if you can recycle the plant material you already have. Can your aisle decorations become decorations for the tables at the reception? Can you reuse the flowers from the rehearsal dinner for the reception or a brunch? Every time you can make

---

[*] Today you can even find wreaths made from recycled fabrics and other surprising materials. See the Eco-Products section of thegreenbrideguide.com for more ideas.

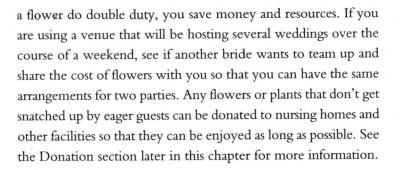

a flower do double duty, you save money and resources. If you are using a venue that will be hosting several weddings over the course of a weekend, see if another bride wants to team up and share the cost of flowers with you so that you can have the same arrangements for two parties. Any flowers or plants that don't get snatched up by eager guests can be donated to nursing homes and other facilities so that they can be enjoyed as long as possible. See the Donation section later in this chapter for more information.

Live Plants

Cut flowers are beautiful, but they have to be arranged, which takes time and costs money. Live plants offer a nice alterative, because they are simple to set up, are equally beautiful, and make nice favors or gifts after the wedding. The following are just some of the live plants that work well at weddings. Ask your local garden center about other hardy species that travel well.

$ Succulents

As someone not keen on watering plants more than once a week, I have fallen in love with succulents. There are many different varieties, each with its own charm, and you can create a pretty centerpiece by clustering a number of small, potted succulents together. For an amazing natural look, pot several succulents in burl wood bowls or mango wood bowls, which are usually crafted from the wood of mango trees that have ceased producing fruit.

$ Bamboo

Small pots of "lucky bamboo" (*Dracaena sanderiana*) have become a reception favorite at Asian-inspired weddings. Lucky bamboo is nice, because it is usually grown hydroponically, so there is no messy soil to spill on the tablecloths or to deal with during transport. As lucky bamboo is a non–native species, make sure your guests know not to plant it outside.

$ Branches

As discussed earlier, you can force branches in winter (by cutting and placing them in very warm water for several days) or use flowering branches in spring to create tall dramatic arrangements. When combined with dried flowers like statice or evergreen cuttings, flowering branches can make vivid and beautiful winter centerpieces. Small branches can also be used in ikebana-style arrangements.

$$ Herbs

Herbs are nice, because you can grow these at home from seed if you start a few months ahead of time. Put a few different types of herbs at every table with a small sign encouraging guests to take them home afterward. You can include your favorite herb recipes (rosemary bread, pesto pasta, etc.) on the back of the menu card.

$$ Flowering Plants

Common flowering houseplants can also make attractive table decor. African violets (*Santa paulia*) in a basket are very charming for a country wedding; ferns work well for a natural look; zinnias create a colorful splash in summer and look great even in low bowls; and pepper plants, with their tiny red, orange, and yellow fruits, are clever additions to any Southwestern-themed affair.

$$$ Evergreens

Place potted evergreens in beautiful ceramic planters or wicker baskets. After the reception, your friends and family can plant these trees in your honor in their yards.

$$$ Terrariums

Perhaps the coolest new addition to reception decor is the use of terrariums. Like bonsai imitating life-sized trees, terrariums create miniature worlds for your guests to explore. You can make your own using glass cookie jars, dirt, pebbles, rocks, moss, succulents, shells, and action figures—really anything that inspires you. You can take it to the next level by including lizards, snails, or hermit crabs for a "wild" feel—just make sure they are transported carefully and are sent to good homes following their starring roles in your centerpieces. Many florists now offer their own versions of a terrarium as well, so be sure to ask around if it is something you are interested in.

Containers

Procuring sustainably grown flowers and plants is important, but the way you present them makes a difference as well. A lot of the materials florists use to hold flowers in place cannot be composted, rendering the post–ceremony or reception cleanup a much more daunting task. Ask your florist to make some of the following changes.

Foam Folly. Green floral foam (aka oasis) is a popular medium for florists to use to create centerpieces of cut flowers, but floral foam is not compostable and not reusable—which means it ends up in the trash. Ask your florist about using small rocks, dried beans (if the flowers do not need water) or marbles instead. These options are nice because in addition to holding the flowers down, they can provide a splash of color if presented in clear glass vases. To see examples, visit the Real Green Weddings section of thegreenbrideguide.com.

Avoid Plastic. Although most plastic containers are technically reusable, when they contain wilting flowers, there is a temptation to chuck the entire lot. Instead, opt for recycled or reusable vessels like the following:

$ Cans

Vintage-inspired peach cans or small tomato-soup cans can add country charm and a homemade feel to a wedding. Ask your friends and family to start collecting them early so that you have plenty to choose from.

$$ Mason Jars

Mason jars are another great option, since they are cheaper than most vases and can be reused again for at-home canning or as rustic drinking glasses.

$$$ Vintage Silver or China Vases

Pull out what you already own, cruise thrift shops, consignment stores, and eBay, and put together a collection of interesting antique items. For our rehearsal dinner, we borrowed and bought twenty antique silver pitchers, tea kettles, and creamers and filled them with plushy autumnal bouquets. The effect was charming. You can give the antiques away after the wedding or resell them online.

Unexpected Treasures. A great way to make your reception memorable is to use unexpected items in the decor. Instead of traditional vases, you can use water-holding items like rain boots (buy them in your bridesmaids' sizes so they can take them home) or large seashells. Traveling in Egypt, we often saw flowers and candles displayed in intricately carved, hollowed-out eggplants, pumpkins, and seasonal gourds. Unusual containers like these can stand alone or become part of a larger themed display.

Donating Flowers after the Wedding

If your experience is anything like mine, there may not be a single vase left after your wedding, let alone flower. If allowed to take them, many guests will happily cart your arrangements away. However, if you do have leftover arrangements, you need to have a plan in place for their disposal. Ideally, you can have someone from your party or one of your vendors drop off unwanted arrangements at a local nursing home, hospital, or care facility that will appreciate them. Corsages, boutonnieres, and bouquets should be disassembled; organic flowers should be composted; non-organic flowers should be thrown away; and the holders should be given back to the florist (or cleaned and stored so that you can reuse or resell them). At the end of a long day, cleanup crews who want to go home often throw everything away, so it is essential that you have a plan and someone to implement it arranged ahead of time.

CHAPTER 7

Going Green— Transportation and Guest Comfort

A lot of wedding planning is coordinating transportation and trying to anticipate your guests' needs. How extensive your plans must be depends on the season, timing, and location of your wedding. The good news is you do not have to reinvent the wheel. This section walks through some of the many green transportation options available to you and offers creative ideas for how to keep your guests happy in (almost) any climate.

TRANSPORTATION

According to the Wedding Report, about 75 percent of couples travel to and from their wedding in a limousine (average cost $674), but there are many alternative forms of transportation that are more fun, more memorable, and better for the environment.

Car Options

Cars, trucks, and buses are the leading producers of air pollution in the form of smog and carbon dioxide, according to the EPA. Smog irritates eyes and causes respiratory problems like asthma, and carbon dioxide leads to global warming. Every gallon of gasoline burned releases 19.4 pounds of carbon dioxide into the atmosphere. While you may not think the few miles you will travel to and from your wedding will make a difference, imagine the impact if every bride and groom chose a form of eco-travel—it would literally save hundreds of thousands of tons of CO_2 from entering the atmosphere. Furthermore, going to and from your wedding is a symbolic journey, and your guests will notice and think about the fact that you chose a greener option.

$ Public Transportation

In addition to being cost-effective and environmentally sound, taking public transportation in full wedding regalia must be a blast. The oohs and ahhs, the smiles and laughs, the sheer amount of attention and excitement would be electrifying. It's probably the closest thing to celebrity we mere mortals can experience. As an added bonus, trolley cars, buses, and subway systems all lend themselves to unique, arty photographs.

$ Carpool

Cars produce almost the same amount of pollution whether they are carrying one passenger or five. By carpooling to and from your ceremony, you decrease the total amount of pollution your wedding generates while enjoying the company of friends and family. Help your guests carpool as well by setting up a ride board on your website or by using a service like TripHub (triphub.com), which allows guests to share maps, itineraries, and travel plans. You can also resort to old-fashioned methods and designate a friend to help coordinate rides. If you plan to use a limo service, ask your attendants to congregate in one place to reduce the amount of driving required to shuttle them to and from the ceremony.

$$ Car Share

Car sharing programs are popping up in major cities across the United States as a clever, flexible way for people to rent cars for short periods of time. These programs are designed to eliminate the need for personal cars, thereby decreasing the waste associated with producing, buying, and maintaining thousands of personal vehicles. Most car sharing programs, like Flexcar (flexcar.com), charge a flat per-hour rate that covers gas and insurance. Unlike regular rental cars, cars are picked up and dropped off all over many U.S. cities, and you can reserve the one closest to you. When you become a member of a car sharing program, you are given a card that is used to start the rental car and to fill the tank with gas. It is extremely clever and convenient, and your membership is good in any participating city, so you can use the program when you travel. To discover which services are available where you live or where you are having your wedding, CarSharing.net offers an updated list alphabetized by city.

$$ Bus and Trolley

If you have a lot of friends or family coming from a specific area or need to transport guests from a ceremony site to a reception venue and back, consider hiring a bus or van to move everyone en masse. If you provide snacks and drinks on board, a wedding bus can be a highlight for you and your guests. See if you can find companies willing to use biodiesel. Another fun option is a trolley. Elegant Trolleys (eleganttrolleys.com) in Chicago offers complete wedding packages, and the Great American Trolley Co. (gatrolley.com) services all of New Jersey and parts of Delaware. If you can find a company that has electric trolleys, it's even better.

$$$ Rent a Hybrid or Alternative-Fuel Vehicle

Instead of renting a limo, rent a hybrid vehicle, which gets better gas mileage by using a combination of gasoline and electric power. Or rent a vehicle that uses clean-burning natural gas or plant-derived ethanol. If you live in California or Arizona, EvRental (evrental.com) rents hybrid vehicles like the Toyota Prius and the Honda Civic. In Los Angeles, Evo Limo (evolimo.com) is a car service that uses converted, clean-burning natural-gas Chevy Suburban SUVs to chauffer

eco-conscious couples around town. If you're lucky enough to live on Maui or are having a destination wedding, Bio-Beetle (bio-beetle.com) rents adorable biodiesel VW Beetles, Golfs, Jettas, Jeeps, and more. For other parts of the country, Enterprise (enterprise.com) now carries Priuses at some locations. This is a fast-growing market, so make sure to check online for new offers in your area!

A Carbon-Neutral Entrance

Depending on where your wedding is and how far you are staying from the ceremony site, you may be able to take a more creative form of green transportation. Make a zero-emissions entrance with some of the following options.

$ Bicycle

If you're an athletic couple, it's wonderfully fun to arrive at and/or leave the ceremony on bikes (or a bicycle built for two). Take it a step further by buying (or registering early for) an even greener bike, like ones made from bamboo by Calfee Design (calfeedesign.com) or Bike Bamboo (bikebamboo.com), or a foldable (and highly transportable) bike, like the ones by Birdy (birdybike.com). If a bike that transforms into a suitcase intrigues you, get your hands on the new Skoot. For a good list with links to every imaginable type of bicycle, see Electro Ride Bikes and Scooters (electric-bikes.com). If you already own a bike you love, you can "bio-bling" it with a new set of impenetrable, puncture-proof, recyclable polyurethane tires from Greentyre (greentyre.com).

$$ Boat

Boats are fun and romantic. If you are getting married at the water's edge, consider renting a rowboat or sailing to and from your ceremony. For a moment of privacy between the ceremony and reception, you and your husband can go out to the middle of the lake or a few hundred feet off shore. Imagine how cool it would be to look back and see all of your friends and family gathered together at the water's edge—and you'll have absolutely beautiful photographs!

$$$ It's Electric!

Electric vehicles are significantly more environmentally friendly than cars that run on gasoline or diesel. Even when you factor in the emissions from the power plants they derive their energy from, electric vehicles put out one-tenth of the pollution and keep the air quality at street level cleaner, because they do not release any smog. A number of companies now rent small electric cars or scooters; look in the Yellow Pages or online for locations near you.

$$$ Horses

For a western- or period-themed wedding, arrive on horseback. If you want to keep yourself pristine but want the fairy-tale romance of a horse, arrive in a horse-drawn carriage or sleigh. Either way you will make a splash with eco-style.

$$$ Skis

Having a mountain wedding in winter? Why not arrive (or better yet make your getaway) on skis, snowboards, or sleds? It's a great way to let the adventure of marriage begin.

Carbon Offsetting

Most vehicles (whether planes, trains, or automobiles) burn petroleum and release carbon dioxide, a greenhouse gas, into the atmosphere. According to the American Public Transportation Association (apta.com), transportation generates 33 percent of the total greenhouse-gas emissions in the United States and produces 6.9 million metric tons of CO_2 annually. Most of that CO_2 comes from cars and light trucks (aka personal vehicles). Trying to reduce your carbon footprint is very important, and you can calculate your footprint and learn about ways to reduce it at Carbon Footprint (carbonfootprint.com), a UK-based company, or on Al Gore's *An Inconvenient Truth* website (climatecrisis.net). Portovert (portovert.com) has also partnered with Native Energy to create a wedding-day-specific calculator (nativeenergy.com/pages/portovert/168.php?afc=portovert).

In addition to trying to reduce your consumption and the carbon footprint of your wedding, you can also "offset" the carbon your wedding adds to the atmosphere in a few different ways. The number of companies offering carbon-offsetting programs is rapidly expanding, so be sure to shop around before selecting the program that is best for you. If you're not sure which type of offsetting you want to participate in, consider doing what my husband and I did and create a diversified "carbon portfolio," putting some money into each of the different offset options. Whatever you choose, make sure to let your guests know about the carbon offsetting by including a small note on your program or inside the seating cards.

$ Tree Planting

Tree planting is the most popular form of carbon offsetting. Trees pull carbon (in the form of carbon dioxide) from the atmosphere and convert it to biomass (aka turn it into more trees). When trees die, they decompose and that carbon, instead of reentering the atmosphere, becomes part of the soil. When you buy trees to offset your carbon, you are planting (by proxy) the number of trees needed to absorb your emissions. Planting trees also has other benefits for the environment, as trees provide habitat, deter soil loss, and help prevent flooding.

There are many different tree-planting companies out there that have programs for reforestation (planting in areas that used to be forest) and afforestation (establishing trees in areas that were not previously forested). You can plant trees in Israel through the Jewish National Fund (jnf.org), support sustainable agroforestry projects in developing countries with Trees for the Future (treesftf.org), or plant trees here in the United States through American Forests (americanforests.org).

$$ Renewable-Energy Credits

Another method of offsetting is to stop carbon that will be emitted in the future from being produced. One way to do this is through investing in renewable (nonpetroleum) energy development, including wind, solar, and hydroelectric power, as well as biofuels. You can buy "renewable-energy credits," which put more renewable energy on the grid, from companies like Carbonfund.org and Native Energy (nativeenergy.com).

$$$ Other Programs

When you start looking, there are many other interesting offsetting programs out there. For example, Co2balance (co2balance.com) reduces the amount of carbon released into the atmosphere from firewood and trash burning by supplying solar ovens in East Africa. TerraPass (terrapass.com) helps farmers install anaerobic digesters, which collect and convert greenhouse gases from farm manure into methane for energy production.

GUEST COMFORT

Part of being a great host is anticipating your guests' needs and planning for their comfort. What your guests will require will depend on the climate, the weather, the location, and the time of day. This section begins with things that apply to most weddings and then addresses specific issues to think about when facing cold, hot, or wet weather. With a little preparation you can help keep your guests comfortable no matter what the conditions are. You may also want to give your guests gifts or treats. Welcome baskets are discussed in this chapter. For favor ideas see Chapter Nine.

General Concerns

No matter where your wedding is, you need to make sure the following items are taken care of—or you will have some very unhappy and disoriented guests.

Good Directions

When looking at different locations, take note of their signage. Are there clear signs at every turn? Is there some sort of lighting for nighttime arrivals? If the answer to either of these questions is no, you will need to pick up the slack. Make sure to provide clear, turn-by-turn directions for your guests on your website (and double check MapQuest directions), and then add signs and lights at every major junction the day before the wedding. For our wedding, which required guests to navigate pitch-black back roads, my husband used recycled picket-fence pieces to make whimsical, wooden wedding signs (the pointed fence tops became arrows), and he planted a solar spotlight at the base of each one.[*] Make sure to test the arrangement out ahead of time to make sure your signs are as visible as you want them to be.

Toilets

Outdoor weddings, weddings in old houses, or weddings in places that rely on septic tanks almost always require additional toilets to run smoothly. The septic tank at my parents' house overflowed during my sister's wedding, and I will not describe what that was like—let's just say it was not pretty. Even if your ceremony is short, not having a working toilet for any length of time is a nightmare for guests. Port-A-Potties are not cheap, but bite the bullet. As of now, renting a composting toilet is not a viable option, but keep your eyes open for future green toilet companies.

---

[*] You can see these signs in the foreground of the picture taken of us (and our dog, Reuben) for the *Hartford Courant* article "Living Green," March 31, 2008—available in the Reading Room at thegreenbrideguide.com.

Baskets of Necessities

While we are talking toilets, it is polite to include a basket of necessities in each bathroom. This basket should include a few over-the-counter meds (for headache and stomachache, at a minimum), tissues, deodorant, tampons (for women's bathrooms), and any lotions, soaps, or other niceties you want to include. For a list of green options, see the Hair and Makeup section in Chapter Three.

Programs

If your wedding guests come from diverse backgrounds, programs can help them feel included by explaining the different customs and symbolic elements of your ceremony. Programs are often used to introduce the friends and family members participating in your wedding and to honor loved ones who cannot attend. In addition, programs are a great place to talk about your social and environmental values without seeming preachy. After all, you have a captive audience with nothing to do but read until the music starts, so take the opportunity to tell your guests about some of the green elements in your wedding. You will want to make sure someone is in charge of handing your programs out (do not put them on the chairs for outdoor weddings or they may blow away) and collecting and recycling them after the ceremony. For ideas on green printing options, see Chapter Five.

Schedule of Events

A schedule of events is particularly nice if you are having a weekend or destination wedding where you have planned a number of different activities to entertain your guests. For our wedding, because we had a number of different properties where guests were staying, we had a chalkboard that listed the activities in the central hall at the primary location, and offered printed brochures for guests to take back to their rooms.[●] To make our program, my brother used Apple's Pages (apple.com/iwork/pages), which he describes as a hybrid of Microsoft Office and Adobe InDesign that is an intuitive program designed specifically for brochure and flyer layout. Using a program like Pages, you can lay out a beautiful, professional-quality brochure and print it from home. You can also use a company like Green Printer (discussed in Chapter Five) that uses soy inks and 100 percent recycled paper and offsets the carbon generated from shipping the programs to you.

Cold Weather

A winter wedding can be cozy and romantic, but unprepared guests (or even guests with good intentions but lacking cold-weather experience) can spend a lot of time feeling miserable. Evening weddings and outdoor weddings can pose the same problems, so consider including some of the following cold-weather comforts at your affair.

$ Hot Beverages

Hot beverages are a must for cold-weather events. Have the caterer heat up local cider or offer a selection of organic teas and coffee. See the Catering Section in Chapter Ten for tips on how to make a complete cold-weather beverage bar.

$$ Socks

If you are having a weekend winter wedding in a historic home or inn, place a basket of bulky wool or cotton tube socks by the front door, and let guests slip into something warm and dry when they come in from the cold. Thick socks can double as your favor if you have enough pairs that every guest can take one. Add a cute welcome note to the basket.

[●] See pictures in the Real Green Weddings section of thegreenbrideguide.com.

$$$ *Pashminas*

Men usually wear formal jackets to weddings, but women often like to dress in slinky, sexy numbers. The result is that many women will show up at your wedding underdressed for cool, let alone truly cold, weather. For a crisp afternoon or evening wedding, a pile of lush pashminas or shawls can help guests feel warm and cared for.

Hot Weather

Hot weather at a wedding is a blessing and a curse. The upside is that you can have activities outside and can wear slinky, lightweight clothing to show off your wedding physique. The downside is that too much sun or stagnant heat can be uncomfortable—and even downright dangerous. Hot weather also brings bugs that can make being outside unpleasant. Make sure your hot-weather wedding is well stocked with the following items.

$ *Water*

In hot weather, dehydration can come on quickly, so it's essential to provide guests with water. It's tempting to offer bottles of water, but in addition to the environmental costs of bottles (see "Better Bottled Water" in the Welcome Basket section of this chapter), bottled water is actually less safe than most tap water. According to a test of 1,000 bottles and 103 brands of water conducted by the Natural Resources Defense Council (nrdc.org), almost one-third of the bottles contained contamination in the form of synthetic chemicals, bacteria, or arsenic. One-third! This is because water that is bottled and sold in the same state—about 65 percent of all bottled water—is exempt from the FDA regulation. Even the bottled water that comes under the jurisdiction of the FDA is subject to less stringent testing and purity standards than water that comes out of the tap. For example, bottled water does not have to be disinfected like tap water does.

If you took away the pretty logos and brand names that make you feel you are drinking directly from glacial runoff, which would you rather drink? My friend Carly, a former event planner for multibillion-dollar companies, firmly believes in offering guests tap water. She notes that in addition to the social and environmental benefits, serving water in glass pitchers with slices of lemons, limes, or cucumber is much more elegant and makes a more enticing display than a tower of plastic bottles. No matter what season you have your wedding in, make sure water is in your service contract, or it may not be out when guests need it.

$ Sunscreen

Sunscreen is a must for the bridal party, and it's polite to have it on hand for guests as well. One bride I know got terribly burned the day before her wedding. The severity of her situation was emphasized by the fact that the burn and her dress had different necklines—creating a horribly embarrassing effect. Make sure that in the week leading up to your wedding, you are more careful than ever (and avoid the temptation to step into a tanning salon!). At any outdoor event, be sure to have a few bottles of sunscreen out for people to use.

$$ Bug Control

For summer weddings, offering your guests bug spray is mandatory. If you don't want your guests smelling like OFF, try fragrant citronella, cedar, lemongrass, rosemary, and geranium antibug balm from Badger (badgerbalm.com). You can also set up or hand out solar-powered mosquito guards from Real Goods (available at gaiam.com) or pots of soy citronella candles, like the ones available from LuminEssent Candles (luminessentcandles.com).

$$ Fans

A nice touch for hot-weather weddings is to put a bamboo fan on every seat. Bliss Wedding Market (blissweddingsmarket.com) offers lovely—and quite effective—woven bamboo and palm fans that can double as favors. Pamela's Parasols (mentioned in the Non-Flower Alternatives section in Chapter Six), also sells sturdy white bamboo and rice-paper fans.

$$$ Shade Tent

Along the same lines, if you plan to have an outdoor wedding, it is essential to have a shade tent erected for guests who want to avoid the sun. Most tent- or canopy-rental companies have them, and they are not very expensive. Our skin actually thins with age, so elderly guests in particular are sensitive to the sun's rays and will be uncomfortable and may feel anxious if forced to sit in direct sunlight for more than a few minutes.

Wet Weather

Although rain is supposed to be lucky on your wedding day, every bride dreads the idea that her guests will be cold, wet, and muddy. If the forecast calls for rain on your wedding day, consider the following options for keeping guests comfortable.

$ Flip-Flops and Towels

If it's going to be muddy, give guests the option of leaving their shoes inside and donning flip-flops instead. You can buy inexpensive flops at any major big-box store, such as Target, and encourage your guests to preserve their shoes by leaving them in a basket by the door. While you're at it, buy some big beach towels so guests can dry off when they come back inside.

$$ Umbrellas or Ponchos

If you plan to have guests outside in a drizzle or will have guests running back and forth between buildings, offer a pile of umbrellas, ponchos, or biodegradable trash bags for them to find shelter under. For your bridal party, you can rent elegant vintage umbrellas from places like Bella Umbrella (bellaumbrella.com) or buy modern umbrellas from a non-profit like the Museum of Modern Art (moma.org).

("Priceless") Rain Plan

It is absolutely essential that you have a rain plan no matter how remote the possibility of rain is. That plan can be a tent with sides or a backup venue and transportation, but it needs to be something. Everyone in charge of making your wedding run smoothly, from the wedding planner to the band leader, should know what to do in case of rain.

Most importantly, you need to come up with a system for letting guests know about a change of plan or venue. You can put the plan on the invitation, or have a phone number guests can call if they are not sure where to go. For our wedding, we gave guests my father's cell phone number and left messages on all of our phones with updated information. When we woke up to an overcast sky (that cleared just in time for the ceremony), I was glad to have a solid backup plan.

WELCOME BASKETS

Welcome baskets are an unnecessary but classy touch, especially if you have out-of-town guests or are having a destination wedding. Welcome baskets offer you a chance to build excitement and to set the tone for your wedding before it begins. Because they are not expected, your welcome baskets can be as simple or as lavish as you want. Most welcome baskets include maps of the area and the wedding itinerary, along with some edible items and one or two seasonal or place-specific goodies. For each of these categories you can use eco-conscious options.

Even a drink and a small box of chocolates or cookies will let your guests know you are thinking about them and care about their comfort from the moment they arrive. When calculating your costs, remember that welcome baskets are typically provided on a per room, not per guest, basis. You should plan to drop off your welcome baskets the day before your guests arrive and leave them at the front desk for delivery upon check-in.

Edibles

There is nothing that makes people grumpier than the stress of traveling, and nothing cures a case of the grumps like a little snack to get the blood sugar back up and running. If you want to give your guests a small gift upon arrival but don't want to spend a fortune, consider some of the following options.

$ Homemade Treats

While homemade treats are less practical if you are having a destination wedding, they offer a sweet way to greet friends and relatives arriving from out of town. One trick is to bake cookies or brownies a couple of weeks before your wedding and freeze them; then two days before everyone arrives, defrost them in the fridge so they taste fresh as new. Place your treats in a recycled-paper bag or one of the unique, earth-friendly containers discussed in the Favors section in Chapter Nine. Add a customized welcome note on recycled or seed paper as a finishing touch.

$$ DIY Organics

If you head down to the local health-food store or the natural-food section of any major grocery store, you can now find a plethora of delicious organic granola bars, chocolates, nuts, fruits, beverages, and more. If you have the time, take a few different items home to sample. Think about your budget and what you would want to have waiting for you upon arrival. If you are using a small health-food store, ask if they can give you a discount if you buy in bulk—or go to the company's website and order directly to save. If you are making welcome baskets for kids, it is nice to include a candy treat as well, like a bag of SunSpire Sun Drops (Inspiredfoods.com), which are an all-natural alternative to M&Ms.

$$ Better Bottled Water

Although in most places the best water around is from the tap (as discussed earlier in this chapter), Americans still love the convenience of bottled water. According to the International Bottled Water Association (bottledwater.org), people in the United States consume 8.25 billion gallons of bottled water a year, or 27.6 gallons per person. The Container Recycling Institute (container-recycling.org) calculates that the amount of oil it takes just to make the bottles could provide enough electricity for 250,000 homes or fuel 100,000 cars. Unfortunately, four out of five bottles end up in the landfill instead of recycling facilities, creating even more waste.

If you want to give your guests bottled water, choose companies like Belu (belu.org) or Biota (biotaspringwater.com), which now sell water in 100 percent compostable corn-based plastic (although the caps continue to be made of traditional plastic and can only be recycled). Or choose a company that is giving back. Belu gives 100 percent of its profits to help provide clean, safe drinking water in developing countries, and Ethos (ethoswater.com) donates five cents to promote water projects for every bottle sold.

$$$ Local Delectables

It is always nice to include a small local food item in your welcome basket. In addition to supporting the local economy, including a regional delicacy in the welcome basket gives your guests a sense of place and hints of all the delicious local foods to come. See the Favors section in Chapter Nine for a list of ideas.

$$$ Prefabbed Eco-gift Baskets

If you don't have a lot of guests or have money to splurge on welcome baskets, there are incredible premade all-natural and organic gift baskets available online. I have used Organic Style (organicstyle.com) on several occasions, because they offer a nice variety at reasonable prices.

Seasonal Necessities

When making welcome baskets for out-of-town guests or for guests attending a destination wedding, it is fun to include a reusable seasonal item that they may need while they are there. The following are just a few green possibilities.

- **Winter.** If you are having a winter wedding, add a pair of unbleached wool socks, a natural chapstick, or a botanical moisturizer to the bag. Give your guests the tools they will need to be comfortable as they run around a winter wonderland.

- **Spring.** Pollen, bugs, and rain are the biggest problems for springtime guests. Offer guests an immunity booster like Emergen-C, a small tin of Badger antibug balm, or a beautiful umbrella.

- **Summer.** For a hot summer wedding, tuck a travel-sized natural sunscreen, a hemp beach hat, or a corn-based Frisbee into the welcome bag. Your guests will know the fun is about to begin from the moment they arrive.

- **Fall.** For a crisp fall wedding, make your guests feel cozy and warm by including a pair of organic cotton mittens, natural hand cream, or a small soy-based candle.

MAKING KIDS HAPPY

If you decide to invite children to your wedding, there are several things you can do to make sure they are well behaved and their parents are happy. There are three steps to (virtually) guarantee success: watch them, feed them, and entertain them.

$ Watch Them

In the great scheme of wedding costs, the extra $10 to $15 per hour to have a teenage baby-sitter on hand is nothing. If you want your ceremony to go smoothly, have a baby-sitter or two hanging around nearby, but not within earshot, of the ceremony location. You can let each parent know about the option personally, or put a well-placed sign near the entrance to the ceremony site. Having a baby-sitter will encourage parents to remove fussy or crying children from the area, because they won't have to miss the ceremony to be with them.

If you have a kids' table at the meal (which provides a nice break for parents), it's wise to have a baby-sitter or two there as well, so the parents don't have to keep hopping up to help their kids order and cut their food into small pieces. If your finances are stretched too thin to hire a sitter, you can get a list of responsible teens in the area through friends, a high school, or local religious groups. Send their information around to all the eligible families, encouraging them to pool together to hire someone if they would like to have a sitter available during the event.

$$ Feed Them

While adults will appreciate that duck confit, most kids—and many teenagers—would vastly prefer classic kid foods, like chicken fingers, grilled cheese, and french fries. If the kitchen or caterer can't come up with something suitably green, you can always supply them with a few boxes of organic pasta and sauce (be sure to negotiate a decreased per child fee if you provide the ingredients!). If you plan on having a champagne toast, offer kids a flute of Martinelli's organic sparkling cider (martinellis.com) or the like so that they feel part of the celebration.

$$$ Entertain Them

Even if you hire sitters, it helps to have things for kids to do during a long dinner and dancing set. The following are a few tricks worth considering. Instead of putting fancy linens down at a kids' table, put down butcher paper and give each child a set of environmentally friendly crayons or colored pencils from EcoChoices (ecochoices.com). If you want kids to sit with their parents, consider setting their places with an educational, washable/reusable coloring placemat from Just a Dream (justadreamonline.com). Instead of a favor, give each kid a small activity bag. This can include things like organic candy, maze or puzzle books, origami instructions and paper, or other educational games and toys. Try to avoid disposables and cheap plastic toys. If you want kids to be enthralled all night long, set up a photo booth or invite a sketch artist to come and draw guests' portraits—watching the artist work will be fun for adults and children alike and will allow guests to take home a memorable souvenir. Just make sure you and your husband get a drawing!

CHAPTER 8

A Ceremony on Earth

Sometimes with the all the rigmarole and frenzy of planning, it is hard to remember what your wedding is all about—your community coming together to witness your vows and to celebrate you and your partner's commitment to one another. Creating a ceremony that reflects your values and beliefs is extremely important, and I highly recommend writing personal vows to each other if your religious tradition allows it. The process of writing your vows and putting together a marriage ceremony can be profoundly insightful and moving. A lot has been written about how to "green" a ceremony with environmentally themed poems, songs, and scripture. Therefore, this chapter focuses on how to "green" the more tangible elements of a ceremony, focusing on technical details like site decoration and the acquisition of ritual objects.

CEREMONY DECOR

In addition to the floral elements discussed in Chapter Six, there are a few aesthetic decisions you need to make about your ceremony setup. This section walks through some of the elements that set the stage on which your ceremony will be performed.

Aisle Runner

Let me begin this section with two horror stories (names will be omitted to spare those involved from having to relive painful memories). Trauma number one: At a beautiful outdoor wedding on a lush grassy hillside, bride and groom decide not to have a runner. The grandmother, a very stylish lady who wears very stylish heels, gets a heel stuck in the ground when she is walking down the aisle and almost topples over, leaving everyone in the audience sweaty and anxious. Trauma number two: At an indoor wedding, the bride decides to put down an ethereal, gauzy, white roll-out runner on top of hotel carpeting. As bride is coming down the aisle, runner clings to her train because of static electricity, and her attendants have to frantically pull it off, making the aisle look askew and sending guests into a panic. The moral of these parables is not "damned if you do, damned if you don't," but rather that aisle runners are something you need to think about carefully. The following are some reliable green options.

$ Petals, Leaves, and Confetti

If you are having an indoor wedding on a non-slippery floor, consider creating the visual effect of an aisle with a natural material like organic rose petals or aromatic herbs. One company with an impressive selection of organic and pesticide-free products is Mountain Rose Herbs (mountainroseherbs.com). You could spread dried lavender and rosemary down the aisle and have your flower girls toss miniature pink rose buds and/or white jasmine flowers. Dried leaves also work well. You can collect them yourself, or buy them wholesale online from companies like Nature's Pressed Flowers (naturespressed.com). For an outdoor wedding with solid footing, Ecoparti (ecoparti.com) makes colorful, biodegradable ecofetti that can add a nice splash.

$$ Heavy Material

Another option is to rent or buy a piece of heavy burlap or canvas, which you can paint to your liking. You can save the canvas after your wedding and use it as a mural on a wall or as a drop cloth the next time you renovate your house. No matter what you choose, make sure your runner is a few feet longer than the aisle; and if you do pick a light fabric, consider placing plywood boards down under it, and do whatever it takes to secure it to the ground.

$$$ Rugs

If you want to have a fabric aisle runner, steer clear of the thin, disposable kind both for environmental and safety reasons. For our hilltop wedding, we used a twenty-five-foot-long Oriental runner from my parents' staircase down the aisle and a second Oriental rug under the wedding canopy. It created a lush and elegant space for the ceremony and looked wonderful in the photographs.◉

If you like this idea but don't have a long rug that will work, you can buy one on eBay and resell it after the event or rent one (search "carpet runner rental" online).

Wedding Canopy

In many religions, it is traditional for the bride and groom to get married under a wedding canopy (or chuppah). These can be as simple as four poles and a piece of cloth or elaborate handmade affairs. Many synagogues and churches have canopies on site, but if you need to provide your own, consider some of the following options:

$ Borrow

If you are getting married in a small town or on a weekday, you may be able to borrow one from a local place of worship.

◉ You can see a picture of the runner in situ on the Real Green Weddings page of thegreenbrideguide.com.

$$ Make

If you have a beautiful piece of fabric you would like to use, like a family heirloom talit, tablecloth, or shawl, it is very easy to make your own canopy using tree limbs or bamboo poles and flowerpots; just search "do-it-yourself directions" online. If you have creative friends, give them the dimensions and ask them to be in charge of making you a natural-material canopy—you will probably be surprised and delighted with the results.

$$ Rent

There are many wedding-canopy-rental companies out there, offering everything from the wrought-iron botanical designs at Under the Chuppah (underthechuppahonline.com) to the wicker gazebos at some of the Classic Party Rentals locations (classicpartyrentals.com). Take your eco-chic style a step further with a canopy made from sustainable materials, like the bamboo-pole versions available from Kelly Scott Designs (kellyscottdesigns.com).

$$$ Buy

You can buy amazing chuppahs online from companies like Chuppah House (chuppah-house.com). When buying a chuppah, try to avoid PVC piping, the production of which releases highly toxic organochlorine compounds (known carcinogens and endocrine disrupters) into the environment. Instead, opt for natural, sustainable woods like cherry, maple, birch, and black walnut. See the Quick Guide to Wood Buying in the Registry section of Chapter Twelve for more sustainable woods options.

RITUAL OBJECTS

Every culture has ritual objects that are used in the wedding ceremony, and I have only included a small sampling here. As you read through this section, think about the ritual objects you will include in your own wedding, and use the suggestions below to help find green versions. It is always sustainable to use things that are already in the family, and incorporating vintage or heirloom pieces makes your wedding even more meaningful. If you want to or have to buy something new, buy high-quality items that you can use again or can keep for your children to use at their weddings. Whenever possible, avoid plastic or petroleum-based products and rely on natural, sustainably produced materials.

Ring Pillow

In many American weddings, a small child (or pet) carries the wedding rings down the aisle on a pillow. A recent green trend is to have the "pillow" made from a bed of moss, a collection of flowers, or other natural material. If you have any sewing skills, fabric ring pillows are relatively easy to make. You can buy a yard of organic satin or cotton fabric and fill it with organic wool or cotton batting from Heart of Vermont (heartofvermont. com). If you are Jewish, you can use the same technique to create a break-the-glass pillow (just make sure to put the glass inside before you sew it up!). When I bought my wedding dress, the train was several yards longer than I wanted. My husband's great-aunt used the extra fabric to make us a gorgeous break-the-glass pillow embroidered with our names and the date of our wedding.◉

Flower Girl Baskets

Basket making is an ancient tradition, and it is great to support local artisans if you can. Visit craft fairs, or look online for heritage baskets, like Nantucket Lightship baskets, baskets made by the Amish, or Native American birch bark baskets. Baskets are also a lot of fun to make if you have the time and interest. I recommend taking a basket-weaving class at your local art center to learn different weaving techniques. You can use all

---

◉ See pictures in the Real Green Weddings section at thegreenbrideguide.com.

sorts of natural materials and can weave in colorful cloth ribbons to create one-of-a-kind pieces. Larger, more elaborate baskets are nice for handing out programs, kippot, or shawls.

Ritual Cup

In many traditions the bride and groom drink from the same cup as part of the ceremony. In Judaism this takes the form of a silver kiddush cup; Pueblo Indians use a handcrafted ceramic wedding vase. Most families keep (and treasure) these ritual items, so ask around for one to use at your wedding. My husband and I were lucky to be able use the same cup my parents used at their wedding in 1976. My grandparents had the cup engraved for my parents, and we had an engraver add our names and the date in a crest opposite the original design, creating a new family tradition. If you want to buy a ritual cup new, support local artists when you can, or buy a vintage piece online.

Broom

For hundreds of years, brooms were thought to have magical powers. Many cultures, including people in Ireland and Africa, used brooms in marriage ceremonies to symbolically sweep away the old life and start a new one. During the time of slavery, African American couples jumped over brooms to symbolize their public commitment to each other. Today brooms are still featured in Wiccan and Roma ceremonies, and are experiencing a resurgence in the African American community as well. If you want to include broom jumping as part of your marriage ceremony, consider using a beautiful handmade Colonial-style or Shaker broom. Warren Olney, who owns the Broomshop. com, is a retired forester and second-generation broom maker who carries a beautiful selection of brooms made from cut branches and natural broom corn.

Rice

Rice, a symbol of fertility for many cultures, plays a prominent role in weddings. At Indian weddings, rice is the first food the bride and groom eat; at some church weddings, rice is thrown as the couple exits. Some environmental advocates advise against throwing rice because it can harm birds, but this is not true. The biggest environmental problem with rice is the way it is grown.

Rice researchers are concerned about decreasing rice biodiversity, pesticide dependence, and the potential negative impacts of planting genetically modified rice varieties (see the International Rice Research Institute at irri.org or Greenrice. net to learn more). If you can, try to find rice that has been grown without the use of petroleum-based fertilizers and toxic chemicals. Avoid buying individually packaged bags and rice that has to be shipped from overseas. Many stores, like Whole Foods, offer organic rice in bulk that you can distribute to guests in a passed pail or basket. You can buy five-pound bags of organic rice grown in the Pacific Northwest from S & W Rice (s-and-wrice.com).

Rice Alternatives

Perhaps out of fear of being pelted with hard rice kernels by feisty teenage attendees, many couples today offer their guests rice alternatives. These include bubbles, birdseed, organic petals, confetti, and even butterflies. Consider a few words of advice on each.

$ Confetti

Paper confetti is always colorful and fun. Use recycled (nonglossy) paper or biodegradable ecofetti (ecoparti.com).

$ Birdseed

Substituting birdseed for rice creates the same visual effect for the photographs and provides a more nutritious treat for the birds. However, it is not a good idea to use birdseed in natural areas, because there is a chance the seed will germinate and introduce non-native plant species. Use seed blends of native species, or keep the birdseed use to urban affairs. Whatever you throw or release, make sure to get permission ahead of time from the wedding venue, park, or wildlife area involved.

$$ Bubbles

They are fun, but most people I know who have had guests blow bubbles at them say they felt slimy and gross afterward, as bubbles are made from soap solution. The other problem is that bubbles can stain your dress. Especially if you are wearing something slinky or satiny, you may want to avoid the bubble route entirely.

$$$ Petals

Silk petals do not biodegrade quickly, can stick to guests' clothing, and can make the ground slippery. Instead of silk, opt for real organic petals, which are soft and beautiful and biodegrade quickly. You can also ask your florist to provide petals from his or her stock, or buy them from the sources mentioned earlier.

SPARKLERS

Sparklers are fun, but they only last a minute and are made from mined metals (such as iron and aluminum, with added barium, copper, and strontium for color). A nice alterative to sparklers is to have guests light and hold reusable soy candles as they escort you to your car. The result is enchanting and more sustainable.

$$$ Butterflies

Butterfly releases have become controversial in environmental circles. Advocates against butterfly release, like the North American Butterfly Association (naba.org), raise the following concerns:

- Captive-bred butterflies could spread diseases and parasites to wild species.

- Captive-bred butterflies and their offspring might not be able to orient themselves properly for migration.

- The market for captive-raised butterflies can create an incentive for poachers to take butterflies from the wild and sell them illegally.

While these are all legitimate worries, the USDA currently allows and regulates the sale of butterflies, and the International Butterfly Breeders Association (butterflybreeders.org) has worked hard to promote sustainable butterfly raising and responsible release. Its members subscribe to a code of ethics, which forbids the shipment of wild-caught butterflies, and its website has instructions for the caring, feeding, and release of butterflies. Many companies, like Swallowtail Farms (swallowtailfarms.com), now offer certified disease-free specimens. To find out which butterfly species are native to your state (and appropriate for release), see Butterflies and Moths of North America (butterflies andmoths.org/map).

CHAPTER 9

The Green Reception

The reception is the most expensive aspect of the wedding, accounting for 50 to 70 percent of the total wedding budget. This chapter covers all aspects of the wedding reception, from significant choices, like the menu and music, to small details, like the name cards and guest book. No matter what your budget or decor, there are ways to make every aspect of your reception more sustainable.

SETTING THE STAGE

Some venues provide all of the basic things you need to throw a party, while others offer only few or none of the basic necessities and leave you to do the heavy lifting, both literally and figuratively. As discussed in Chapter Two, there are advantages and disadvantages to having complete control at your location. This section walks through some of the basic items you may need to procure for you event, such as lighting, tables, glasses, plates, etc., and offers green choices in every category.

Tents

If you're having an outdoor wedding, you will almost certainly need a tent. Tents come in many shapes and sizes, and you can find tent-rental options in your area in the phone book or online. Some companies allow you to cancel your rental with little or no penalty if you give forty-eight hours' notice, so if the five-day weather forecast is excellent or you live in a part of the country where it rarely rains or gets cold, you may be able to duck this necessity. However, even for daytime weddings in sunny places, it is wise to have a small shade tent where your guests can seek shelter from the sun, as discussed in the Guest Comfort section in Chapter Seven. To decrease the environmental impact of your tent, make sure to choose one that is large enough to accommodate your guests, but no larger. The larger the tent, the more energy it will take to set up, heat, and light.

Lighting

As researchers will tell you, lighting affects mood—so lighting design should not be overlooked when thinking about ambiance. For daytime weddings, you will probably not need a lot of additional light, although be sure to check out the natural light in the space you will use for your ceremony and reception in advance and to have a backup plan for an overcast day. Late afternoon and evening weddings—or tented weddings—can be illuminated in many different ways. If the facility offers overhead lighting, make sure it works on a dimmer if you want to add any of the following items.

THE RULE OF FIVE

When buying candles for your reception, make sure they have a "burn time" of at least five hours, and more if you think your party will continue into the night.

$ Candles

Illuminating a room with candles creates an extremely romantic atmosphere and saves electricity. However, most candles you see in stores are made from paraffin, which is a petroleum product.

In addition to being a non-renewable resource, paraffin contains as many as eleven documented toxins and two EPA-recognized carcinogens—benzene and toluene. Additionally, the chemical fragrances added to candles are not regulated, even though you breathe them in as the candles burn. The key, therefore, is to find candles made from natural sources, like soy or beeswax, which are scented with essential oils. Natural candles are available in many shapes and sizes.❂

Soy, palm, and beeswax candles are clean burning (emitting 95 percent less soot than paraffin candles) and often last longer, so you get more for your money. When burned, these candles release essential oils, which can add enchanting seasonal scents to the air. Country Light Candle (countrylightcandle.com) has pillar candles made from palm oil that reveal their crystalline design when lit. Way Out Wax (wayoutwax.com) offers soy aromatherapy candles, including scent blends like Escentual Love and Citrus Harmony. USA Soy Candles (usasoycandles. com) is a good source of colorful 2.5-ounce votives, and Bee Natural (beenatural.com) has beautiful botanical candles and bulk beeswax for do-it-yourself enthusiasts.

You can add essential oils to wax or pour scented oil directly into ornamental diffusers. Both oils and diffusers are available online from Aura Cacia (auracacia.com). If you decide to use soy tea lights, available scented and unscented in bulk from Country Light Candle Company (countrylightcandle.com), consider displaying them in recycled-glass or bicycle-gear tea-light holders, like the ones available at Greenfeet (greenfeet. com). You can also have candles double as favors. GreenSpace Candles (greenspacecandles.com) sells soy candles in personalized wedding tins. Finally, for an outdoor wedding, bug-repellant

---

❂ See the Quick Guide page in the About the Book section of thegreenbrideguide. com for a list and description of common types.

citronella-scented candles, available in seventy colors from LuminEssent Candles (luminessentcandles.com), might be the way to go. Whenever you have candles burning, make sure there is a fire extinguisher on hand.

$$ Lamps and Lanterns

Lamps and lanterns make wonderful reception decor. You can use olive-oil lamps (which have been around since biblical times), ornate candelabras, or cut-tin or iron Moroccan-style lanterns on the tables. For luminous light from above, string up colorful rice-paper lanterns, available with bamboo ribbing from Cherry Blossom Gardens, (cherryblossomgardens.com), solar lanterns, or strands of Christmas-tree lights.

$$ Solar Lighting

There are now great solar-lighting options available in big-box stores like Target and Home Depot and online from retailers like Gardener's Supply Company (gardeners.com). Solar lights have built-in batteries and are charged with solar panels that absorb sunlight and convert it to energy. They come in many different shapes and sizes, from small path lights on posts to intricate lanterns that can be hung from trees to floating, illuminated lily pads. You can even get solar-powered Christmas lights. You will need to charge solar lights at least a day ahead of time by leaving them out in full sun. Not all solar lights are created equal—the new ones that utilize LED technology can be almost twenty times brighter than the older models. The LED solar lights cost more but will last for thousands of hours, meaning you can use them at home after the wedding or resell them.

$$$ Rechargeable Candles

You should check to make sure candles are permitted at your venue, as some locations restrict or prohibit their use. The good news is that you can now get the feel of flickering candles without a flame. My husband and I first discovered rechargeable candles at a local Indian-food restaurant in town and fell in love with them. Instead of being cheesy as one might expect, they are remarkably charming and are also safe for kids. A few popular kinds include square tea lights by Philips Aurelle (nam.lighting. philips.com), Viatek (viatekproducts.com) tea lights that come with separate votive holders, and Brookstone's (brookstone.com) scented "Flameless Wax Sensor Candles," which are pillar candles that run on AA batteries (rechargeable batteries not included). Because the LED lights last for thousands of hours, these are good products to buy used if you can find them.

Cups, Bowls, Plates, and Utensils

There are many different ways to create green table settings. For a small wedding, you can use items you and your friends and family already own. For a larger wedding, you can buy and resell things made from natural and recycled materials, rent them, or purchase disposables. If you are inclined toward one-time-use tableware, opt for biodegradable or compostable versions. There are now products available that look and feel like traditional plastic but are actually made from cornstarch, potato, sugarcane (aka bagasse), bamboo, and other natural materials.

A good source of sustainable tableware, hot and cold cups, corn-based straws, and "to-go" containers is Excellent Packaging and Supply (excellentpackaging.com). For our casual rehearsal dinner, we bought EarthShell (earthshellnow.com) plates and bowls and were very satisfied with their construction. For a more sophisticated event, you can find compostable, certified organic woodlike plates and utensils made from biodegradable bamboo from Bambu (bambuhome.com). If composting is not an option, you can get colorful 100 percent recycled, machine washable, and recyclable plastic plates, cups, and even toothpicks from Recycline (recycline.com).* Because many of these products are indistinguishable from their less sustainable counterparts, make sure to let your guests know they are eating on green goods with a small sign at the bar or a note on the menu.

Chairs, Tables, Etc.

If the venue you are using does not provide chairs and tables, you will have to rent them. While it is hard to find chairs and tables made from natural and sustainably harvested materials, some companies, like Classic Party Rentals (classicparty-rentals.com), offer a few green options, like bamboo chairs and burlap tablecloths.

Tablecloths and Linens

Vibrant colors and sophisticated patterns are the new rage for wedding table linens. Putting beautiful fabric down can really make a table pop, but if you don't find green linens to rent, consider making or purchasing more sustainable versions and selling them after your big day. If you are good with a sewing machine, you can buy organic fabrics by the yard from companies like Heart of Vermont (heartofvermont.com). For our rehearsal dinner, we bought natural jute cloth from Jo-Ann Fabric (joann. com) that could be cut to size and was heavy enough to not need edging. For a more refined look, you can find premade, colorful 100 percent hemp linen napkins, placemats, and table runners from Rawganique (rawganique.com).

Most fair trade companies, like Ten Thousand Villages (tenthousandvillages.com) and World of Good (worldofgood. com), offer a nice selection of hand-woven textiles to liven any table. For something different and chic, try the polished-stone placemats and table runners at VivaTerra (vivaterra.com). Top

---

* Recycline offers a 15 percent wedding discount. The company also makes Preserve recycled plastic kitchenware, which is available at Whole Foods.

your organic look off with recycled glass, metal, or bamboo napkin rings (see fair trade store eShopAfrica.com for a variety of options), or place a small twig, fern, polished rock or bundle of lavender from Lavender Green (lavendergreen.com) on each napkin or plate for an elegant eco-chic look.

ORGANIZATIONAL ELEMENTS

When you walk into a reception, there are a number of organizational items to help you navigate through the space. Each of these elements offers a unique opportunity to be creative and green.

The Present Table

Besides the obvious generous gesture, it's nice when guests bring gifts to the wedding, because gifts delivered in person tend to have less packaging and therefore generate less waste. To help make sure you do not have "orphan" gifts, include a roll of Scotch tape and a sign asking guests to secure their cards to their presents. You would be amazed by how many unidentified presents you can end up with at the end of the night. It's also a good idea to designate a friend or family member (preferably one with a large van and a strong back) as the official end-of-evening present mover. If you have a lot of different people taking gifts back for you, one or two presents are likely to get lost in the shuffle. If your culture gives money as a gift, set up a recycled (and decorated) shipping box with a slit for envelopes, or hang an elegant vintage birdcage where guests can leave cards or write well wishes.

The Guest Book

A guest book takes little effort and yields great rewards. The "book" itself can be anything from a simple blank book in which guests write congratulatory notes to a laundry line with clothespins and note cards. No matter what form your guest book takes, it gives guests a chance to express their happiness for you and gives you something special to enjoy long after the party has ended. If you are using a videographer, your guest book can be confessional-style. Otherwise, think about using one of the options below.

$ Make Your Own

If you are crafty, you can make your own paper from recycled envelopes, flyers, or junk mail, or buy premade natural paper and bind it into a book. See Chapter Five for tips on making your own paper—you can buy everything you need to make paper and bind a book from Arnold Grummer's, a family owned and operated paper-making supply business (arnoldgrummer. com). For illustrated instructions on hardcover bookbinding and a list of necessary supplies, see Bookbinding for Beginners (bookbindingfb.com).

$$ Recycled and Natural Paper

Everyone has a vice, and mine is beautiful handmade journals. I love them so much that if I see a stationery store further up the block, I actually cross the street in order to avoid it. The wonderful textures, the crisp pages, and the smell of handcrafted paper are true delights. A wedding is a great excuse to buy an exquisite journal to use as a guest book. Like a childhood journal, your guest book will be something you cherish for many years, and is something your children and even your grandchildren can enjoy. A trip to your local papery will yield ideas aplenty. You can find beautiful blank books and albums online, made from recycled and organic papers, from companies like Creative Papers Online (handmade-paper.us) or Of the Earth (oftheearth. com).

$$ Fair Trade Paper

Many sustainable tree-free papers are harvested in tropical countries, so you can find beautiful albums and books made from banana leaves, rice straw, and other natural materials. Browse fair trade stores like Novica (novica.com) and Global Exchange (store.gxonlinestore.org).

$$$ Creative Alternatives

Instead of using a traditional book, you can let the theme of your party and your imagination dictate something unique. Have guests use fabric markers to sign squares of organic cotton and turn them into a quilt. Place an album next to a digital-photo booth and printer, and encourage guests to put on funny hats. Set up a video-confession booth and ask each guest to record a memory of the two of you together. The possibilities are endless.

A PEN(NY) FOR YOUR THOUGHTS

Although not necessary, it's always nice to put out a fancy pen for guests to use to sign the guest book or write you well wishes. Botanical Paperworks (botanicalpaperworks.com) has a nice selection of glass pens and soy inks. For handcrafted, American-wood ballpoint pens, you can find one-of-a-kind treasures like the ones offered by artisans Dana and Hank DiPasquale at Sculpted Forest (sculptedforest.com)

The Seating Chart

A seating chart lets your guests know which table is theirs. The same company that prints your invitations may offer matching seating-chart designs (see Chapter Five for more information). For a homemade version, you can buy a large sheet of recycled paper or card stock and bring a PDF file down to a local printer—or write the names out by hand. You can also use the ideas below to create fun displays, with each guest's name and table number on or next to a natural or recycled object.

For our wedding my husband used a picket fence to create a peg-board with vintage keys. Each slat had a table number on top, and I wrote the guests' names next to keys that they took to their tables to find their seats. It was fairly elaborate but easy to make and it looked really cool.[*] A friend of mine used an old map of the world as her seating chart, and guests located their table by finding the one that bore the name of the region where their name was written on the larger map.

Name Cards

Name cards are another place you can have fun developing the theme of your wedding. For sustainable paper options, see the Paper Correspondence section of Chapter Five. For enticing three-dimensional ideas, consider some of the following.

$ Natural Objects

There are many beautiful objects in nature that can be turned into elegant place cards. For a summer wedding, you can paint guests' names onto smooth river stones, perfect shells, or sea glass. For a fall wedding, you can use milk- or water-based paint to write names on fallen leaves, small branches, or miniature pumpkins. After the wedding, you can turn these items into permanent displays in your home or return them to whence they came.

$$ Dual-Function Objects

Many table decor elements can double as place settings. Use special glass paint to put guests' names on small tea lights or hurricane candles. The lights not only create a romantic ambiance but also can double (or in this case triple) as favors. You can also use the same edibles discussed in Chapter Five as place markers.

---

[*] You can see a picture online in the Real Green Weddings section of thegreenbrideguide.com.

Think how delightful it is for guests to find their seats with personalized cookies or mini chocolate bars guiding the way! You can also create more elaborate personalized cupcakes, or for an inexpensive and healthier version, write guests' names on small toothpick flags, and put a piece of ripe seasonal fruit at each place setting.

$$$ Recycled and Reusable Objects

One cute idea for vineyard weddings is to make place card holders from wine corks. If you start early and spread the word, you can probably collect enough corks to make these yourself, or you can buy reusable resin ones from Bright and Bold (bright andbold.com). Many favors, like miniature recycled-paper journals or vintage picture frames, can also double as place cards with the quick addition of a name label.

TABLE DECORATIONS

Most receptions take place over the course of several hours, and your guests will spend a great deal of that time sitting at their tables, drinking, eating, and generally schmoozing. Therefore, both for the overall ambiance of the room and to give your guests something to look at while they sit, it is nice to have some kind of centerpiece in the middle of each table (or all along the table, if you are sitting banquet-style). Traditionally, couples have chosen to use flowers (discussed in Chapter Six), but non-floral options are becoming increasingly popular. Non-floral decorations work particularly well for theme weddings, as they allow you to express the essence of the idea in artistic ways. Almost anything can act as the centerpiece if you let your interests, your aesthetics, and your imagination be your guide.

Nature-Themed Ideas

There are so many ways to capture the beauty of the natural world. In the weeks leading up to your wedding, look around and see what the landscape has to offer for inspiration.

Rivers and Tides

For our wedding, my husband made fountains in glass vases filled with stones from the beach outside our house. While a bit of a nightmare to transport, they were beautiful, and the sound of trickling water made the view of the scenic Hudson River come to life. (The stones were returned to the beach, thanks to some very generous friends!). For a less involved water display, you can set out large, flat bowls of water and float candles and/or petals in them.

Shells, Fish, and Sea Glass

In addition to making displays on a bed of sand, you can incorporate shells, sea glass, and driftwood. If you are worried about combing the beach, you can buy manufactured "sea glass," made from recycled glass bottles, from Mega Glass (megaglass. com). You can also display live goldfish or beta fish in glass bowls and allow guests to take them home afterward. However, be sure you have a way to return or donate unwanted fish (or are willing to have quite a collection yourself), because store-bought fish cannot be released into the wild. If you want live fish at an event, it is also important that you consult a breeder or knowledgeable pet store employee about how to transport and care for them. Fish are fragile; they cannot be put into tap water, cannot be exposed to extreme temperatures, need to be in containers that allow for high rates of oxygen exchange, and cannot travel long distances.

Seasonal Beauty

Every season has its bounty. For example, you can capture the romance of crisp autumn days by creating displays with dried leaves, pinecones, gourds, pumpkins, apples, berries, horse chestnuts, or bales of hay. Add dramatic candelabras or "honeypot" candles with pressed leaves inside, available from Bee Natural (beenatural.com). In addition to the flowers at our rehearsal dinner, we scattered nuts, pale green pinecones, and red pears down the centers of the tables. In winter, create a magical landscape with Christmas lights, ice sculptures, potted evergreens, flowering branches, pinecones, and bowls of nuts (flanked by elegant nutcrackers). Winter wreaths intertwined with tall, white pillar candles and winterberries can be very dramatic as well.

Objects of Interest

It is not necessary to have a nature theme in order to have an eco-friendly reception. Recycling decorations and supplies, repurposing and reusing unexpected elements, and incorporating reusable objects are all great ways to be green.

$ Ribbons

Curled and colorful ribbons are another element that can transform the mundane. You can use inexpensive, clear-glass hurricane lamps, bowls, or vases and wrap them in layers of lush ribbon. Ribbons can also be used to create a colorful bed for candles or flowers to rest on. For something wild and festive, hang ribbons off lanterns like strings—so that the whole party is under a canopy of streamers. If possible, try to use ribbons made from organic cotton or biodegradable materials that have been dyed with soy inks.

BEWARE OF BALLOONS

Most balloons are made out of either latex (a product manufactured from rubber-tree sap) or foil (aka Mylar), made from thin layers of nylon and aluminum. Because they are made from natural rubber, latex balloons break down much more quickly (decomposition time is about six months) than Mylar balloons and therefore have less impact on the environment. Mass balloon releases are illegal in several state and municipalities now, and for good reason. As discussed in the introduction, if they are released, both types of balloon can find their way into the water, where whales, sea turtles, and other marine wildlife may suffer illness or death from ingesting them. If you choose to use balloons, be sure to choose the rubber variety, tie them with cotton ribbon, and dispose of them properly.

$$ Objets d'Art

One idea I love but did not get a chance to use at my wedding was placing a unique collection of objects on each table—little "still lifes" that would be interesting and meaningful. Perhaps it stemmed from my desire to clean out our basement, but I still think it would be cool to make arrangements that included antique or miniature books, pottery, swatches of unique fabric, glass beads, vintage buttons, feathers, small iron objects, and all sorts of junk-shop collectables. Because you will be far too busy before the reception to set the table up, the hitch would be that you would have to trust your friends or florist to arrange the tables to your liking. One way to do this would be to put each table's treasures in a separate crate along with a photograph of the layout. It might not come out exactly according to your plan, but it would still be neat.

$$$ Paper Flowers

You probably made them as a kid, but the paper flowers you can make (or buy) as an adult put a new twist on the fanciful. For an example, look at the work of Jude Miller (judemiller. com), who creates sprigs of ultra-realistic wildflowers from paper. According to an article from *Garden Illustrated,* Jude taught herself to make paper flowers using the book *How to Make Flowers with Dennison Crepe Paper* (republished in 2007 by Kessinger Publishing Company). Perhaps you can learn to make your own beautiful paper flowers, too.

Edible Decorations

Instead of the usual flowers or candles, why not have your center-pieces double as dessert? You can offer healthy arrangements with fruits and vegetables or towers of chocolate, cupcakes, or cookies. No matter what they are made of, edible centerpieces are sure to be a hit.

$ Candies

Candies are colorful and come in so many shapes and sizes that you can make beautiful, creative (and yummy) displays for your guests to enjoy. You can also hand out goodie bags at the end of the night for guests to take home any leftovers.

$$ Nuts

Nuts look great when placed in tall glass vases or scattered around the base of an autumnal display. If you want guests to eat them, be sure to leave out nutcrackers and receptacles for shells, or put shelled nuts in small silver appetizer bowls. You can buy bulk organic nuts in many health-food stores and online from companies like Braga Farms (buyorganicnuts.com), or you can buy organic nut sampler baskets from places like Diamond Organics (diamond organics.com) or Organic Style (organicstyle.com).

$$ Cupcakes

Cupcakes on cake stands or in shallow tiers make fun and delicious centerpieces, especially when you add a flourish like an edible flower on top of each one. You can make sure that they match your color scheme with custom icing, or you can put one at each place setting with a guest's name in place of seating cards. Cupcakes often take the place of a wedding cake these days, which is another way to slim down expenses. For more whimsical ideas, see the Small Cakes section in Chapter Ten.

$$$ Fruit

Fruit is always beautiful. You can make pyramids of seasonal fruits like oranges, apples, or pears. Blood oranges and pink grapefruit are particularly gorgeous when sliced, and lemons, limes, and grapes look lovely when mixed with live flowers. When you use fresh fruit, anything that goes uneaten can be used to make juice for breakfast, baked into pies, or used at the bar. Plan ahead with the kitchen at your reception location to see what kinds of leftover fruit would work best for them. If they cannot provide it, you can buy organic fruit at the supermarket, at a local farmers market, or online.

If you want to offer your guests diversity and do not want the hassle of self-assembly, you can buy organic fruit gift baskets from companies like Gourmet Gift Baskets (gourmetgiftbaskets. com) for less than the cost of the average table arrangement. You can also buy "arrangements" of cut fruit from companies like the Fresh Fruit Bouquet Company (ffbc.com) and Incredibly Edible Delights (fruitflowers.com), although neither company offers an organic version yet.

$$$ Chocolate

It is very hard to go wrong with chocolate. Fondue fountains have been extremely popular wedding fare (for obvious reasons).

For a retro centerpiece/dessert, consider placing individual s'mores roasters and the necessary accoutrements in tempting displays.* You can also incorporate chocolate by placing tiers of truffles, chocolate-covered strawberries, or hand-dipped fortune cookies on every table. Your guests will be sweetly surprised.

FAVORS

Favors are a relatively new phenomenon and, according to *Brides New York* magazine, despite what the industry may try to tell you, they are still entirely optional. You should not feel obligated to give your guests anything—after all, you are throwing a gigantic, expensive party for them! Therefore, you may want to do yourself a favor and just skip favors, because when you think back on it, can you remember a single favor you received at a wedding you attended more than five years ago? Or have you ever said, "Well, the food was okay, and the bride looked good—but man those *favors*!"

In the long run, no one is likely to recall what you do in the favor department unless it is awful or truly unique. Before you shell out several hundred dollars, think carefully about whether you want to go down the favor road at all.

Favors tend to go in and out of style like clothing. For example, matchbooks with the couple's names were very popular in the 1980s. A few years ago, candy emblazoned with pictures of the bride and groom seemed to be the rage. More recently there was the year of the personalized CD. Before you buy these things just to have something to give, think about the wonderful, more meaningful alternatives that are available. Pick items that can be reused, are made from recycled materials, employ local businesses, or support a cause you believe in.

---

* If you want to capture the classic s'mores taste, Hershey's now offers organic chocolate bars!

This section will provide you with a few ideas, but think about your values, your hobbies, or the way you met, and try to find something that is unique and meaningful for the two of you. Depending on what you choose, you can put favors on your guests' plates, in a basket by the door, in goodie bags, on chairs at the ceremony, or give them out at any other time during the wedding.

Recycled and Reusable Favors

The best way to ensure your favors do not end up as orphans is to give your guests something they can—and will—use again. If these things can be made from recycled materials all the better! If it's not possible to find what you're looking for in a post-consumer version, look for natural materials or buy from a reputable fair trade company.

$ Something Small

If you want to give a token gift but don't want to spend a fortune, skip the plastic diamond rings and stick to simple, useful basics. For a modern twist on the 1980s matchbook, you can now get personalized, pocket-sized Soduku game packets on 100 percent recycled paper. For golf enthusiasts, you can buy corn based biodegradable tees and balls from Eco Golf (ecogolf. com). For chefs and bakers, put together a small book of your favorite recipes attached to a heart-shaped metal cookie cutter with a ribbon. If you have a green thumb, give guests a packet of seeds with your names and wedding date on it or a matchstick garden from Brooklyn 5 and 10 (brooklyn5and10.com)—they offer wedding discounts, so be sure to ask! For western-themed weddings, a cloth bandana can double as a napkin and a favor. For Asian-themed dinners, give each guest a set of beautiful chopsticks from Ten Thousand Villages (tenthousandvillages. com) or another fair trade company. No matter what style wedding you are planning, you can find a small, appropriate gift your guests will enjoy using long after the celebration is over.

$$ Plant a Tree

For a green wedding, a tree is a wonderful favor. Trees clean the air of toxins, prevent soil erosion, and sequester carbon from the atmosphere. The Arbor Day Foundation (arborday.org) allows you to find tree species appropriate for your area by zip code, and you can buy small evergreen saplings in favor-ready packages online from Tree Beginnings (plantamemory.com). For larger, more established saplings, contact your local nursery. Small trees can do double duty as decorations if you put them in beautiful pots. You can then use tags or stickers on the pots in lieu of place cards.

For out-of-town guests, or for a more portable tree favor, consider the "Advice from a Tree" seed packets available from Your True Nature (yourtruenature.com). The company offers a mix of Blue Spruce, Ponderosa Pine, and Douglas Fir seeds packaged in a 100 percent recycled paper packet depicting a tree and offering a life lesson. Another great option is a tree starter kit from Tree in a Box (treeinabox.com), which contains a plantable pellet and a miniature information book about the tree species. If you do give a tree favor, be sure to choose a native species and to include a set of tree-planting instructions.◉

$$ Pot a Plant

If you have a lot of friends who live in city apartments with no backyards, you may want to opt for potted plants instead of trees. Ferns, violets, even potted cacti make nice gifts and can double as table decorations. If you are worried about guests having to fly home with their plants, offer them small terra-cotta

---

◉ To see sample tree-planting instructions to include with your favors as well as more tree- and seed-favor designs, visit the Eco-Products section of thegreenbrideguide.com.

pots or even shot glasses with prebagged soil and seeds or a single bulb. Organic seeds are available online from Seeds of Change (seedsofchange.com). You can also give them something lighter and easier to pack, like a seed-imbedded paper ornament from Botanical Paperworks (botanicalpaperworks.com) that they can plant when they get home.

$$ Personalized Gear

If you are having a large wedding, a number of companies, like Print Globe (printglobe.com), now provide 100 percent recycled products from coffee mugs to T-shirts personalized with the logo of your choice for a few dollars each. You can also buy organic clothing, hats, blankets, socks, etc. and iron on a design at home using transfer sheets for your home printer, available through Amazon and at many computer and paper stores. To find quality organic items of all kinds, search a green-product directory like GreenPeople (greenpeople.org).

$$ Wax Poetic

Many decorators incorporate tea lights or pillar candles into wedding-reception decor, because candles make a table feel more intimate and enhance the romantic mood. Instead of buying tea lights en masse, buy slightly larger soy candles in individual containers that your guests can take home at the end of the evening. If you are having a sit-down brunch or a Victorian wedding, consider a soy candle in a reusable teacup from Roses and Teacups (roses-and-teacups.com). For a harvest dinner, pumpkin-pie candles in reusable ceramic mugs from Pieces of Vermont (piecesofvermont.com) are fun. For a natural look, try a palm-wax river-rock candle from Sassy Herbs (sassyherbs. com). Whatever your wedding style, there are wonderful natural-candle favors to complement your decor.

$$$ Eco-Design

If you are having a small wedding or have a bit more to spend, consider unique recycled or natural-material items, like the ceramic pop art coasters from Robot Candy (robotcandy.com) or a colorful recycled-glass vase from Uncommon Goods (uncommongoods.com). For a destination wedding, pass out luggage tags made from recycled circuit boards from Eco-artware.com. You can also find a lot of unique high-design items from Etsy (etsy.com). Just be sure to order as far ahead of time as possible and to double-check that the quantity you want will be available.

For a Cause

It's always nice to give a gift that gives back, and you can show you care while supporting important environmental and humanitarian causes by either donating to the charities directly or by buying gifts whose proceeds benefit a worthy cause.

Donations in Honor

Because favors are not required but are just icing on the proverbial (wedding) cake, consider giving a donation in honor of your guests in lieu of a tangible favor. According to the Better Business Bureau (bbb.org), 80 percent of the money charities raise comes from individual donors.

If you don't have a charity in mind already, or want to learn more about charities in your area of interest, here are a few useful tools. The American Philanthropy Institute (charity-watch.org) has used the financial records of hundreds of charities to come up with a grading system based on the percent of the money they raise that goes to programming versus administrative expenses. Charity Navigator (charitynavigator.org) also ranks charities and allows you to filter information about charities by focus, location, size, and other useful criteria. Give.org is a website maintained by the Better Business Bureau that has data on thousands of charities and a list of the charities that were awarded the National Charity Seal.

It's appropriate to donate one to two dollars per guest and to let your guests know about the donation on the inside of their place card or on a separate piece of paper. There is no need to mention the dollar amount, but it is nice to add a personal note about why you picked the specific charity with a general description of its mission.

$ Carbon Offsetting

For our wedding, my husband and I offset our guests' travel in lieu of favors and put a note inside the seating cards.[*] If you want to give your guests something tangible that accomplishes the same goal, you can do what one couple interviewed by *Sierra* magazine (May/June 2004) did and give each guest a compact fluorescent lightbulb.[* *] Because compact fluorescents (CFCs) produce the same amount of light with less electricity, replacing a 50-watt bulb with an 11-watt CFC keeps 685 pounds of carbon dioxide from being emitted. Reducing future emissions is another form of offsetting that is a nice (albeit unconventional) way to spread the environmental message while decreasing the impact of your wedding. For extra punch, include a fact sheet that shows your guests the monetary and environmental savings of switching all of the bulbs in their houses to CFCs.

$$ Gifts That Give

If you want to support a charitable organization but want to give your guests something tangible as well, The Rain Forest Site, The Hunger Site, The Breast Cancer Site, the Child Health Site,

---

[*] You can see a picture of the place cards we made and learn more about carbon offsetting at thegreenbrideguide.com.

[* *] For pictures of their wedding and their light bulb favors see the Real Weddings page at thegreenbrideguide.com.

The Literacy Site, and The Animal Rescue Site have all linked together through greatergood.org to sell jewelry, clothing, and fair trade wares to support their causes. (The web address for each of these sites is the same format, e.g., www.thehungersite. com.) Additionally, almost every non-profit generates money by offering T-shirts, mugs, and other gear with its logo or other environmental slogans online.

Edible

It's hard to go wrong when you give your guests a small, edible treat they can enjoy while they are celebrating or take home for later. A perfect chocolate-covered strawberry can be eaten for dessert, a small jar of marmalade pocketed for another day. Whether you choose a favor for now or a favor for later, you will have happy guests who know you care.

$ Bulk Tea and Coffee

Everyone loves a gourmet cup of tea or coffee. If you want to give a personal favor on a budget, buy organic or fair trade loose-leaf tea or shade-grown organic coffee and repackage it into single-serving sizes. You can customize tea bags by adding a personalized label from your home computer or from a company like Doing Personal Favors (doingpersonalfavors.com). For loose-leaf tea, check out Inspired Brew (inspiredbrew.com). It offers fair trade and organic tea, uses recycled shipping materials, and donates a portion of each purchase to an international humanitarian effort. The Republic of Tea (republicoftea.com) is another good source of high-quality tea and tea accessories. For coffee, Green Mountain Coffee Roasters (greenmountain coffee.com) has an amazing selection of eco-coffees, including alluring flavors like Wild Mountain Blueberry and Pumpkin Spice, although you can also buy regular flavors and add your own cinnamon, hazelnut, or ground-up peppermint stick to create unique tastes. Package your tea or coffee in muslin tea bags to make single-serving favors, or larger recycled bags for take-home gifts.

$ Homemade Hospitalities

If you are a good cook, are crafty, or have some extra time (ha), nothing beats a homemade favor. For my brother's wedding, he used a simple recipe to make truffles that he rolled in coconut, cinnamon, chopped nuts, and cocoa powder and gave each guest a set of four. Another friend of mine went to a pick-your-own strawberry field, and she and her mom made petite homemade jams for each guest. Sugar cookies and cupcakes are simple treats that can easily be personalized with frosting or by using edible inks to print from your computer onto wafer paper (for more information and to buy supplies see sugarcraft.com). Almost any homemade goody can be turned into a favor with the right presentation.

$$ Chocoholic Heaven

Chocolate is an unfailing crowd pleaser and comes in many forms. You can buy single-serving organic hot chocolate or cocoa from Canterbury Organics, available online from Conifer Specialties (conifer-inc.com), or adorable and tasty fair trade organic ladybugs from Rapunzel (rapunzel.com). For the sentimental, try organic chocolate hearts in your wedding colors from Sweet Earth Organic Chocolates (sweetearthchocolates.com). For animal lovers, consider Endangered Species organic chocolate bars available at www.chocolatebar.com. Lake Champlain's Dark Spicy Aztec chocolate has quite a pop, and its small Milk/Sea Salt/Almonds squares are great for those who enjoy the combination of sweet and salty tastes (lakechamplainchocolates.com). Finally, for something simple, inexpensive, and classic, Equal Exchange (equalexchange.com) has dinner-mint-size dark chocolates.

$$ After-Dinner Mints and Gum

Ensure your guests have good breath by giving them small tins of gourmet mints. VeganEssentials (veganessentials.com) sells Organic Chimp Mints, which are individually wrapped mint chocolates, and their profits go to support the Jane Goodall Institute (janegoodall.org). Sencha sells sugar-free fair trade Green Tea Mints through Amazon. For all-natural gum from the rainforest, try Glee Gum (gleegum.com)

$$ Vegan Versions

There are a number of companies that specialize in vegan products, like VeganEssentials (mentioned earlier), which carries everything from truffles to cookies. Most dark chocolate, like the organic squares we used for our wedding from Green and Black's (greenandblacksdirect.com), are naturally vegan. Some health-food companies, like St. Claire's (stclaires.com), specialize in all-natural dairy-free products and carry a wide selection of vegan breath mints. If you are intentionally seeking vegan products, make sure to highlight that fact to your guests by including a small write-up about why a vegan option is important to you.

$$ Organic Options

As with the welcome baskets, favors are a nice time to include any number of delicious organic treats. If you are Greek or just like nuts, a small bowl or beautiful box of organic almonds is nice (although if you give ones covered in chocolate, be careful about nut allergies). One couple I know made organic trail mix from the bulk bins at Whole Foods and gave out little bags at the send off that read "Happy Trails." Another friend of mine used different types of fruits instead of table numbers and had a fresh piece on each person's plate. It was simple, elegant, and delicious! You can find many organic options these days from local farms, big food chains, and online (buyorganicnuts.com).

$$$ Local Delicacies

If you are having your wedding in a state or region that has specialties, favors are a fun way to share the local "flavor" with your guests. Possible options include jars of local honey from a farmers market, small bottles of organic maple syrup, miniature bottles of local wine, jams or jellies, regionally famous BBQ sauce, cheese curds, a hot Cajun spice mix, jalapeño jelly, or sharp cheddar. Personalize these gifts with a homemade label or a note from the two of you.

Handmade Favors

For artists and crafters, making small favors can be a wonderful way for you to add a personal touch to your reception. If you want to make your own favors, it is essential that you start early and stay realistic. As an amateur (but dedicated) potter, I wanted to make each guest a miniature vase. However, when the numbers climbed toward 160 and I was still working to complete my twenty-fifth vase three months later, I had to scrap the idea. I just couldn't spend five hundred hours working on the favors, even though I thought they would be great. I have heard of brides who spent the last week before the wedding frantically crocheting mittens or canning homemade jams. While I am sure their efforts were appreciated, the time before your wedding is precious, and you do not need added stress. If you do take on a project, choose something simple, start as early as possible, and have a backup plan in mind.

Containing Your Favors

Whether you make your own favors or buy something new, even simple gifts can be transformed into something special with the right packaging. Although small organza bags may be tempting, they are made from petroleum and are not environmentally sound. For more sustainable, more unique favors, consider some of the following ideas instead.

$ Jazz It Up

Enter the world where Martha Stewart lives—get out the tools and get creative. Plain paper bags can become fancy favors with a little help from funky scissors, a unique hole punch, and some pretty ribbon. Buy an interesting stamp or have one made to your specifications from RubberStamps.net. You can also use a silkscreen kit from EZScreenPrint (ezscreenprint.com) to create a motif throughout your wedding for embellishing napkins, seating cards, and programs. With special inks, you can decorate natural elements as well, including stones, shells, driftwood, and leaves. Search online or in magazines and wedding books for inspiring images, and have fun!

$$ A Twist on Tradition

If you like the look of traditional favor containers, look for similar items made from sustainable materials. For example, Bliss Weddings Market (blissweddingsmarket.com) offers colorful jute drawstring bags and raffia CD cases. Instead of a white paper box, use a recycled paper box exquisitely embellished with dried flowers, like the ones available from Ecopapel (catgen.com/ecopapel/EN/). If you have an idea for a gift, see if you can find an eco-friendly alternative before you buy.

$$$ Unexpected Bags and Boxes

Although you can certainly buy prefabricated recycled bags and boxes in all shapes and sizes, there are many options out there that will highlight your creativity and delight the recipients. Buy mixed lots of unused origami paper on eBay, and construct miniature boxes to put truffles or small cookies in. If you can sew, buy lots of vintage fabric or remnants from the local fabric store to make small, reusable cloth pouches. For a simple design, place your treat in the center of a small fabric square or bandana

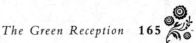

and bring the ends together to create a pouch you can tie with a piece of ribbon. If you are not the crafty type, pick small reusable objects, like mini-flower pots, decorated mason jars, or plantable seed-paper boxes from Botanical Paperworks (botanicalpaperworks.com).

CHAPTER 10

Gastronomically Green—Food and Drink

According to the Wedding Report, the average couple spends over $10,000 on food and another $3,000 on beverages and bartending. Because food and beverages make up nearly half of the typical wedding budget, this is an area where your choices can have a lot of impact. If every bride committed just half of her food and drink budget to buying local and organic foods, it would generate an additional $15 billion worth of green business! The impact of your choice can make a huge difference. Before you sign your catering contract, consider some of the following ideas and alternatives.

Less Is More

In the 1980s, when a non-fat diet was the rage, my mother used to bring home large boxes of fat-free raspberry strudel. It was just awful. When I queried whether she wouldn't prefer to have one small decadently rich, full-fat brownie instead of half a tray of the tasteless pastry, she said when it came to dessert, quantity was more important than quality. I disagreed then and disagree now. Quantity is *not* the most important factor in making your guests happy, and food is *not* the place to skimp in your wedding. Delicious food is so memorable (and so rare at weddings) that a scrumptious meal will make a truly lasting impression on your guests.

If money is tight, there are a number of ways to decrease the quantity of food you will need so you do not have to sacrifice taste. For example, instead of having a full dinner, plan a gourmet brunch buffet, luncheon, or dessert reception. If you want to have dinner, decrease the number of courses you serve. In the summer, offer a salad and skip the soup. In the winter, offer hot soup, and skip the salad and intermezzo. Offer three passed appetizers instead of six, or opt for appetizer-stations (with cheeses, fruit, olives, etc.), which require fewer waitstaff. There is so much food at weddings that no one will notice these changes, and you will save a lot of money.[note]

DIY Cooking

While most couples would never dream of cooking their own wedding feast, there are benefits to doing it yourself if you are having a small or informal affair. When you cater your own event, you have complete control of the recipes and the ingredients, and you *will* save money. However, even if you are having a relatively small wedding, creating a complete menu from scratch can be a Herculean task—and will take up a lot of time you may not want to spend in your final days of pre-wedding preparation. If you have specific recipes you want, a good compromise is to look for a caterer who is willing to follow your orders. If you have a signature entrée or dessert or two you want to make, sign yourself up for those, but I highly recommend leaving the rest of the cooking, serving, and cleanup to professionals. Even if you could, you don't want to spend your wedding day making sure the mushroom puffs are hot enough—and it is not polite to ask any of your guests to take on these chores. If you are still adamant that you do not want a caterer, consider spreading out the responsibility for cooking by having a potluck or BBQ and

[note] For a list and description of different serving styles see the Quick Guide page in the About the Book section at thegreenbrideguide.com.

designate friends and family members to be in charge of setup, serving, and cleanup.

Something Different

A great way to save money and have delicious food is to avoid the classic wedding caterers entirely and have your wedding feast supplied by your favorite restaurant. Weddings are a nice opportunity to honor your heritage or just your favorite ethnic cuisine. Chinese, Mexican, Israeli, Indian, Thai, and even sushi restaurants can almost always beat the going wedding rates and can provide sumptuous and memorable spreads.

CATERING

Some reception venues come with in-house caterers, and others allow or require you to bring in your own. There are advantages and disadvantages to each arrangement. In-house caterers are familiar with the setup, timetable, and general style of the venue but may be less flexible with menu selections. A private caterer can be less expensive, because you can shop around, and will probably be more willing to make substitutions, but he or she may not be familiar with the location or arrangements at the venue. Before you sign off on any caterer, ask about some of the following ideas and options. You can also use the Sustainability Worksheet: Questions to Ask a Caterer at the back of this book to help you compare different vendors. For serving styles, see the Quick Guide at thegreenbrideguide.com.

Organic Food

Some caterers, like Back to Earth (backtoearth.org) in Berkeley, California, or Greg Christian (gregchristian.com) in Chicago, offer organic and natural-food catering. You can find certified green restaurants by state through the Green Restaurant Association (dinegreen.com), in Green America's Green Pages (coopamerica.org/pubs/greenpages), or from your state's organic-growers association or certifying agency. Sometimes you have to work backward by asking organic-growers associations or members of the Slow Food Movement (slowfood. com) which restaurants they sell organic produce to.

Although it may take more work to locate an organic caterer, when you choose one you know you are supporting green business. Rest assured that your work will pay off when you guests are served a fresh, delicious meal. Because organic caterers buy in bulk and have worked hard to develop relationships with local suppliers, you may be surprised at how reasonably priced they are. Good organic caterers will also work with you to develop a menu for your budget. If you can't find a caterer who specializes in organic food, see if any caterers are willing to substitute some organic ingredients for your meal.

GMO-Free Foods

Although you hear less about it these days than just a few years ago, genetically modified foods are ubiquitous. These foods are produced from genetically modified organisms (GMOs), organisms that have had their genes altered through genetic engineering to produce desirable traits. GMOs are extremely controversial, and scientists and policy makers have been debating the potential benefits and dangers since the 1990s. Groups like the Organic Consumers Association (organic consumers.org) and Greenpeace (greenpeace.org/usa) have worked hard to have products that contain GMOs labeled, but so far they have not been successful. Certified "100 percent organic" products cannot contain GMOs, so insisting on 100 percent organic ingredients is a good way to avoid them. If you plan to provide some of the ingredients to your caterer, you can find labeled GMO-free products at many health-food stores and natural-food retailers like Whole Foods.

Local and Seasonal Foods

Have you ever done a blind taste test of a freshly picked tomato from the garden and one shipped from overseas? Although they may look similar, the one from the store will often taste blanched and fishy. This is because produce that is shipped from abroad has to be picked before it's ripe. Importers often spray produce with artificial ripeners to make it look appealing on the store shelves. Fruits and vegetables picked fresh not only taste better, but studies now show they may be better for you as well. In an age when the average American meal travels fifteen hundred miles, buck the trend and serve your guests a feast of fresh local delicacies. When you buy local food, you keep money in your community and support local farmers; decrease the carbon footprint of your meal, because the food does not have to be shipped thousands of miles; and get to enjoy the taste of fresh, high-quality food.

Incorporating regional foods into your menu is a great way to give your wedding local flavor, literally. As the French say, you want your guests to "eat the view." If you can't create a full menu of local foods, try to showcase your region's finest. For example, if you are having a wedding in New England, offer lobsters or clam chowder. If you are having a southern affair, have a BBQ with locally raised meat and fresh corn. You can find local farms and restaurants that work with community-supported agriculture groups (CSAs) and regional organic farmers at Local Harvest (localharvest.org).

Vegetarian Food

While buying locally grown, pasture-raised organic meat saves resources and addresses some of the ethical concerns associated with large-scale farming operations, it still takes a lot more energy and water to produce meat than it does to provide vegetarian fare. Factory farming in the United States has taken a devastating toll on the environment. Not only does livestock production consume 70 percent of our grain, but the waste from Concentrated Animal Feeding Operations (CAFOs) often sits in large manure lagoons and pollutes land and water alike. Meat production has also been associated with deforestation, climate change (both from methane production from the animals and from the oil used to transport meat around the globe), and depletion of water resources (it takes two hundred times more water to produce a pound of beef than a pound of potatoes, and half of the water consumed in the United States is used for livestock production).

Needless to say, there are a lot of good reasons to be a vegetarian or to host a vegetarian event. Offering your guests vegetarian fare almost always saves money as well and gives guests a chance to experience how delicious vegetarian cuisine can be. Friends of mine put a spin on the vegetarian theme by offering a Middle Eastern buffet with intricate spreads of baba ghanoush, hummus, and lentils. If you are an avid meat eater or just don't think a wedding would be the same without the meat—perhaps you are afraid guests will walk around all night saying, "Where's the beef?"—compromise. It is traditional to include at least one vegetarian entrée and one or two vegetarian hors d'oeuvres and appetizers.

At my wedding, the pear and brie pastry purse was the first thing to go—so you might be pleasantly surprised at how well the vegetarian food is received. To find restaurants that specialize in vegetarian cuisine, the Vegetarian Resource Group (vrg.org) has a good directory, which is searchable by city and state. A search of the local Yellow Pages usually offers a few options, or you can ask at one of the natural-food stores listed in *The Tofu Tollbooth* by Elizabeth Zipern and the folksinger Dar Williams, an atlas for locating natural-food stores around the country.

Vegan Fare

If you or your fiancé are vegan, your wedding is a nice opportunity to demonstrate how delectable your lifestyle choice can be. If you are worried about hosting a 100 percent vegan event, you can provide a few well-marked vegan options and encourage everyone to try them. Though we are not vegan, some of our guests do not eat meat or dairy products. As part of our celebration, my husband baked a vegan chocolate-chocolate-chip pound cake, which was the hit of the party.

Fish

Fish are a great source of protein and make yummy entrées, but there are a number of human-health and environmental problems you should be aware of before choosing which fish to serve at your wedding. The main concerns are mercury exposure, overfishing and bycatch, and fish farming (aka aquaculture).

Mercury Exposure. When toxins that are stored in fat, like mercury, lead, and DDT, are released into the environment, they are absorbed into the bodies of fish and other marine species. When large fish eat small fish, the large fish absorb the toxins in the small fish. Therefore, as you move up the food chain, the amount of toxins increases—a phenomenon known as bioaccumulation.

Unfortunately, many of the fish we eat today contain dangerous levels of mercury, which is released into the environment by coal-burning power plants. The risks are especially high for young children and unborn fetuses, so pregnant woman or nursing mothers need to be particularly careful. The Sierra Club offers an updated list of high-risk fish (sierraclub.org/mercury/guide.asp), and the EPA recommends that at-risk populations limit their intake of fish to one meal per week.

Overfishing and Bycatch. Fishing today is rarely done with a rod and hook. Most fish are caught in gigantic nets that pull in tons of fish at a time. As a result, we are quickly depleting the ocean's resources. The sad fact is that many of the fish caught in industrial nets are never eaten. According to the Food and Agriculture Organization of the United Nations (fao.org), one in four sea creatures caught in fishing nets dies unnecessarily. Nets also take the lives of dolphins, sea turtles, seals, sharks, and whales. We have all heard of dolphin-safe tuna, but there are now fishing techniques that protect other at-risk species as well. The Monterey Bay Aquarium in California tracks these technologies and offers an updated list of safe and unsafe fish choices on its website (monterey bayaquarium.org/cr/seafoodwatch.asp).

Fish Farming. It used to be that only people who lived near the sea ate fish regularly, but today you can find fish on the menu at restaurants across the United States. As wild populations have diminished, fish farming has become increasingly popular, and today about half of the seafood in the U.S. comes from farms. But farms are not the panacea we hoped they would be. Many fish farms still depend on wild populations for their stock, use antibiotics to control disease (which creates "superbugs"), and pollute nearby water with the discharge of fish fecal matter. There are also concerns about GMO fish escaping into wild populations. That said, in some cases choosing farmed fish or seafood is better than eating their wild counterparts. Use the guide by the Monterey Bay Aquarium mentioned earlier to make safe selections. The Aquarium puts out wallet-sized watch lists by region, and if you want to distribute them at your wedding, they will send them to you for free. You can also download a similar list distributed by the National Audubon Society in PDF-format and print them out on recycled paper at home (audubon.org/campaign/lo/seafood).

Humane Meat and Poultry

You can educate friends and family about the benefits and improved taste of sustainably grown meat and poultry if you choose to serve them at your wedding. Most meat produced in the United States today comes from factory farms, where thousands of animals are crowded together and are pumped up with growth hormones and antibiotics. A lot has been written about the perils of factory farming, from the inhumane treatment of the animals to the significant environmental and human-health consequences associated with the practice. What has gotten less press is the fact that even "free-range" animals often live in abominable conditions.

The best thing to do is to buy organic, grass-fed/free-range meat and poultry from a small farm in your area. If you can go to the farm and see the animals, then there is accountability, which is your best guarantee of quality. Many high-end restaurants and caterers have relationships with reputable organic or biodynamic (kind of superorganic) farms. Ask about the source of the meat and poultry being offered by your caterer, and if it is not to your liking, ask about the possibility of substitution.

In addition to the resources listed in the organic and local food sections earlier, a good source of sustainable meat is Heritage Foods USA (heritagefoodsusa.com). They offer humanely raised, antibiotic-free genetic varieties of poultry, pork, beef, lamb, and even bison—the farming of which combats the monoculture breeds of factory farming. To address the issue of accountability, Heritage Foods USA offers traceable labels, which track the farm that produced the meat, the conditions in which the meat was raised, the feeding history, and more. They even have a "turkey cam," where you can see your birds live on the farm before processing.

Kosher Meat and Poultry

The word *kosher* means clean or "fit" in the context of Jewish dietary laws. To be certified kosher, animals must be raised, killed, and processed under standards that are stricter than those required by the USDA. For example, kosher meat must be hormone-free, and animals that have broken bones, punctures, or visible illness cannot be eaten. Kosher animals are hand-slaughtered with a single cut, and the use of stun guns and sledgehammers (which can scatter brain and nerve particles— the source of mad cow disease) is not permitted. The meat is processed in salt water, which helps kill lingering bacteria.

The demand for kosher meat is growing because of the perceived quality and health benefits. Because kosher meat has been around for literally thousands of years, you can find it at almost any supermarket. Some companies, like Wise Organic Pastures (wiseorganicpastures.com), sell dual-certified kosher/ organic chicken, turkey, and beef in stores across the United States and online.

Beverages

As the twist on an old saying goes, eat, drink, and be married. The selection and styles of drinks you offer will depend on the time of day, the location, the season, your culture, and your religious beliefs. Unless you have good reasons not to offer alcohol, it is nice to provide your guests with a selection of both alcoholic and non-alcoholic beverages. Beverage selection and bartending may be included in your venue, provided by your caterer, or left to your discretion. If you are not providing the beverages yourself, see if you can negotiate for some of the following green options before signing a beverage service contract.

Juice and Soda

Whether served alone or accompanying a full bar, it's nice to have a selection of juices and sodas available for your guests. The best is fresh squeezed juice from organic fruit. If you live in a part of the country that specializes in citrus or are having a brunch reception, nothing beats fresh squeezed orange juice. If you have to buy canned or bottled juices, there are many delicious organic options available at local health-food stores, large health-food retailers like Whole Foods and Trader Joes, and even major supermarket chains like Stop and Shop. Some companies, like Elite Naturel (organicjuiceusa.com), even offer exotic organic juice flavors, like Honeydew Melon, Quince, and Black Mulberry.

Any fountain soda could be considered green on a certain level, because it is not sold in individual packages. However, if you or your caterer will be using canned or bottled sodas, consider an alternative like Blue Sky's organic soda line (drink bluesky.com), which offers flavors like Orange Crème and Black Cherry in addition to the usual Cola, Ginger Ale, and Root Beer. The company has an even wider selection of natural sodas, which do not contain artificial color, flavors or preservatives. If you feel too attached to Coke or Pepsi to make the switch, buy the largest bottles you can, and make sure they get recycled after the big day.

ALCOHOL-BUYING GUIDELINES

The amount of alcohol you need at a wedding can vary significantly. Generally speaking, daytime receptions require less alcohol than nighttime events, and younger crowds drink more than older crowds. You know your guests best, so you will be the best judge of how much (and what) they are likely to drink. A general rule of thumb is to provide your guests with one drink per person per hour—or four to five drinks per person for an evening affair. If you want to offer a limited bar with wine, beer, and champagne, use the rule of five to calculate how many drinks you need, then divide the total using the following guidelines:

- A bottle of champagne = 6-8 flutes
- A bottle of wine = 5 glasses
- A beer = 1 drink
- A liter of liquor = 18 drinks

Many liquor stores allow you to return unopened beverages, which means you can err on the safe side without penalty. If you are having a full bar, use the following buying guidelines per 100 people:

- Beer = 2 cases (48 beers)
- Champagne = 1.5 cases (18 bottles)
- Red wine = 1 case (12 bottles)
- White wine = 1.5 cases (18 bottles)
- Whisky = 1–2 liters
- Bourbon = 1–2 liters
- Gin = 2 liters
- Scotch = 3 liters
- Light rum = 1 liter
- Vodka = 6 liters
- Tequila = 1 liter
- Dry vermouth = 2 bottles
- Sweet vermouth = 2 bottles

Beer

Most guests will drink either wine or beer, and there are many quality "green" beer options available on the market today.

$ Do-It-Yourself Beer

Like wine, beer is something you can make at home. There are a number of DIY kits that give you everything you need to start making your own brew. Mr. Beer (mrbeer.com) offers a kit that allows you to brew and bottle two gallons in two weeks. It even has a brew-your-own root beer kit! For a kit made by a famous Australian microbrewery, try the All-in-One Brewing Kit from Cooper's Brewery (makebeer.net), which comes with an instructional video.

$ Bulk

Although it limits the selection of beer you can offer, buying beer in a keg or pony keg saves resources and costs less. If the idea of a keg harkens back to your college days in a bad way, remember that the keg can stay behind the bar and that your guests will not be walking around with red plastic cups. If you want to have beer available on the tables, you can always have the bartender decant it into pitchers. Ask your local beer distributor about available varieties.

$$ Microbrews

Why give your guests Miller or Bud Light when there are so many worthy microbrews? Take your bridal attendants out for a beer tasting and let them choose their favorites! You can search for microbreweries by city and state at the Brewers Association (beertown.org).

$$$ Organic

There are also a number of excellent organic breweries with wide distribution. Wolaver's Organic Ales (wolavers.com) is a popular choice. The Vermont-based company uses locally produced wheat and other ingredients in its small-batch brews. Another notable beer maker (and my sister's favorite) is Fish Brewing Company (fishbrewing.com), based in Olympia, Washington. It offers organic ales and German-style lagers and provides web links to fish-conservation groups, like Save Our Wild Salmons (removedams.org) and Trout Unlimited (tu.org), on their website. My father, an ale connoisseur, recommends the Nut Brown Ale from Peak Organic (peakbrewing.com).

Wine

Even a limited bar usually includes one red and one white wine. When buying wine, cut down on waste by purchasing larger-quantity containers. In addition to magnums (equal to two bottles) and boxes (equal to four bottles), you can get bottles containing up to 30 liters (40 bottles of wine). Not only do these huge bottles have wonderful biblical names like the Salmanazar (9 liters), the Balthazar (12 liters), and—for all you *Matrix* fans out there—the Nebuchadnezzar (15 liters), but they also look really cool! In the months leading up to your wedding, do a taste test of a number of different companies and varietals until you find a few you love. In many states you can have wines shipped directly to your home. If local law does not permit direct shipping, ask a local wine store to import for you. When making your selection, consider some of the following options.

$ Make Your Own Wines

As I write, there are somewhere between fifty and one hundred bottles of wine aging in my basement. My upstairs neighbor Honor is an oenephile and brews her own wines using fruits and flowers from our garden and the nearby park. Although I have never done it myself, she insists it is an easy process. There are a number of how-to books and DVDs that offer step-by-step instructions for those who want to try it at home.

There are also some wineries that allow you to make your own wine (under supervision) using their grapes and equipment. Some places, like Make-N-Take Wines in Jacksonville, Florida (makentakewines.com), offer packages that include bottles, personalized labels, and a wine-tasting party. What a nice way to bring your families together to celebrate your engagement— and you can share the "fruits" of your labor on the big day. No matter where you get your wine, you can personalize it with your own label (see winelabel.com for examples).

$$ Local

If you live in an area that grows wine, it is nice to support a local vineyard. If you are having a vineyard wedding, the wine will probably be part of the package, but even if you are having your wedding somewhere else, you can ask for or provide locally grown wine. There are a few search engines, like the Wine Directory (winedirectory.org), that list wineries by state. You can look in the yellow pages for vineyards in your area or run a Google search for "vineyard" or "winery" plus the name of your state. Many states also have wine trails or vineyard tours posted online that can help you locate wineries of interest.

$$ Fair Trade

Because grape harvesting is arduous work often done by laborers in developing countries, it is important to support fair trade ventures. One company, Etica (eticafairtrade.com), offers fair trade wines from Argentina, South Africa, and Chile.

$$$ Organic

Grapes are one of the most pesticide-heavy crops in the world. In the conventional grape-crushing process, some of the chemicals that have been added to the grapes find their way into the final product, meaning when you drink conventional wine, you are drinking trace amounts of dangerous chemicals as well. Organic wine is made from grapes that have been grown without the use of chemical pesticides, fertilizer, and herbicides. Most organic wines also have fewer sulfites, because they cannot add additional preservatives, which is good for people who are prone to wine headaches. Many wine stores now carry a few organic varieties, so next time you go, ask about organic options. Set up a wine tasting with your friends, and you may soon be a convert.

In sampling wines for our wedding, my husband and I fell in love with Gewurztraminer, an organic version of which is now available from Frey Wine (freywine.com). Frey's 2006 Pinot Noir was applauded by the *Wall Street Journal*. Fetzer (fetzer.com) makes a magnificent Riesling, and it is not surprising that it was named Winery of the Year nine times by *Wine & Spirits* magazine. Fetzer also won a number of EPA awards for green business practices. Bonterra (bonterra.com) is another well-known California organic winery. It offers a nice selection of organic wines, including a delicious Chardonnay. Frog's Leap (frogsleap.com) in Napa Valley has a popular Cabernet Sauvignon. For an online selection of organic vegan wines, try the Organic Wine Company (theorganicwinecompany.com).◉

$$$ Biodynamic

Biodynamic wines (aka BD wines) are wines made from grapes grown using biodynamic techniques, which are similar to organic but contain a spiritual element and are considered to be even stricter, or more natural, than traditional organic farming. Ask for biodynamic wines at your local wine store. You can also buy biodynamic wines direct from a number of certified vineyards, like Cooper Mountain in Oregon (coopermountainwine.com), which is certified by the largest biodynamic certifier, Demeter (demeter-usa.org). Frey, mentioned earlier, also carries biodynamic wine.

Champagne

Organic champagnes are still hard to find, but a few do exist. If your local wine store does not carry one or cannot get

◉ More organic wines are available every day—see the Eco-Products section of thegreenbrideguide.com for a wider selection of options.

you the variety you want in time, try K&L Wine Merchants (klwines.com), which has a reliable organic champagne selection. You can also use sparkling white wine in place of champagne (which can only come from the Champagne region of France). You can find organic, biodynamic, and vegan champagnes and sparkling wines at Diamond Organics (diamondorganics.com). In a pinch, LVMH Group, which owns the leading champagne producers Möet and Chandon, uses integrated pest management (IPM) techniques to keep grape moths off their vines. For guests who can't drink the bubbly, you can get "champagne-style" organic sodas from Santa Cruz Organic (scojuice.com) or organic sparkling apple cider from Martinelli's (martinellis. com), available online and at many grocery stores.

Hard Alcohol

Although it is perfectly acceptable to offer only beer and wine to your guests, it is also nice to have a full bar. If the bar is not included in your catering contract, or you want the flexibility of buying your own alcohol, use the buying guidelines outlined earlier in this chapter to estimate the quantities you will need. Even if the bar is included, you can often negotiate substitutions, so consider some of the following organic products. Square One Vodka (squareonevodka.com) is a female-owned company that offers certified 100 percent organic rye vodka in a cool, angular bottle. Tru Vodka (truvodka.com) is made from American wheat, and Vodka 360 (vodka360.com) is not organic but sells its vodka in a reusable 85 percent recycled glass bottle with a 100 percent post-consumer recycled paper label. The company offers interesting tips and useful environmental information (like a list of recycling centers by state) on its website. Maison Jomere (maisonjomere.com) is a good source of imported organic spirits, including Highland Harvest Organic Scotch Whisky, Juniper

Green Organic London Dry Gin, and Papagayo Organic Spiced Rum. For an American gin made with organic ingredients, try Bluecoat (bluecoatgin.com).

For tequila, 4 Copas (4copas.com) uses 100 percent organic blue agave to create several award-winning tequilas sold in hand-blown, artisan blue glass bottles. Use the (low-glycemic) organic agave nectar to mix perfect margaritas. In 2006, the distiller Gordon and MacPhail released the first certified organic single-malt Scotch whiskey—Benromach Organic (benromach.com)—with "sweet, charred oak aromas" laced with fresh fruit notes of banana and pineapple. It is my husband's new favorite. For something a bit different, try VeeV spirits (veevlife.com), made from vitamin-rich açaí berries, prickly pear, acerola cherry, and ginseng. VeeV's spirits contain no artificial additives, and the company has undertaken a number of green initiatives, from using post-consumer materials and wind energy to donating money to the Rainforest Action Network. Finally, pick up some Modmix Organic Cocktail Mixers. You can get martini, margarita, and mojito mixes online from BTC Elements (btcelements.com).

EXPERT ADVICE

H. Joseph Ehrmann opened the first certified green bar in the United States, Elixir, in San Francisco (elixirsf.com). When buying for his bar, he has three categories of "green spirits": (1) certified organic, (2) made with organic ingredients, and (3) green. He tries to buy liquor from category one whenever possible, because he believes that companies should make every effort they can to be sustainable and worries about "greenwashing." When choosing green beverages, make sure to read labels carefully and try to promote the companies that are doing the most to protect the environment.

Hot Beverages

Coffee and tea are standard fare at most weddings, but a hot glass of cider or a mug of mint cocoa can transform a fall or winter wedding into a cozy event. No matter which hot beverages you offer, there are eco-friendly options available.

$ Coffee and Tea

The latest coffee statistics show that Americans consume 400 million cups of coffee a day (146 billion cups a year), and tea in the United States is a $6.5 billion industry! All of these delicious beverages come at a cost. "Conventionally grown" (aka non-organic) teas and coffee destroy rainforest, reduce soil fertility, contaminate water, and expose workers to toxic chemical pesticides. If you want to include sustainably produced beverages in your wedding, offer a selection of organic coffees and teas—they are easy to find, relatively inexpensive, and taste great.

When choosing coffee and tea, ask for specific certifications— fair trade, organic, and shade grown. A number of companies now offer coffees with all three, including Grounds for Change (groundsforchange.com), Green Mountain Coffee Roasters (greenmountaincoffee.com), and Equal Exchange (equalexchange.com).⊚ These companies also carry fair trade organic teas, so you can have everything shipped together. Green Mountain Coffee Roasters also sources fair trade-certified coffee for Newman's Own Organics, and about 20 percent of the packaging is made from a sugar polymer.

⊚ For more eco-friendly coffee and tea options, see the Eco-Products section of thegreenbrideguide.com.

THE SCOOP ON SHADE-GROWN COFFEE

Coffee was traditionally grown in the shade of native trees. Shade-grown coffee has a richer flavor, requires fewer pesticides and fertilizers to grow, and provides habitat for migrating songbird species. Hybridized full-sun coffee plantations were introduced in the 1970s as a way to produce more coffee in a shorter amount of time. The nitrogen-fixing shade trees were cut down, and farmers began relying on chemical fertilizers and pesticides to produce decent yields. Certified shade-grown coffee is a return to nature and diversity. According to the U.S. Fish and Wildlife Service (fws.gov), in some parts of the neotropics, shade-grown coffee is the only remaining forestlike habitat left. Help support them buy purchasing certified shade-grown brews!

$$ Hot Chocolate

For little kids and winter weddings, nothing beats a hot cup of cocoa. Lake Champlain (lakechamplainchocolates.com) sells a sampler set with six different varieties, and Dagoba (dagoba-chocolate.com) makes a zesty version with chilies and cinnamon called "xocolatl" that your adult guests are sure to love.

$$$ Cider

If you are having a fall wedding, buy gallons of fresh-pressed cider from a local orchard, and add cinnamon or clove for a scrumptious seasonal treat. You can also give guests packets of Simply Organic's Mulling Spice and let them add it to taste.

Hot Beverage Essentials

Don't forget to top your coffee and tea bar off with organic milk and at least one variety of organic milk substitute (e.g., soy or rice milk)—available in most large supermarkets and health-food stores. For sweeteners, offer honey, certified organic European-style sugar packets from Wholesome Sweeteners (available at organicsugars.biz), packets of unrefined blond cane sugar from Sugar in the Raw (sugarintheraw.com), and/or fair trade sugar packets from Equal Exchange (equalexchange. com). For a natural, calorie-free sweetener, try SweetLeaf Stevia (sweetleaf.com), available at Whole Foods and the Vitamin Shoppe, which you can also get in drop form with aromatic flavors like English Toffee. According to the FDA, the use of bleached coffee filters is a primary way people ingest carcinogenic dioxins. Therefore, you should also provide your caterer with unbleached coffee filters, like the ones available from Natural Brew, which you can find in big-box stores like Sam's Club. Don't forget to add extra spoons or compostable wood stirrers.

CAKE AND DESSERT

A good wedding cake is magical, but there are many other delicious options. From cupcakes to petit fours, today's "wedding cakes" can take many forms and can be more sustainable and more delectable than traditional wedding cake. Frosting is a big part of cake texture and taste.◉

Cakes

Open any bridal magazine and you will see picture after picture of sumptuous-looking, multitiered wedding cakes that seem to defy the laws of physics in their construction and grandeur. According to the Wedding Report, the average wedding cake (including cutting fees) in America today costs almost $600. If only they all tasted as good as they look! I cannot tell you how many times I have watched a wedding cake cut in great anticipation, only to find myself looking into my coffee and thinking about the

---

◉ See the Quick Guide page at thegreenbrideguide.com for a list and description of different frosting options.

chocolate bars I keep stashed in my car. If you want a traditional cake, don't sacrifice flavor for looks. Make sure your baker offers samples and/or has wonderful references before signing the dotted line. If you want a traditional cake, the following are a few ideas on how to make your cake more environmentally friendly—how to have your cake and eat it too, so to speak.

TOP THIS!

Instead of buying a onetime-use cake topper, consider using something with personal meaning. Whether a *Star Wars* action figure, a porcelain sculpture from your collection, or an elegant fan, displaying something personal tells your guests something about you and makes the cake more interesting. If nothing you own calls to you, consider skipping a topper and having the baker make something decorative with fondant, piping, edible flowers,* or other natural elements. For our cake my husband I had the baker use natural-colored ribbons and pressed ferns from our garden. I have also seen cakes topped with marzipan fruit, candles, and fresh strawberries. For a Christmas wedding, top the cake with a homemade gingerbread bride and groom—for an autumn wedding, perhaps miniature bride-and-groom painted gourds.

One cool idea (adapted from Danny Seo's *Simply Green Parties*) is to ask a bakery that makes cakes with scanned images on them to use natural elements, like colorful autumn leaves and flowers, to create an edible frosting sheet for you. Your baker can then cut up the frosting sheet to make lifelike edible embellishments to top a cake or cupcakes.

$ Small Cakes

It's often easier and less expensive to buy several small organic cakes than one large "wedding cake." For half the cost of a

---

* It's important to note that if you use edible flowers like nasturtiums, hibiscus, roses, orange blossoms, pansies, marigolds, or squash blossoms in *any* dish, they must be pesticide-free, or they can be hazardous to your guests.

wedding cake, you can buy fifteen or twenty different kinds of organic cake to create a mouth-watering display. Organic bakeries like Ghalia Organic Desserts (ghaliaorganicdesserts. com) in Los Angeles create everything from dark chocolate coconut cake to blood orange custard cake, allowing you to offer everyone at your wedding something he or she will enjoy. Even if you have to buy cakes made with conventional ingredients, offering a selection of flavors usually results in fewer leftovers. Another fun option is to put a miniature (six-to-twelve-person) wedding cake on every table, like the picture-perfect ones made from local and organic ingredients by Miette in San Francisco (miettecakes.com). For a more personalized (and nostalgic) version, give each guest an organic chocolate cupcake or "Goldie" made by New York baker Sarah Magid (sarahmagid.com). Sarah also makes full-sized organic wedding cakes with intricate whimsical decorations.

$ Fake Layers

If you have your heart set on a five-tiered extravaganza but don't have enough people coming to your wedding to eat it all, save money and decrease leftovers by having the chef add several fake tiers. It has become quite common for bakers to frost a layer or two of cardboard (recycled if possible) to make a cake seem bigger. You cut and serve the real layers, so your guests never know!

$$ Vegan

There are a surprising number of vendors offering vegan weddings cakes. One notable Philadelphia bakery, Lotus Cake Studio (lotuscakestudio.com), has creative theme cakes that are true works of art—perfect as a wedding cake or a groom's cake. I was able to locate vegan bakers in almost every state by googling "vegan cake directory" and following the link to About.com.

SLICE THIS

Like corkage fees that some restaurants charge when you bring your own wine, some reception sites will have a per-person "cutting fee" if you bring your own cake or cakes. Be sure to ask about this before you sign a contract. You may be able to negotiate it away if they are not able to provide you with organic or vegan options.

$$ Organic

Making an organic cake is relatively easy, as most of the key ingredients are readily available in organic varieties at large chain supermarkets. Some bakers and bakeries specialize in organic wedding cakes, but if there isn't one in your area, ask around to see if any are willing to make ingredient substitutions. Even if a baker can only get organic flour and sugar, it's worth the effort.

Non-cake Dessert Options

Wedding cakes are large, expensive, and often do not taste as good as other desserts—so why not jump aboard the new trend of non-cake cakes? At weddings these days, you find everything from magnificent dessert buffets to cake-shaped towers of treats. Non-cake options are also clever ways to dodge pricey cake-cutting fees, which they can't charge you if there is no cake. The following are a few fun ideas, but you should let your imagination—and your stomach—be your guide!

$ Candy Station

One charming idea is to fill different-sized glass containers with your favorite natural and organic candies and chocolates and give guests recycled-paper bags to fill as though they are in a candy store. You can create a colorful display or go for a dramatic monochrome effect—either way you will delight your guests. The best part is that the goodie bags can double as wedding favors.

$ Something Small

Sometimes a personal treat (in a portable container) is the best option, because your guests may be so sated from the meal they are not hungry for dessert. See the Favor section in Chapter Nine for a few ideas in this category.

$$ Tower of Treats

A recent trend reflected in magazines from *Brides* to *Readymade* is to create a cake-shaped tower of treats. These can be anything from gourmet powdered truffles to kitschy Ho-Hos. You can also display cupcakes on tiered trays for a similar effect. Towers of treats are a bit more interesting than a regular cake, and if you choose your favorite items, you won't mind taking home the leftovers at all.

$$$ Dessert Buffet

If you're not a cake lover, opt for an array of small, delectable desserts, such as tarts, pies, and éclairs, instead. A dessert buffet is a nice choice, because all of your guests can find something they like; small desserts are easier to take home; and a dessert spread costs less and looks delightful. As long as you include both chocolate and fruit options, it is hard to go wrong. If you want to have part of your wedding done potluck-style, asking everyone to bring a dessert is a nice way to go. One couple I know had everyone bring a pie, which created an impressive and flavorful buffet.

$$$ S'mores and Fondue Fountains

Interactive desserts are all the rage. For the taste of camp without the campfire, put an individual s'mores roaster on every table along with the fixings, and let your guests roast their own. Fondue fountains with fresh local or organic fruit are always fun. You can rent large ones for a buffet from some catering companies or can buy (and resell) smaller fountains for each table.

CLEANUP

Before you know it, the party will be over, and it will be time to clean up. If you are smart, you and your husband will be long gone, off to enjoy your honeymoon (or off to the after party with your friends). To have the cleanup run successfully without your oversight, you need to have a cleanup plan and the man power to carry it out. You can probably make arrangements with your caterer or reception venue for things like garbage disposal, composting, recycling, and food and flower donations. You will need to employ friends and family members to take gifts, leftover cake, and anything else you have supplied. In addition to the discussion "The Importance of Communicating Your Vision" in the Introduction, following are some tips on how to smoothly execute your wedding-day cleanup.

Composting

It's hard to compost unless the venue you choose is already set up to do it. Sometimes you can rent a compost bin and bring your compost to state-run or local facilities. You can also offer to help places like country clubs and hotels set up composting facilities, but it may be a tough sell. If composting is an option, try to design a menu that lends itself well to composting, which means either eliminating meat, raw dairy, and oily foods or having these items served on separate plates. If composting is not an option, you have to focus on minimizing waste. Consider having a buffet reception (which can make food easier to reuse or donate depending on the laws), or give your guests Tupperware or recycled-paper takeout containers at the end of the night for them to take uneaten food home with them.

Recycling

It may surprise you to know the EPA estimates that, despite decades of campaigning and education, only 5 percent of plastic and 22 percent of glass in this country actually gets recycled. Some states and municipalities have now enacted laws that require businesses like hotels and restaurants to recycle, but not all have, so make sure to ask venues and caterers ahead of time what, if anything, they recycle. If the place you choose does not have recycling bins on the premises, see if it is willing to collect all recyclable goods from your wedding, and ask a friend or family member to pick up the slack. If the venue uses canned sodas or bottled beers, there could be a hefty financial incentive for your volunteer.

Trash Bags

It is so easy and inexpensive to get trash bags made from recycled or biodegradable material these days that there is little excuse not to use them. If your request is not met, you can buy a roll at most supermarkets or online from Kokopelli's Green Market (kokogm.com), and ask the caterer or reception to use them.

Detergents

The same strategies mentioned earlier for trash bags apply to detergent. If you are using rented dishes or linens, or if they come with your venue, ask if the company already uses or is willing to use non-toxic chlorine and phosphate-free detergents. Seventh Generation (seventhgeneration.com) has a line of effective products in scents like Blue Eucalyptus and Lavender.

Donating Food

While most states have restrictions on food donations (ask your caterer; he or she should know), you may be able to donate some of your leftover or uneaten victuals to food banks or hunger-relief programs in your area. Some caterers have relationships with churches and shelters and will take care of the donation for you, although you should make sure the donation is part of your contract before you sign, to be safe. If you need to find a shelter accepting donations in your area, America's Second Harvest, the Nation's Food Bank Network (secondharvest.org), is the country's largest hunger-relief organization and has food banks and food-rescue member organizations in every state, the District of Columbia, and Puerto Rico. You can search for a location to donate to in your area by zip code from the website's main page. The website also offers instructions on how to safely pack and store all kinds of leftovers for proper donation, which you can print out and give to your caterer. If your caterer is not willing to make the donation, make sure you designate someone to transport everything in a timely manner.

Green Music and Memories

At its core, a wedding is a great party. Many brides report that their wedding was the best party they ever went to. This makes sense, because every detail of your wedding is exactly how you want it to be. You choose the food, the people, the decorations, and the music. Whether you have live music, a DJ, or use an iPod, you are sure to have a wonderful event. If done correctly, you will have Grandma up and shaking her booty, and you will not want to miss it, which is why this section also discusses documentation and the small things you can do to make sure your photography and/or videos are as green as can be.

MUSIC

Nineteenth-century German philosopher Friedrich Wilhelm Nietzsche once wrote, "Without music life would be a mistake." While Nietzsche's sentiments may seem a bit drastic, it is true that good music can make a good party *great*. For your wedding you will need to make two big decisions about the music: what kind of music you want and how you want to have it played. The choice of music that's appropriate will depend on your culture, your taste, and the nature of the event. Whether you use live musicians or recorded music will depend on your budget, your preferences, and your priorities.

Some green wedding resources advocate for "unplugged" music, but supporting local musicians has greater social value, and the amount of electricity that bands require for their equipment is minimal when viewed in the larger context of a wedding. Running an iPod and speakers takes more energy than strolling violinists, but the violinists have to drive to the site and will need dinner, which takes energy to prepare. The bottom line is that there is no "right" answer. If you like a cappella, classical guitar, or harp music, go for it, but otherwise, either stick to a computer/iPod or get the DJ or band of your choice, and don't worry about it. Consider some of the following options and choose what works best for you and your fiancé.

Unplugged

Whether played while you walk down the aisle or as background music at a cocktail party or low-key reception, acoustic music is a nice addition to any wedding. The following are a few popular kinds worth considering.

$ Strolling Violins

Strolling violins are usually associated with fancy Italian restaurants. They are good for small, intimate venues with good acoustics where table-to-table romance will be appreciated.

$ Acoustic Guitars

In Morocco this year, my husband and I ate at a restaurant that featured a live acoustic guitar/sitar duo. The music the two men played was breathtakingly beautiful, reminding me how skilled musicians can enliven a room. Acoustic guitar offers a melodic, ethereal sound that will captivate your guests.

$$ Chamber Music Ensembles

Wedding ceremonies are elegant affairs, so it's not surprising that classical music or chamber music (a form of classical music meant to be played for intimate gatherings) is the most popular accompaniment. Chamber groups can include many different arrangements but usually have two to five musicians playing violin, viola, cello, flute, piano, oboe, or clarinet.

EXPERT ADVICE FOR OUTDOOR WEDDINGS

Part of being green is reducing waste—both physical waste and economic waste. Too often well-intentioned couples book musicians to play at their outdoor wedding, only to be disappointed when the musicians have to cancel because of weather or cannot be heard because of the layout. Ginny Bales, the lead vocalist and business manager for Bales and Gitlin Music (balesgitlinmusic. com) is working on a new book called *I Sang at Your Wedding: A Practical Guide to a Wedding that Works.* Based on twenty-five years' experience in the field, she offers brides who want to have an outdoor wedding the following tips:

1. Acoustic music works best outside if the wedding is small (less than a hundred people) and the site is sheltered from the wind.
2. Most musicians will not play if it is too cold (less than 55 degrees), too hot, or too wet (including a thick fog or mist) for fear of damaging their priceless instruments. Make sure to read your music contract carefully to find out what the parameters are. To be safe, give your musicians a shelter with roll-down sides, prepare to have space heaters on call, and always have a plan B.
3. Certain instruments are hard to play while walking, so if you want a parade, make sure to ask the musicians what will be possible ahead of time.
4. For amplified music, make sure that the band has plenty of time and space to set up equipment and that it has its own designated outlet to plug into. (Don't assume that the band

can share the same electrical circuit with your tent lighting, a videographer, or coffeepot, since this often doesn't work.)

A good band can read a crowd and improvise in tough situations. An excellent band can build on and focus the energy of your guests to create a more intense feeling of celebration than is possible with recorded music. Hiring live musicians also creates important employment for artists. So before you jump to the iPod, consider hiring a live band!

$$ A cappella

In New Haven, where I live, a popular restaurant called Mory's offers live a cappella music from the Yale singing group the Whiffenpoofs. Anyone who has been there can attest to how much fun it is to see them perform, as they twirl and jig and bring classic tunes to life. Not everyone likes a cappella, but a good a cappella group can be great fun, putting on a dinner show your guests will surely remember.

$$ Steel Drums

For a tropical wedding, nothing makes guests feel like they are on vacation like a steel-drum band.

$$$ Klezmer

Klezmer music is traditional Jewish music with roots in the fifteenth century. Klezmer bands are fun for getting the old folks up and moving with horas and polkas.

$$$ Mariachi

Mariachi music originated in Mexico and mariachi musicians often come in full costume, including silver-studded outfits and wide-brimmed hats. Most bands have a wide repertoire, from dance music to lugubrious serenades.

> **Average Cost of Music by Provider***
> Ceremony:
> Musicians = $500
> DJ = $900
> Band = $1,500
>
> Reception:
> DJ = $800
> Musicians = $1,200
> Band = $3,200
> *Data from the Wedding Report, rounded to nearest $100.

Plugged In

Although many couples still choose acoustic music for at least part of their wedding, wedding music on the whole is evolving, and electronica is now in vogue. The following are a few pros and cons of common electronic choices, as well as tips for getting the most out of your wedding music.

$ iPod

It doesn't take many hours of feverishly massaging the numbers into the wedding calculator to realize that if you decide to have an iPod wedding, you can take that number in the "entertainment" line and make it a big fat $0. If you are crunched for cash or are confident you can create a rockin' wedding on your own, an iPod may be the way to go. For our wedding, my husband and I split the difference. We had my childhood violin teachers play for our ceremony and used an iPod for the reception. Here are a few keys to making an iPod work for you.

- **Setup.** Make sure that the venue you are using has the speakers and amplifiers you need and that they will work with your iPod/computer. Test whatever system you plan to use ahead of time, and buy or borrow missing and backup parts. The speakers at many venues are meant for speeches only and will not work for a rockin' dance party—and your home speakers may not be enough in a noisy setting. Make sure to research your speaker needs carefully, and buy or rent what you will need to fill the space.

Diversity. Remember that the songs you like to listen to in your living room may not work for a party. Apple's iTunes Essentials offers many tried-and-true wedding song collections for less than $75 apiece. You can also do what we did, and ask your guests to include their favorite dance songs in the RSVP. When they hear the songs they picked, they are more likely to get up and dance, and it helps you gauge your audience. To accommodate everyone, we ended up making a number of thirty-minute mixes so we could have different types of music over the course of an evening. We went to the eclectic extreme for our wedding, with chamber music for the ceremony, jazz for the cocktail hour, Israeli dancing music for the first set, schmaltzy lounge music for dinner, and salsa and 1980s rock for the dance party. It was a blast.

Taking Charge. If you use an iPod or any form of DIY music, it is absolutely essential that you designate a competent family member or friend to be in charge and to act as a master of ceremonies. The flow of every party is different, and you will need someone to tell guests that it is time to eat, while changing the music to a mellower mix. That someone should not be you.

Backup. Always always always have your playlists backed up on CD, and consider bringing a system that can work if the power goes out. That backup doesn't have to be a generator, just another way of keeping the party going. When the power went out at one friend's wedding, the groom's family took out African drums and created a drum circle, which was a lot fun and very memorable.

$$ DJ

The upside of having a DJ is that DJs are usually less expensive than a band and can keep a party moving all night long. The downside is that a bad DJ can make your party turn from fun to cheesy in two seconds flat, and many DJs today use iPods (which may leave you feeling like "for $500 I could do that!"). If you decide to go with a DJ, be sure to give him or her a "do not play" and a "favorites" list ahead of time. Also make sure he or she comes with equipment and that you retain the volume controls. Ask your DJ what the backup plan is in case of a power outage.

$$$ Band

The upside of a good band is that they can be flexible, fun, and give off great energy. Many bands play recorded music during their breaks or can do "continuous music," rotating which members are on break. Bands often charge more for this service, and it is probably unnecessary, as parties need space to breathe and a CD works just as well. The downside of having a band is that bands inherently have a more limited repertoire than the infinite universe of digital music, so you may not be able to hear your favorite songs unless you request them ahead of time. Bands can also get lost; someone can fall ill; or an instrument can break. Finally, unless it is in the contract, bands will not usually stick around into the wee hours. As with all music plans, you should make sure to have a backup plan ready and a good mix to put on between sets. To save electricity, ask the band to skip all of the fancy lights and accessories.

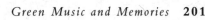

PHOTOGRAPHY AND VIDEOGRAPHY

As the old Jewish joke goes, "Oh, the kids are cute, but you should see the pictures!" Pictures are an important aspect of any wedding, and an entire "shadow industry" has developed around our desire to capture our weddings on film. In addition to expensive photography packages (average price about $2,500), the industry now pushes disposable cameras, videographers, professional photo booths, and more. The following are a few simple ways to make your photography more green.

Hiring Photographers—Amateurs Can Work

If you have friends or relatives who are good with a camera, you can save a lot of money by hiring them to document your wedding. If you have a friend or multiple friends take pictures, you can upload all of them onto a site like Kodak Gallery and let everyone buy the prints they want for just pennies apiece. If you do hire a photographer, give him or her a list of the pictures you would like taken, and be sure to include the rights to the images in the contract. Most photographers charge outrageous prices for printing and do not let you keep the negatives or digital files. You should also consider hiring a professional photographer who does weddings on the side. If the photographer has another source of income, he or she may be more willing to negotiate the contract price and image rights. An MFA graduate student may be similarly flexible. Contact a local art institute and ask for a list of people who are at the top of their class.

MONEY-SAVING TIP

Most photographers and videographers work on an hourly basis. You can save money by scheduling the toasts, cake cutting, first dance, and other must-have-documented moments immediately after dinner so the photographer and/or videographer does not have to stay until the end of the party.

Stay Digital

Although some photographers are still wed to film-based photography (and may try to convince you it is better), digital technology has evolved to the point that the vast majority of professional photographers—including those for *National Geographic*—use digital cameras. Film processing requires toxic chemicals, takes a long time, costs more, and does not yield higher-quality results. By staying digital, your photographer can quickly and easily delete unwanted images, provide you with proofs, color correct, and post all of the photos on the web. With digital photography, only the pictures you want are printed, saving additional resources. It is clearly the green choice du jour.

If you do hire a film-based photographer, ask him or her to only print proofs of the best pictures (perhaps a few hundred out of the thousands). In addition to being better for the environment, this will save additional money—as proofs are expensive to produce.

Avoid Disposable Cameras

Although it's a fun idea to have a disposable camera at every table (or these days disposable video cameras), usually guests only take a few shots before moving on. Because of the way these cameras are designed, images are often underexposed; the film is expensive to process; and the cameras are not easily recyclable. If you want to make sure you get lots of candid shots, ask a few of your friends to bring their digital cameras with them and to be "on duty." They will be happy to do it, and the pictures and short video clips you will get will be a lot better. If you decide you really want disposable cameras, be sure to buy ones that have been recycled (available online at americanbridal.com).

Hiring Videographers

Almost everything that was said earlier about photographers also applies to video—if you have a few friends take videos you can upload them and edit them yourself with iMovie or a similar program. You can also try to find a videographer who is willing to edit amateur video, so the final product will have a professional feel. That said, if video is important to you, hiring a professional guarantees a certain level of quality. Be sure to lay down clear lines about what you do and do not want recorded and how close the videographer can get. I went to a wedding where a man was lurking in the bushes about fifteen feet from the bride and groom during the ceremony. It was distracting, to say the least.

CHAPTER 12

Giving and Receiving Green

Like many celebratory occasions, weddings are a time of gift giving and receiving. It has become customary for brides to give their attendants and parents thank-you gifts, either at the rehearsal dinner or right before the ceremony. Depending on your vision, your budget, and the overall scale of your event, you may also want to prepare welcome baskets for your guests (discussed in Chapter Seven) or give your guests small favors (discussed in Chapter Nine).

Then there is the matter of gift getting. Soon you will realize that getting married is like hitting the love and gift jackpots in one fell swoop. Unless you get your registry up and running quickly, random gifts will start pouring in, and soon you and your fiancé will have to expand the kitchen to create enough storage for all of the new decorative bowls you will acquire. This chapter offers green ideas for each gift-giving opportunity and provides ideas and resources for creating a diverse, meaningful, and useful registry.

THANK-YOU GIFTS FOR THE WEDDING PARTY

It has become traditional for the bride and groom to give the members of their wedding party thank-you gifts, either at the rehearsal dinner or sometime before the ceremony. According to the Wedding Report, couples spend about $750 on these gifts—almost twice what they spend on favors. Traditional attendant gifts for women include spa baskets or gift certificates, silk or flannel pajamas, stationery or journals, jewelry, fancy soaps, and scented-candle sets. For men, couples often choose cufflinks, money clips, Swiss Army knives, cigars, lighters, and flasks. For parents, many couples wait until after the event and give them a portrait from the wedding in a beautiful frame. For any kind of gift you want to give, there are green versions. There are also a lot of less traditional items which are worth considering, because how many money clips can a man use after all?◉

Recycled Gifts

Recycled materials, including glass, metals, paper, and electronics, are now being crafted into beautiful gifts. The following are just a few of the many recycled items available in the marketplace today.

$ Recycled and Vintage Glass

Only 20 percent of the glass in the United States is recycled, so finding creative ways to reuse broken and discarded glass is important. A number of companies now make gorgeous recycled-glass earrings, necklaces, and pendants for less than $20. Christy Fisher Studio (christyfisherstudio.com) has simple but elegant designs using round glass drops and stained glass in every color of the rainbow. Austin Design Jewelry (austindesignjewelry.com) uses recycled-glass beads to make luminous bracelets that would make any mom happy, and you can find unique crushed-glass and recycled-marble pendants at Fiddlehead Studio (fiddleheadstudio.com). Beautiful and unusual rings designed from antique and vintage Swarovski crystals and semiprecious stones

---

◉ See the Eco-Products section of thegreenbrideguide.com for a large selection of green gifts for moms and maids, men, children, babies, and even pets!

are available from companies like Seraglia (seraglia.com). For non-jewelry gifts, look at Gaiam (gaiam.com) and Aurora Glass (auroraglass.org), which sell recycled-glass wind chimes and sun catchers. For a nature lover, you can find elegant recycled-glass hummingbird feeders at National Geographic (nationalgeographic.com) and on Amazon.

$$ Metal Matters

For traditional groomsmen gifts like flasks and pocket watches, look at vintage stores and auction sites online. You can find antique silver and gold items, often for less than the cost of new ones. Bring your found treasures down to a local jeweler to have them personally monogrammed and polished. Vintage jewelry, powder mirrors, and antique perfume bottles also make excellent gifts for bridesmaids, mothers, and grandmothers.

$$ Paper Pleasures

It is absolutely amazing how beautiful discarded magazines and newspapers can be when subjected to an artist's touch. Give your bridesmaids funky recycled-paper clutches or bracelets, like the ones available from Ecoist (ecoist.com) and your groomsmen recycled rice-sack messenger bags from Wedge Worldwide (wedgeworldwide.coop). Charm your attendants with an intricate fair trade recycled-paper jewelry box from Novica (novice.com), or a beautiful twig, leaf, and recycled paper journal from World of Good (worldofgood.com).

For a summer wedding, give festive totes from Reusable Bags (reusablebags.com), made from recycled juice containers. Throw in a pair of raffia flip-flops and an organic beach towel. Want to frame a picture for your parents? Put a photo in a colorful recycled-paper frame from Wonders of the World (wondersof theworld.net). Recycled-paper gifts abound, from the whimsical to the elegant; there is something for everyone on your list.

$$ Pottery and Beads

Broken to Beautiful (broken-to-beautiful.org) is an organization that supports victims of domestic violence. The broken-china earrings and angel ornaments (available at roses-and-teacups. com) would make wonderful bridesmaid gifts. Although not for charity, VerdeRocks (gwen-davis.com) uses sustainable materials like bamboo, recycled metals, and vintage beads and crystals to create funky sustainable jewelry. The beaded cocktail rings are particularly cool.

$$ Vintage Finds

Cruise antique shops for beautiful pieces of vintage jewelry, watches, hats, and more. You can take dingy pieces to a local jewelry store for a professional cleaning or use a number of natural cleaning tricks. For example, gemstones usually sparkle up with a five-minute soak in vinegar, a gentle scrub with an old toothbrush, and a quick warm-water rinse.

$$$ Gizmos and Gadgets Turned Gifts

There are so many reasonably priced, cool gifts out there made from recycled computers, outdated technology like cassette tapes, and common goods that wear out or are usable only in complete sets. Eco-Artware (eco-artware.com) sells handsome money clips and business-card holders made from recycled circuit boards, and Uncommon Goods (uncommongoods. com) carries men's cufflinks made from typewriter keys, watch works, and even seats from famous baseball stadiums. They also sell duct-tape wallets—a sure winner with any teenager—and guitar-pick necklaces. For women, Acorn Studios (acornstudios. ca) offers a computer-part pendant, circuit-board mini photo album, and floppy-disc notebook. Greenfeet (greenfeet.com) sells coasters made from discarded LPs, bike-chain eyeglass frames, and record cuff bracelets.

Natural Ideas

For a green wedding, nothing is more "natural" than giving gifts made from nature's bounty. In addition to textiles made from organic cotton and bamboo, you can now find natural versions of many surprising things like sports equipment and sunglasses. If there is something you want to give that is not listed below, search online for a sustainable version—you may be pleasantly surprise by the many green options available in the marketplace today.

$ Cotton and Hemp

Give your bridal party matching organic cotton or hemp T-shirts, hats, or bags. Green America offers an extensive directory of organic- and hemp-clothing stores. You can buy plain items online and personalize them with iron on transfer sheets, or buy something that can be professionally monogrammed, like luxurious organic cotton bath towels from Pottery Barn. If you want to give your maids a lip balm and a few other small beauty products, tuck them in to a stylish cosmetics bag like the ones from Global Girlfriend (globalgirlfriend.com), which supports women's cooperatives and literacy programs around the globe.

$$ Bamboo Buys

As discussed earlier, bamboo can now be made into soft, lush fabric. For a spa-quality gift, try organic bamboo robes from Shirts of Bamboo (shirtsofbamboo.com). If you have fishing fanatics in your bridal party, a bamboo fishing hat from Eco-Fabrik (ecofabrik.com) might be just the thing.

$$ Mother-of-Pearl

Mother-of-pearl is a smooth, iridescent material found on the inside of mollusk shells. It is beautiful, natural, and relatively inexpensive. You can find mother-of-pearl earrings from a number of fair trade jewelry companies, like Moonrise Jewelry (moonrisejewelry.com). Mother-of-pearl is also used to create elaborate inlaid boxes, which you can give as stand alone gifts or can use to present other treasures. Search for mother-of-pearl online in fair trade stores like Global Exchange (store.gxonlinestore.org) and Ten Thousand Villages (tenthousandvillages.com).

$$ Sizzling Scarves

Scarves and pashminas (which are made from the soft wool of the pashmina goat) are always fashionable. They can double as a unifying decor down the aisle for bridesmaids or act as a fashionable layer for a cool evening reception. You can find shawls made from many different kinds of sustainable materials, including alpaca (circleofthesun.org), colorful recycled silk (greatergoodsonline.com), and elegant hemp-flax linen (rawganique.com). A warm, soft shawl is a wonderful gift that your friends and family can enjoy over and over again.

$$ Sporting Equipment

If you have athletic friends or want to have the guys and gals toss the old pig around before you wed, Fair Trade Sports (fairtradesports.com) now makes a line of eco-rubber fair trade athletic equipment.

$$ Fabulous Flowers

Do you have a relative or friend who is into gardening? A gift of a flowering plant or seed set is always appreciated. Taraluna's Pocket Gardens and Garden-in-a-Bag collection (taraluna.com) make for easy indoor greenery, and Red Envelope's Year of Seeds (redevenlope.com) come in charming, reusable pots.

$$ Spa Sets

Everyone loves luxurious bath and body products. If you are crafty, you can make your own soaps, candles, and bath salts. You can also buy individual items from companies like Pacifica (pacificacandles.com), which carries natural soaps, body butters, and a collection of divine perfumes (all "made in the USA") to create your own themed baskets. If you want to piece together deluxe toiletry sets for a destination wedding, there are some great travel-themed products online, like the natural soaps wrapped in reproduced maps of Paris, Rome, and New York from Saipua (saipua.com) and candles in travel tins from Er'go Candle Company (ergocandle.com).

If you would rather buy a preassembled set, EcoExpress (ecoexpress.com) offers a robust spa basket and Lavender Green (lavendergreen.com) has a delicious lavender scented spa kit. Dr. Hauschka (drhauschka.com) sells lavish preboxed body care, face care, and aromatherapy bath sets and has partnered with Heifer International (heifer.org), a non-profit that provides chickens, goats, and other domesticated livestock to families in need. Finally, Gilden Tree's organic foot-soak kit is the perfect way to pamper sore feet after a night of dancing, available from Taraluna (taraluna.com).

$$$ Solar Solutions

Alternative energy doesn't just come in the form of huge solar panels anymore. Forgo the funny-looking ties and shot-glass gifts, and splurge on useful solar toys and gadgets. You can now find solar flashlights, radios, portable freezers, even self-cooling hats that recycle the sun's energy. Global Merchants has a good selection (global-merchants.com/home/solars.htm), but you can find many solar options on Amazon and eBay as well.

$$$ Wooden Wonders

If you are having a summer wedding and really want to splurge, buy your bridal party pairs of fabulous, sustainably harvested wood sunglasses from iWood (iwoodecodesign.com). For a spring wedding, Brelli (thebrelli.com) makes a bamboo and biodegradable plastic umbrella shaped like a delicate parasol.

Experiences

Instead of giving the members of your bridal party more stuff, consider giving them experiences they will remember forever. You can work with local vendors or use online sites to give your attendants gift certificates for massages, facials, horseback riding, dinner, golf, and more.

$ Movies

If you have movie fans in your party, you can buy movie theater vouchers online at Fandango.com, purchase a Blockbuster gift card, or give an unlimited monthly rental subscription to Netflix (netflix.com) for less than $10 a month.

$$ Restaurants

If your wedding party will be in town for a few days before or after your wedding, give a gift certificate to your favorite restaurant or coupons for drinks at a local bar. You can also buy discounted gift certificates to participating restaurants by zip code at Restaurant.com.

$$$ Adventures

If your friends and family live in or near select cities, you can purchase gift certificates for cool things like private surfing classes, ninja classes, and DJ-ing lessons through Cloud 9 Living (cloud9living.com).

Edibles

The bottom line is you cannot go wrong with food. Instead of trinkets or jewelry or soft scarves, consider giving your bridal party baskets of treats or fancy bottles of wine. You can also give gifts that keep on giving with "of-the-month" clubs. A few examples follow.

$ Wine

If you have oenephiles in your party, pick up an extra bottle of any number of organic or biodynamic wines (see the Catering section in Chapter Ten). Present the bottle in a lively fair trade reusable wine bag from Global Girlfriend (globalgirlfriend.com), a modern-design jute wine bag from Hemp Fair (hempfair.com), or a recycled thermal bag from Reusable Bags (reusablebags.com).

$ Chocolate

Show your thanks with delectable collections of fair trade and organic chocolates. The fair trade store Equal Exchange (equalexchange.com) offers a reusable bamboo basket filled with miniature chocolates. For the ultimate in extravagance, give your bridal party gourmet chocolate truffles in an edible chocolate box from Charles Chocolates (charleschocolates.com). Its tea-infused truffles with Chinese characters would also work well as favors.

$$ Beer

Although it is not generally considered appropriate to give a six pack of your favorite beer no matter how pretty the bag is, it is totally acceptable and fun to give your buddies a subscription to a beer-of-the-month club. A microbeer-of-the-month gift (beermonthclub.com) supports small brewers across the United States and you can give between two and twelve months, depending on your budget. For something a bit more hands on, give a brew-your-own organic beer kit from Seven Bridges Cooperative (breworganic.com) or one of the microbrew kits mentioned in the Catering section of Chapter Ten.

$$ Coffees, Teas, Jams, and Local Delicacies

As with favors, coffees, jams, and local delicacies make wonderful gifts—the only difference is scale. Instead of giving a single serving of deliciously scented jasmine tea or raspberry jam, give a sampler set or preassembled organic gift basket.

$$$ Treat of the Month

In addition to the beer-of-the-month club, there are clubs that send cookies, fruit, nuts, and even fair trade organic coffees. EcoExpress (ecoexpress.com) has a nice but pricey selection of clubs for wine, beer, fruit, and baked treats. Organic Style (organicstyle.com) offers roses and other flower-of-the-month programs, and for coffee lovers, Grounds for Change (groundsforchange.com) offers an "explorer" option, with three-, six-, and twelve-month fair trade organic coffee samplers.

Charity

There are a number of different ways to support your favorite charities. Most charities sell cards, T-shirts, and other memorabilia to raise money, all of which make thoughtful and appropriate gifts. If you want to make a direct donation in lieu of gifts, the same websites discussed in the Favors section on page 154 will help you find and rank charities. If you feel awkward presenting your attendants with "in your honor" cards, you can always pair a charitable contribution with a token-themed gift. The following are a few ideas to get you started.

Animals

Pair a donation to pro-animal causes like the Humane Society (hsus.org), the Wilderness Society (wilderness.org), or the Conservation and Research for Endangered Species project at the San Diego Zoo (cres.sandiegozoo.org) with a subscription to a wildlife magazine like *National Wildlife* (nwf.org/national-wildlife) or *Birds & Blooms* (birdsandblooms.com).

Arts

Couple a gift to MOMA (moma.org) or an arts foundation with a beautiful recycled-glass magnet or paperweight. If you want to support musicians and raise money for grassroots environmental projects at the same time, buy albums from groups like Musicians United to Sustain the Environment (musemusic.org).

Cancer
In addition to a direct donation for cancer research, give one of the many "pink" goods, whose profits go to support the cause, like a tin of "Sip for the Cure" pink grapefruit tea from the Republic of Tea (republicoftea.com).

Children
A donation to an organization that supports children, like UNICEF or Save the Children, goes well with a stylish organic plush toy from Sage Baby (sagebabynyc.com).

Education and Literacy
On a bookmark made from seed paper, print information about a gift to a local library or DonorsChoose.org, an organization that raises money for school supplies and educational field trips for public schools.

Environment
If you decide to donate to an environmental charity like the Rainforest Action Network (ran.org), the Nature Conservancy (nature.org), the National Resources Defense Council (nrdc.org), or the Wildlife Land Trust (wlt.org), consider giving a nature-themed gift like a box of rainforest chocolates or a small sapling with planting instructions.

Health
A gift to the American Heart Association (americanheart.org) or the American Diabetes Association (diabetes.org) goes well with a tin of Stress Soother from Badger (badgerbalm.com) or an aromatherapy set.

Homelessness

Pair a gift to Habitat for Humanity (habitat.org), the National Coalition for Homeless Veterans (nchv.org), or Mercy Corps (mercycorps.org), an organization that aids displaced families in need, with a festive new doormat made from recycled flip-flops or polypropylene from Green Living (green-living.com).

Hunger

Celebrate a donation to America's Second Harvest (second-harvest.org) or Bread for the World (bread.org) with a small jar of locally made organic preserves, honey, or syrup.

GIFT WRAPPING IDEAS

Everyone likes to open presents, but tubes of shiny wrapping paper can't be recycled. Here are a few ideas for wrapping your gifts in creative, cool, and sustainable ways.

- **Perfect Paper.** Newsprint, especially the comics section, is always fun, but there are more traditional-looking recycled and alternative-fiber wrapping papers as well. For big, colorful recycled-paper sheets printed with bold, modern designs, try Fish Lips Paper Designs (fishlipspaperdesigns.com). For something different, Forest Saver Designs (forestsaver.com) offers gift wrap made from reclaimed NYC subway and topographical designs. Paporganics (papaorganics.com) offers hemp-blend paper printed with vegetable-based ink, and Paper Mojo (papermojo.com) has a large collection of natural-fiber wrapping paper and tissue paper made from banana leaves, recycled cotton rag, and recycled silk. All of its papers are exquisitely embellished. Finally, you can find plantable, seed-infused wrapping paper at Bloomin' (bloomin.com).
- **Unusual Boxes.** Cruise pawnshops, thrift stores, and smoke shops for coffee tins, bamboo steamers, Russian nesting dolls, cigar

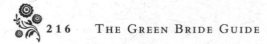

boxes, inlaid-wood boxes, and felt-lined dentist cases. There are so many reusable containers that are much more interesting than plain store-bought wrapping paper!

- **Cloth.** Give two gifts in one by using an antique lace doily, bandana, or scarf bound with a beautiful, biodegradable ribbon from Paporganics (paporganics.com) or with a natural-fiber ribbon like raffia. Lucky Crow (luckycrow.com) sells organic cotton gift bags with organic cotton ribbon closures in three sizes and offers bulk discounts. You can also tuck your gift into reusable, industrial-strength hemp or organic tote or grocery bags from Reusable Bags (reusablebags.com).

- **Cellophane.** Although some cellophane is made from plastic film, the original, or "natural," cellophane is made from regenerated cellulose (a plant-derived material). You can buy natural cellophane bags from Green Earth Office Supply (greenearthofficesupply.com).

- **Packing Materials.** You should not need to buy packing material for your wedding if you save the shipping peanuts from all of the gifts you receive before the big day. By the time my husband and I got married, we had ten trash bags full of peanuts stashed in our basement. When we still had seven bags after the wedding, we listed them on Craigslist and picked up a few extra dollars. If you want to use natural packing materials, you can ship most things in a nest of pine needles or dried leaves. You can also buy a cheap paper shredder and turn your junk mail into colorful confetti.

Kid Gifts

What is appropriate for adults may not work for your flower girls, ring bearers, bellboys, etc. The following are a few green ideas that will keep the kiddies happy without breaking the bank.

$ Fair Trade Finds

For just a few dollars, you can give the kids in your bridal party a gift that will last, while supporting communities in need. Search fair trade clearinghouse websites like Global Crafts (globalcrafts. org) for a wide selection of wooden snakes, animal pens and pencils, mobiles, and more. A Greater Gift (agreatergift.org) is another good source and has embroidered children's backpacks, wood fridge magnets, and kites.

$ The Solar Scoop

Solar toys aren't just for adults. Check out the color-changing beads and solar-powered bugs and race cars from Sundance Solar Products (store.sundancesolar.com).

$$ Natural Clothing and Toys

There is a huge selection of natural kids clothing available online or through Green America's Green Pages (coopamerica. org/pubs/greenpages.org). If you are looking for something natural but a little bit less ordinary than the classic T-shirt or pair of sweatpants, consider buying the kids in your bridal party pairs of colorful tie-dye socks from Maggie's Organics (maggiesorganics.com). For teenagers, World of Good (worldofgood.com) offers fair trade recycled cotton hacky sacks. Delightful organic plush toys abound. Peaceful Company (peacefulcompany.com) has a nice selection, as does Our Green House (ourgreenhouse.com).

$$ Activity Kits

There are a number of fun, "natural" activity kits that make good gifts for kids. Kate's Caring Gifts (katescaringgifts.com) has some intriguing options, including a Make Your Own Gummies out of Seaweed Kit and Make Your Own Chewing Gum from the Rainforest Kit. You can buy organic modeling clay sets with strong, fruity scents from Totally Organic (totallyorganic. us). Another great idea is a Kid's Kit to Save the Planet from Sustainable Bags (sustainablebags.net). It includes two organic cotton shopping bags, Crayola fabric markers, an educational booklet about plastic bags (e.g., "Did you know that the resources it takes to make 14 plastic bags can power a car for mile?"), and more.

$$ Monthly Mags

Support environmental education and give the kids in your party a gift that will give all year with a subscription to a children's magazine like *Ranger Rick* (rangerrickmagazine.com), *National Geographic Kids* (nationalgeographic.com), or *Cousteau Kids* (cousteaukids.org).

$$$ Adopt an Animal

Children love feeling connected to animals and will benefit from learning about a species you adopt on their behalf. Most programs, like Adopt-A-Whale at College of the Atlantic (coa. edu/html/adoptawhale.htm), provide photographs, histories, a certificate of adoption, and annual, semiannual, or monthly newsletters. Charismatic megafauna are the most popular— dolphin, manatees, pandas—but if you know a child who is into critters, you can adopt everything from red rat snakes to black vultures at places like the Calusa Nature Center and Planetarium in Florida (calusanature.com). Couple your gift with a new twist on the pet rock, the Nyokki, an egg-shaped animal that grows grass for hair from Brooklyn 5 and 10 (brooklyn5and10.com).

REGISTRY

Weddings come with a lot of perks. In addition to hosting one of the best parties of your life, you are literally and figuratively *showered* with gifts. First there are the engagement presents— wedding books, picture frames, high-tech wine openers, and of course, bowls. Then there are the shower gifts—frying pans, ice buckets, a Kitchen-Aid mixer if you're lucky, and more bowls. And then there is the main event. It really is phenomenal. Because the gifting begins so soon after you get engaged and doesn't end until months after you've tied the knot, creating a good, diverse, and well publicized registry early is essential to getting things you and your fiancé really want. The general rule of thumb is to have a registry set up six to nine months before the wedding, but I think the sooner you can do it, the better.

Most bridal magazines include a registry guide, which lists all the "registry essentials" including six types of glasses (water, juice, red wine, white wine, champagne, and martini) and two complete sets of dishes. Before you get sucked into registering for your twenty-fourth "accent" plate, take a step back for a moment and think about what you will actually need and use regularly. Because the average age of marriage in the United States today is twenty-seven, almost all brides- and grooms-to-be already own at least one full set of dishes, and other kitchen essentials. If you feel compelled to upgrade, ask yourself if you really want twelve $150 place settings. Maybe four-ounce juice glasses are a bit antiquated in the age of the Big Gulp and the sixteen-ounce "small" soda. Just because it's on the "essentials" list does not in fact mean it is "essential." Plus, if you think about the total number of gifts you will receive, aren't there a lot of other things you would be more excited about getting?

If you find yourself thinking "but we have more stuff than we need already!" it's appropriate on the invitation to print the line "Your presence is your gift to us" or to ask for donations to a specified charity in lieu of gifts. However, most friends and relatives will *want* to give you something and may feel awkward coming to your wedding empty-handed, so this may not be as effective as you hope. Look around your kitchen, think about your hobbies and favorite activities, and see if there are things you could use. You don't want to end up with fifteen salad bowls and twelve vases because you didn't register (and trust me, it will happen). If you still feel adamantly that you do not want any more *stuff*, at least set up a registry of experiences in addition to a charity registry. After all, salsa lessons do not harm the environment and make a great gift. This section offers innovative ideas and useful information for creating registries for things, experiences, and donations.

Things

Wedding guests in America spend $19 billion every year on wedding gifts. Think about what a difference it would make if all of that money went to support worthy causes and sustainable businesses. By choosing green products like organic towels and sustainably harvested wood furniture, or by registering for elegant, durable, and versatile products through a donation site, you can make the money spent on gifts for you also support the environment and communities in need. It's common to set up a few different registries so that you don't have to rely on any one approach. Remember to put links to all of your registries on your wedding website.

Appliances

If you're going to register for a large appliance like a kitchen mixer, air conditioner, or washing machine, choose energy-efficient designs that are built to last and come with extended or lifetime warranties. Environmentally friendly items not only decrease your household footprint but save you money as well. Conveniently, the government has created a comprehensive website for its Energy Star program (energystar.gov) to help consumers make more environmentally and financially sound product choices. Look for and compare the yellow Energy Star labels when shopping. If you bring your utility bill to the store with you, you can use these labels to calculate long-term costs and savings on the spot. If you like the idea of registering for a

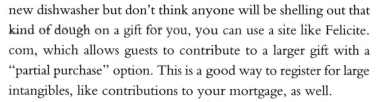

new dishwasher but don't think anyone will be shelling out that kind of dough on a gift for you, you can use a site like Felicite. com, which allows guests to contribute to a larger gift with a "partial purchase" option. This is a good way to register for large intangibles, like contributions to your mortgage, as well.

Workable Wood

The great thing about wood furniture is that if it is well constructed and properly cared for, it can last for hundreds of years. But not all woods are created equal. Many of the popular hard woods come from endangered tree species harvested in a way that destroys habitat, pollutes water resources, and displaces the local people and wildlife. While one bed or dresser set is not going to ruin the world, according to the World Bank (worldbank.org), the cumulative impact of the market for these wood products results in the destruction of 1.25 million acres of rainforest every year. To combat the problem, a number of watchdog groups and third-party certifiers are now monitoring the wood-furniture industry. The Forest Stewardship Council's (FSC) certification program is the one endorsed by the most prominent environmental groups. For more information and for a list of responsible businesses, visit credibleforestcertification.org.

QUICK GUIDE TO WOOD BUYING

In addition to buying FSC-certified products, if you want to be sure the furniture you register for is environmentally sound, a general rule of thumb is to avoid tropical woods and stick to locally grown and harvested timber. Here is a quick buyer's guide:

BAD: ebony, iroko, teak, lauan, mahogany, meranti, merbau, ramin, redwood, rosewood, and zebrawood. Any wood that has been "pressure treated" is also hazardous to your health, because the process employs highly toxic chemicals (including arsenic, creosote, and pentachlorophenol).

OKAY: ash, beech, birch, cherry, elm, hickory, maple, oak, pine, (yellow) poplar, spruce, stika, sycamore, and (black) walnut.
GOOD: Antique wood, recycled wood, driftwood, and bamboo.

Futuristic Furniture

Thanks to creative eco-conscious designers, a number of companies now carry top of the line furniture upholstered with 100 percent organic fabrics. Before you hand over that hard-gifted cash for any old love seat, check out Furnature (furnature.com) and A Natural Home (anaturalhome.com). For extremely modern furniture designs made from all manner of recycled materials, including corrugated cardboard and leather belts, see Branch (branchhome.com). Whit McLeod (mcleodchair.com) makes marvelous and remarkably comfortable folding chairs from recycled wine barrels and VivaTerra (vivaterra.com), which has a registry option, carries a sizable selection of high-end eco-furniture, from railroad-tie bookshelves to timber-block stools. For wild-looking driftwood tables, lamps, and mirrors, check out Driftwood Fine Art (driftwoodfineart.com) or the website where artist Carl Woodland sells his work (alldriftwoodfurniture.com). Even Crate and Barrel, through its spin-off company CB2, now offers green home goods, like recycled-leather bar stools.

Recycled Rugs

Many different products are being recycled into rugs these days. In addition to the recycled flip-flop doormat mentioned earlier, you can find lush recycled T-shirt shag or colorful soda-bottle rugs from companies like Gaiam (gaiam.com). For a more earthy look, try an organic hemp throw rug from Rawganique

(rawganique.com). Soft, washable organic Egyptian cotton floor mats are available from Kushtush Organics (kushtush. com), where you can even find an organic pet bed for your pup to sleep on. For more recycled rugs, and for a host of other recycled home furnishings, the blog Haute Nature (hautenature. blogspot.com) is an excellent resource.

Green Glass

If you want to register for recycled glassware, Riverside Design Group (riversidedesigns.com) makes elegant plates, serving dishes, bowls, and trays from colorful, postindustrial recycled glass. GreenSage (greensage.com), which has a bridal registry feature, offers a nice collection of colorful tumblers and goblets that can be decoratively frosted. The Green Glass Co. (greenglass. com) also makes lovely goblets from recycled wine bottles and festive tumblers from Mexican beer bottles.

REGISTRY TIP

In addition to things you would like for your home, you can also register for items you want to use at your wedding or on your honeymoon. For example, you might want to include items like a recycled-glass lemonade stand, a digital camera and photo-booth printer, or a home-brewing kit. Some websites have ways for you to prioritize the items so that you can indicate to your guests which items you would like them to buy first.

Better Bedding

It is common for couples to register for new linens and bedding. People like gifting comfy flannel sheets, fireside throws, and thick winter blankets to couples for their new nest. Most large retailers now offer some of these items in natural and organic options, but there are a number of specialty stores that offer a wider selection. For example, Heart of Vermont (heartofvermont. com) not only offers a wide range of bedding but also sells organic pillows, mattresses, and even shower curtains. Although it only offers gift certificates and does not have a registry, Poppy Cotton (poppycotton.com) is a cool company that uses 1970s fabrics to create decorative pillows and lampshades, and Bodrum Linens (bodrumlinens.com) has gorgeous organic table linens, dish towels, aprons, and oven mitts.

Adventure Gear

There's a whole world of eco-adventure gear now available. Pair a recycled plastic kayak from Walden with an organic life vest from REI (rei.com). If you are hikers, ask for matching eco-fleece vests and hats from Blue Ice Clothing (blueice clothing.com) and Patagonia Eco Rain Shell Jackets (patagonia. com), which are made from recycled polyester.

Other Fabulous Finds

As you search for specific items made from natural or recycled materials, browse the other products eco-companies carry. In my research, I came across a number of interesting items for the home, including three-dimensional recycled contemporary wallpaper tiles at Chiasso (chiasso.com) and a chimney-free ethanol-burning fireplace from Lekker (lekkerhome.com). A reasonably priced and wonderful gift we got for our wedding was a club soda maker from Soda-Club (sodaclub.com). It allows you to fill reusable bottles with tap water and carbonate at home. Because I am addicted to fizz, I think this gift has reduced my environmental footprint more than anything else.

Local Artisans

Set up a registry or wish list with a local artisan or craftsperson. This is a wonderful way to acquire one-of-a-kind handmade ceramic plates, blown-glass vases, and other household essentials. Attending local craft shows and open studios is a great way to

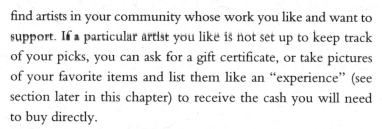

find artists in your community whose work you like and want to support. If a particular artist you like is not set up to keep track of your picks, you can ask for a gift certificate, or take pictures of your favorite items and list them like an "experience" (see section later in this chapter) to receive the cash you will need to buy directly.

Fair Trade

As with favors and thank-you gifts, your registry is another great opportunity to support fair trade. A number of fair trade organizations, including Global Exchange (store.gxonlinestore.org), Green Living (green-living.com), and Ten Thousand Villages (tenthousandvillages.com), allow you to set up traditional online gift registries.

Art for a Cause

Although some guests will probably give you artwork you did not register for (a risky practice that yields mixed results), you can help your art enthusiast friends and relatives pick something you truly want and support a good cause at the same time. There are a number of artists and charity groups who raise money to support victims of violence, prisoners, abandoned animals, and other marginalized groups by selling artwork. For example, Prison Art (prisonart.org) helps talented prisoners earn extra money for stamps and other commissary items by selling their artwork and jewelry. Through Painting 4 Paws (painting4paws.com), artist Karen Derrico raises money for animal rescue programs. For art posters that support the Red Cross, check out the Hurricane Poster Project (thehurricaneposterproject.com).

Experiences

Instead of or in addition to tangible gifts, it is now possible to register for all kinds of events, adventures, lessons and experiences. Using the sites below, your guests can buy you a spa treatment, tickets to a Broadway show, or a scuba package for your honeymoon. Let the fun begin!

Honeymoon Travel

The cool thing about honeymoon registries is that guests can contribute directly to your adventure. Most of the honeymoon registry sites (honeyluna.com, sendusoff.com, afterthe weddingday.com, and thebigday.com, to name a handful) work the same way. They generally offer two options. In option one, they act as your travel agent, book your honeymoon, and give you the registry service for free or for a reduced rate. In option two, you book your own trip, use their website template to create your registry, and they charge you 6-9 percent. Because either way they are taking a commission, and because my husband and I wanted to go on an ecotour, we decided to go with option two, which allows you more flexibility. However, no matter which option you choose, your guests will love giving you an experience you will remember forever.

Classes, Adventures, and More

In addition to registering with local businesses such as dance studios and day spas, you can now register for any number of hand-picked adventures from companies like Could 9 Living (cloud9living.com). If you love to cook, register for cooking classes and a produce subscription with a local community-supported agriculture group (CSA).

The Sky Is the Limit

When setting up a honeymoon registry (discussed earlier), I quickly discovered that you can use the templates registry sites provided to register for virtually anything you can think of. Not only did we use the registry for our four-day mini-moon in Vermont, but we added all kinds of other experiences, including pottery classes, theater tickets, dinner at a green restaurant in New York City, camping passes for the RockyGrass Festival in Colorado, and more. It was great! You can even use these websites to register for larger gifts, like a bedroom set or mortgage payments for a new house.

Charity

It has become fairly common for eco-conscious couples to encourage their guests to donate to charity, and there are a number of ways to do this. You can ask for general donations to charity instead of gifts on your invitation and website. You can link your website to specific charities you want your guests to support, or you can set up a pledge page or a fund in your name. Not everyone will feel comfortable making a donation in your honor, so to ensure that a percentage of every gift bought benefits charity, register using a charity portal site. Using one or a combination of these techniques, you can be sure that your wedding gift giving will give back.

Direct Donations

You can either link directly to your favorite charity or use a charity clearinghouse site like JustGive (justgive.org), which allows you to select a few of your favorite charities and local organizations and present them all on one page.

Pledge Pages

Organizations like Be the Change (bethechange.org) and FirstGiving (firstgiving.com) enable you to create fund-raising pages for the cause of your choice. Using their online tools, you can ask friends and family to sponsor a run, raise money to build a garden in your neighborhood, or help support a friend or family member with cancer. These websites allow you to post pictures and additional information to help get your message out.

Fund in Your Name

Many groups, like community foundations, local housing authorities, and local schools, allow you to set up a fund in your honor. Once you establish a fund, you can continue to watch it grow over the course of your lifetime.

Portal Sites

The idea behind a portal site is simple. Large retailers like Amazon, Linens 'n Things, Cooking.com, and REI donate a specified percentage of every purchase your guests make in exchange for being listed as a member of the portal site. Retailers win because they get your business. You win because your guests can buy something you want while supporting a cause you believe in. There are a number of these sites available, and you should choose the one that fits your taste best. My husband and I registered with the I Do Foundation (idofoundation.org), where retailers donate between 4-8 percent to the charity of your choice.

CHAPTER 13

Planning an Eco-fabulous Honeymoon

*Y*our honeymoon is a special time. It's a chance for you and your new husband to escape the chaos of your lives and the rigors of planning a wedding and focus on each other. It is a chance to unwind and to enjoy your new status as a married couple. The good news is you no longer have to go camping to have an eco-friendly honeymoon—although you still can if you want to! Now there are green honeymoon options for everyone. In addition to ecotourism companies, which outfit adventure travel in almost every country, there are green hotels, green cruises, and even local retreats that you can enjoy without significantly impacting the environment. Whether you want to go abroad, explore the United States, or stay close to home, this chapter offers ideas for every kind of couple.

GENERAL PLANNING TIPS

No matter where you decide to go, there are a few things you should consider before making plans that can save you time and money.

Timing

If your vacation schedule permits, consider taking your honeymoon during one of the "shoulder" weeks, the few weeks right before and right after the peak season for your destination.

The weather will be similar to the peak season, but you will not have to fight through the crowds to enjoy it. According to Smarter Travel (smartertravel.com), choosing a shoulder week can also cut 40 percent off the price of your trip.

Booking Air Travel

When booking air travel, stay over a Saturday night to yield cheaper fares. Similarly, use search engines like Kayak.com and Cheaptickets.com to search nearby airports, which can halve the cost of your trip. If you want to fly green, be sure to offset the carbon emissions from your flight. For more information, see the Transportation section in Chapter Seven.

Paying for It

One easy way to get the most bang for your buck is to pay for absolutely everything you can with a credit card that earns flyer miles. It is even better if that card also provides automatic trip insurance, which will save you additional money and hassle.

Portal Sites

While it's preferable to choose one of the eco-friendly honeymoon options discussed in this chapter, if you have your heart set on going with a more traditional package, booking your trip through a portal site like the I Do Foundation (ido foundation.org) will ensure that a portion of your package price goes to support the cause of your choice.

Insure It

According to the Wedding Report, the average honeymoon costs about $4,000. With this in mind, why not spend a few extra dollars and fully insure your trip? There are many different sources of travel insurance, including homeowners' policies, airline companies, and tour outfitters. It's important to read the fine print before you select a policy, because coverage can vary significantly.

MINIMAL-IMPACT TRAVEL

If you plan to visit ecologically sensitive areas, it is very important that you practice minimal-impact travel. I have included a short list of guidelines for reefs, trekking, and wildlife safaris below, but there are minimal-impact protocols for almost every kind of wilderness experience. Be sure to research the habitats you plan to visit and to ask your outfitter for tips on how to lessen your impact before you leave.

Reefs

Scuba diving and snorkeling are thrilling sports and wonderful ways to commune with nature. The beauty of the underwater world and the ability to explore colorful coral, swim with schools of fish, and find lurking moray eels can take your breath away. However, despite their best intentions, many divers cause permanent damage to reefs by accidentally stepping on or otherwise touching coral. If you go scuba diving or snorkeling, always follow these five rules:

Do not disturb the coral. Even the lightest touch of a finger or the stirring up of sand nearby can kill or permanently damage coral. To avoid unintended contact, make sure you only go in places with deep enough water that waves do not make you accidentally bump the ground below. *National Geographic News* reports that sunscreen also contributes to coral bleaching, so avoid lathering up before diving in.

You can find a list of common travel-insurance terms in the Quick Guide page of the About the Book section of thegreenbrideguide.com.

- **Do not feed the fish.** Although it's exciting to see the fish up close, feeding them can destroy their natural eating habits and tamper with the natural balance of the reef.
- **Do not take plants, coral, or shells.** Empty shells and scattered plants provide shelter for crabs and small fish. Don't steal their homes!
- **Do not use Styrofoam or plastic cups or plastic bags while on a boat or at the beach.** When these items blow into the water, they fall to the sea floor and can kill wildlife.
- **Do not support reef damage on shore.** Stay away from all coral, starfish, and other souvenirs harvested from the sea. Buying these items encourages others to plunder fragile habitat.

Trekking

If you love to hike and spend time together in the outdoors, trekking can be a fun honeymoon option. While trekking or backpacking, be sure to follow these steps to decrease your impact on the surrounding environment.

- **Walk in the footsteps of others.** Literally and figuratively—you should stick to well-worn trails and campsites whenever possible so that no pristine wilderness is disturbed.

- **Leave no garbage.** Make sure you take everything with you from your campsite when you go, including food scraps, sanitary supplies, and packing materials. Everything that came in should go out, down to the last twist tie.

- **Follow fire protocol.** Use pre-existing fire pits whenever possible. Keep your fires small, use only dead or fallen wood, and make sure the fire is completely out (with water, not just ashes or soil) before you move on.

- **Properly dispose of human waste.** If you plan to hike for more than a day or two chances are you will need to, um...do some business in the woods. If you are a purist, you can use what rock climbers use—the charmingly named PVC "Poo Tube." Alternatively, and this is what most hikers do, you can dig a hole. If you go with option two for your number two, make sure you are at least three hundred feet from the closest source of water before you dig down six inches and cover thoroughly.

- **Keep your distance from wildlife.** It is always exciting to find a hawk's nest or come across a deer, but try to keep your distance from the wildlife. Leave nests, burrows, creek beds, meadows, and other nursery areas alone. Bring a good pair of field glasses so that you can get close without disturbing the fauna.

- **Support the community.** If you decide to do a trek with an outfitter, especially in a developing country like Nepal or Tanzania, ask what percent of the money goes back into the local community. It is important that local people profit from the wilderness around them, or there is less incentive for them to protect and preserve it.

Safaris

A wildlife safari can be the adventure of a lifetime. Watching some of the world's most exquisite wildlife in its natural habitat is fantastic. In addition, park fees are often used to protect and maintain infrastructure and habitat for threatened and endangered species. Through revenue sharing programs in places like Kenya, the park's revenue is also used to mitigate the financial burden of migrating wildlife on surrounding communities. Tourist dollars are essential for conservation, but tourism can also destroy the very places people are trying to visit—the so-called "traveler's paradox." Overbuilding in sensitive areas leads to erosion, flooding, and habitat deterioration. If you are planning a "wild honeymoon," be sure to take the following measures to minimize your impact on the environment and the wildlife.

- **Choose a reputable ecotour operator.** If you are taking a packaged safari tour, choose carefully. The proliferation of travelers, SUV sightseeing vehicles, and trekkers can displace wildlife and cause erosion, pollution, and deforestation (as wood and other forest resources are used to build, heat, and maintain guest lodges). Especially if you plan to travel to pristine areas, it is essential that you work with a reputable ecotourism outfitter and practice minimal-impact travel. Select a tour operator like Rainbow Tours (rainbowtours.co.uk), which offers stays at leading eco- and fair trade lodges and has helped build recycling facilities and schools in the local communities.

- **Keep a good distance.** Many safari drivers will try to pull up as close to the animals as possible. When I lived in Kenya, I saw lions driven off a kill by careening tourists. Let your driver know that you want to keep enough distance not to disturb the animals—and bring a great pair of field glasses and/or a high-powered telephoto lens to make up the difference.

- **Watch out for the wind.** If you are in a vehicle with an open roof for viewing, be sure to keep all wrappers, bottles, and camera straps inside a zipped bag in the car. Litter not only makes parks unattractive for the next guests but also can be dangerous for the animals.

- **Visit places that give back.** A lot of wildlife areas, especially in Africa, are run by or now work in partnerships with the local communities. Try to pick locations that benefit the local populations so that they see the parks as an asset and work to protect the wildlife.

- **Buy gifts with care.** Stay away from products made from bone, exotic-animal hide, and endangered wood species (see the Quick Guide to Wood Buying in Chapter Twelve). Even if the sellers claim to be using sustainably harvested inputs, trade in these products can inadvertently support the black market.

HONEYMOON ABROAD

A honeymoon is a wonderful opportunity to go somewhere you have always dreamed of visiting. If you can't go immediately after your wedding, you can always do what my husband and I did—take a "mini-moon" (just a few days off following your wedding) locally and plan a bigger trip when you have more time. The following are some wonderful ways to enjoy a green honeymoon in any country.

$ Volunteer Vacation

While not for everyone, volunteer vacations allow you to make a difference while traveling abroad. (As an added bonus, most trips are either heavily subsidized or tax deductible). Companies like Cross-Cultural Solutions (volunteervacation.org) do not require any previous experience and offer one- to twelve-week programs working in clinics, homes for the elderly, schools, and day-care centers around the globe. For slightly pricier but exciting trips, look at the Earthwatch Institute (earthwatch. org) Expeditions section, where you can search by date and continent to find a wide range of trips, from collecting butterfly data in Vietnam to documenting folk songs and dance in Russia. Along similar lines, the fair trade site Global Exchange (store. gxonlinestore.org) offers reasonably priced, educational Reality Tours to politically complex countries like Cuba, Brazil, and China and, for the brave of heart, volatile areas like Iran, Afghanistan, and North Korea.

$$ Ecotourism

The International Ecotourism Society (TIES), the industry's watchdog group and third-party certifier, defines ecotourism as "responsible travel to natural areas that conserves the environment and improves the well-being of local people." In sum, ecotourism represents the following social, economic, and environmental values.

- **Social Values.** Ecotourism respects the culture and traditions of the local people and works to promote cultural understanding. A key tenet of ecotourism is the idea that local people have the right to make decisions about how to use their land and resources.

- **Economic Values.** With most all-inclusive tours, 80 percent of the revenue goes to airlines, hotels, and international companies—not to local communities. Ecotourism outfitters are committed to supporting the local economy by employing community members as guides, drivers, interpreters, cooks, and guest lecturers and by having guests stay in locally owned and operated accommodations. Ecotourism supports fair trade and discourages the purchase of souvenirs made from wild-animal products (including skins, shells, and bones) and from endangered woods. These items are often poached and endanger the population of the species they are taken from.

Environmental Values. Ecotourists minimize the effect of their travel on natural surroundings while supporting conservation and the appreciation of the natural world. Ecotourists practice minimal-impact travel and do not overtax an area's capacity with their presence.

You can find thousands of eco-trips and places to stay online at Responsibletravel.com. For ecotours in South America, Eco-Index Sustainable Tourism (eco-indextourism.org) is a wonderful resource. If your plans are flexible, TIES hosts an annual eco-holiday auction (ecotourismgala.org), where it sells more than fifty amazing eco-holidays each year.

When you are searching for an ecotour, it is worth noting that in addition to providing ecotourism services, a number of companies are going a step further by donating a percent of the money they earn to local non-profits or by starting their own sustainable development and conservation initiatives. For example, International Expeditions (ietravel.com) donated $60,000 to help start the Amazon Center for Environmental Education and Research (aceer.org) in Peru. You can find a list of certified ecotourism outfitters on the TIES website (ecotourism.org) by doing a general search online, or by picking up a book on ecotourism like *Code Green* by Lonely Planet, which offers well-researched ecotourism destinations on every continent. For certified green beaches, see the Blue Flag website (blueflag.org).

$$$ Food Tourism

One of my favorite parts of traveling abroad is enjoying the local cuisine. Now there are outfitters that specialize in gastronomic adventures with packages that offer a wide range of food themed experiences. There are trips where sampling a large array of local delicacies is the focus, like the vegetarian culinary tours of

India and Malaysia offered by Veg Voyages (vegvoyages.com). There are packages where learning to prepare the local cuisine is the goal, like the hands-on culinary adventures offered by the International Kitchen (theinternationalkitchen.com). Finally, there are activity-based trips, like skiing in Europe or cycling in England, which provide specialty diet foods along the way, like the vegetarian organic-food vacations featured at Vegetarian Vacations (vegetarian-vacations.com).

However, you don't have to go abroad to enjoy a culinary retreat. For couples who want to learn more about healthy American cuisine, the Conscious Gourmet (theconsciousgourmet.com) offers havens where guests spend several days taking yoga classes, attending lectures, and learning to prepare vegetarian, low-carb, or raw foods. All are good options for the epicurean couple.

$$$ Foreign Castles, Estates, and B&Bs

Whether you want to have a destination wedding or a unique honeymoon, there are a number of fantastic properties, including castles, manors, and chateaus, for rent all over Europe. Some of these properties come with staff, like butlers and cooks. You can even find old estates that are run like inns that offer locally grown organic vegetables and meats. Google "wedding in a castle," or visit clearinghouse sites like Celtic Castles (celticcastles.com/weddings.asp), which lists hundreds of venues by location and amenity.

$$$ Cruises

The cruise industry is booming. A cruise is an attractive honeymoon option because cruises are "all inclusive." From the moment you leave port to the moment you return, you do not need to worry about money, food, or entertainment. The best part about a cruise is that you only have to unpack once, and you can still visit a number of exotic locations. But the cruise industry has a dark underbelly. Cruise ships typically carry between two thousand and five thousand passengers, who, according to the Blue Water Network (bluewaternetwork.org) produce an average of 210,000 gallons of raw sewage per voyage. Because of international law, as long as a ship is three miles off shore, it is not subject to most environmental regulations, and many cruise companies dump their raw sewage directly into the ocean. Additionally, a number of large cruise companies, like Carnival and Royal Caribbean, have been cited for illegally dumping oil, garbage, and toxic waste. For an updated list of violations see Cruise Junkie (cruisejunkie.com).

As if the environmental problems were not enough, cruise ships have also been dubbed "sweatshops at sea," because many employees are paid less than minimum wage and work eighty-hour weeks for ten to twelve months at a time. The industry gets away with this by registering its boats in countries like Panama and Liberia so that they are essentially exempt from U.S. environmental and labor laws, as well as the U.S. tax code. So what are two honeymooners to do? Instead of going on a large cruise ship, consider booking a trip with an eco-conscious group like the World Wildlife Fund (worldwildlife.org) or National Geographic (nationalgeographic.com), both of which offer sustainable, nature-oriented adventures. You can also find small ecotourism boat trips through sustainable-travel clearing-houses like Planeta.com.

$$$ Eco-resorts and Eco-lodges

For every Club Med out there you can find another, smaller, all-inclusive eco-resort or lodge that offers luxury accommodations, spa experiences, and the like, but that will also provide ecotour options like bird-watching, safaris, and kayaking. Pair terms like "all-inclusive resort" with "organic" "eco" and "green" in your favorite search engine to find a list of options. You can also find lists of eco-resorts featured in books like Fodor's

Green Travel: The World's Best Eco-Lodges & Earth-Friendly Hotels.
If you want to go to a larger "club" resort, Beaches and Sandals
are now Green Globe 21 certified (ec3global.com) and offer
all-inclusive beach vacations and wedding packages.

HONEYMOON IN THE UNITED STATES

We live in one of the largest and most diverse countries in the
world. Unless you live in Alaska or Hawaii (in which case you
should seriously consider the at-home honeymoon described
later in this chapter), you are just a few hours away from deserts,
mountains, beaches, canyons, and even ice floes. It's all here,
waiting to be enjoyed. Whether you are a couple that likes
to camp or a couple that likes to stay in four-star hotels with
indoor and outdoor pools, there are now green options for
every style.

$ Volunteer Vacation

You don't have to go abroad to have a volunteer trip. A
number of organizations now offer service-oriented travel
here in the United States. For example, the American Hiking
Society (americanhiking.org) runs a hundred one- to two-week
Volunteer Vacations where participants hike backcountry areas
of national forests and rebuild cabins, shelters, and footpaths.
The Student Conservation Association (thesca.org) offers a
range of volunteer opportunities in national parks, forests, and
wilderness areas from coast to coast.

$ National Parks

Take advantage of our country's amazing natural and cultural
resources by visiting a national park. Last year the national parks
had 273 million visitors. The keeper of our parks, the National
Park Service (NPS), has been around since 1916, but today it
is delightfully high tech. The NPS website (nps.gov) provides

a comprehensive directory of the 391 parks, which cover 84 million acres in 49 states. Using its database, you can search by name, location, activity type (biking or camping, for example), or topic (like fossils or the Civil War) and can easily retrieve beautiful color pictures as well as directions, hours of operation, and fee and reservation information. Let the NPS help you plan your trip with its suggested itineraries based on interest and region, available in the For Travelers section of its website. You can do everything from auto touring and rock climbing to hunting and horseback riding. You can even visit coral reefs, caverns, and canyons.

QUICK GUIDE FOR GREEN CAR TRAVEL

For every gallon of gas you burn, you release about twenty pounds of carbon dioxide into the atmosphere. If you take a one-thousand-mile road trip, this adds up to ten tons of CO_2 pollution. That is why getting good gas mileage, especially on a long road trip, is so important. If you are planning on doing any serious driving for your honeymoon, the following tips can help you get better gas mileage and decrease your overall environmental footprint.

- **Get a tune-up.** Before you hit the road, take your car in for a full tune-up. According to *The Green Consumer Guide* by Elkington, Hailes and Makower, a well-tuned car can get 10 percent better gas mileage than a poorly tuned one.
- **Inflate your tires.** Before you leave and at least once while you're on the road, check your tire pressure. A study done by the U.S. Department of Transportation found that more than 25 percent of cars are driving with at least one "substantially underin-flated" tire. In addition to being hazardous, low air pressure can decrease gas mileage by 5 percent. Over long distances, this can really add up, causing more pollution and costing you money.

- **Shed winter weight.** Unless you plan to drive through snowy areas, the lighter your car is the better in terms of gas mileage, so take those bricks out of the trunk before you leave.
- **Responsibly change your oil.** Just one quart of oil, when poured down a storm drain, can kill fish and other aquatic life and contaminate up to 2 million gallons of drinking water. Instead of changing your own oil by the side of the road, take your car to a reputable business.
- **Get better roadside assistance.** Instead of using AAA, join the Better World Club (betterworldclub.com), which provides the same services: emergency roadside assistance, insurances, and free maps to both motorists and bicyclists. The difference? The Better World Club doesn't spend your money lobbying congress for lower emissions standards.
- **Use alternative fuels.** If you have a diesel car, find a station that sells plant-derived biodiesel. If you're traveling in California, Nevada, or Arizona, you can find fueling stations for all kinds of alternative-fuel vehicles with the Clean Car Maps (cleancarmaps.com/home).

$$ Bed-and-Breakfasts

Every year I try to take at least one trip out to Cape Cod to visit my aunt and cousins who own the Nauset House Inn, a quaint B&B in East Orleans. The inn is just minutes from the dune-lined beach, and each room is decorated with homemade quilts and hand-painted furniture. The whole inn is full of nooks and crannies with treasures waiting to be discovered. Obviously I am smitten.

I believe that B&Bs are one of this country's greatest assets. Each one has its own distinct personality, with a decor and menu that reflect the personal taste of the owner. B&Bs are like small bookshops and novelty stores—they have personality. When my husband and I decided to take our four-day mini-moon in Vermont, I immediately began looking for the perfect B&B.

There are a number of guidebooks specifically for B&B travel, including Fodor's *America's Best Bed & Breakfasts*. If you want to support B&Bs that are also working to be more environmentally sound, BnBscape (bnbscape.com) offers an online directory of earth-friendly and certified green inns and B&Bs in the United States and Canada. If you want to bring your pets or children, be sure to ask ahead of time. Inns have different policies regarding kids and animals. If one inn can't help you, be sure to ask for another recommendation.

$$ Reliable Restaurants

If you want to avoid "supersizing" your way across the country, there are a number of excellent resources for finding healthy restaurants and food stores. You can buy a book like *Healthy Highways: The Traveler's Guide to Healthy Eating,* by Nikki and David Goldbeck or the classic *Tofu Tollbooth*, by Elizabeth Zipern and the folksinger Dar Williams.

$$$ Green Hotels and Resorts

If you and your spouse prefer the comfort of hotels, there are a number of green hotels and resorts popping up all over the country. To find one in your area, search online or use the resources outlined in the Green Hotels and Resorts section of Chapter Two.

$$$ Ecotours

You can use many of the same resources from the Honeymoon Abroad section to find ecotours in the United States. The International Ecotourism Society website (ecotourism.org) is a wonderful place to find ecotourism outfitters who offer a wide variety of local adventures. Green America's Green Pages (coopamerica.org/pubs/greenpages/) is another excellent resource. From packaged trips to quick excursions, support sustainable businesses here at home.

CARBON OFFSETTING AIR TRAVEL

Most travel abroad includes air travel. Air travel has gotten much less expensive in recent years, opening up opportunities for more and more couples to explore the globe. While this has many benefits for local economies and for international trade, one downside is that air travel has more environmental impact than almost any other form of travel. Airplanes burn fossil fuels and add water vapor and heat-trapping gases to the atmosphere. According to the International Ecotourism Society, airplanes account for 10 percent of human impact on climate change! As discussed in Chapter Seven, you can decrease the impact of your travel by offsetting your carbon emissions. Some companies, like Travelocity (travelocity.com), allow you to buy carbon credits as part of your online booking. To figure out the carbon emissions for a particular route, use the calculator at ClimateCare (climatecare.org).

EMISSION-REDUCTION TIP

To further decrease the impact of your honeymoon, choose a destination where you can "stay put" for a few days, instead of taking a road trip or a cruise where you are shuttled from place to place. Once you have landed in your destination country, try to use public ground transportation—buses, rail, etc.—as much as possible.

Honeymoon Locally

One of my favorite books growing up was *The Treasure* by Uri Shulevitz. The story is a tale about a poor man named Isaac who has a dream about finding treasure in the capital city. It's only after a long, arduous, and fruitless pilgrimage that he returns home to discover the treasure buried beneath his own home. Almost every place in the United States has hidden treasures that we do not find, because we do not take the time to look for them. Instead of traveling abroad, consider taking your honeymoon close to home. Not only will you decrease your carbon footprint and support the local economy, but you may also have a more relaxing, better vacation than if you go abroad. At a minimum you will have a longer vacation, because you will not have to spend any time in transit.

$ The At-Home Honeymoon

Honeymooning is a state of mind. The most affordable, sustainable, and perhaps most enjoyable option is a hunker-in honeymoon. Tell your friends and family you are going on your honeymoon for a few days. Turn off your phones. Turn off your computer. Get out the oils, take baths, order food in, take long walks with the dog, rent movies, go to the theater, or do whatever you feel like doing to decompress. Honeymooning is not about exotic travel, it is about spending quality time together—just the two of you—right after the wedding. Although this seems so simple as to be absurd, in our fast-paced, all-access-all-the-time world, the best vacation you have ever had may be the one you take at home.

$$ Local Vacationing

Similar to the at-home honeymoon, consider sleeping in your own bed but spending your days exploring nearby haunts. Do all the things you would do if you found yourself in a small village in Italy for four days. Try new restaurants; take a long hike; see a play; and explore local boutiques. Look at the chamber of commerce page for cities and towns nearby to find out about festivals, craft shows, theater performances, concerts,

and interesting museum exhibitions. The best part is, if you find a new restaurant you love you can visit it again anytime—no need to book another flight to taste that soufflé.

$$$ Just a Day Away

If you are looking for something different but still low-key, stay somewhere that is far enough to feel away but close enough that you can get there in half a day's drive. We live in Connecticut and took our four-day mini-moon in Vermont—where we sat in a hot tub watching the leaves change, went antiquing, took a hawking lesson, and ate decadently. It was fabulous. By choosing a destination close to home, you will not only reduce the amount of fossil fuel used in transportation but will also save time and avoid jet lag, leaving you more time to enjoy the thrill of having just pulled off a wedding. See the Honeymoon in the United States section earlier in this chapter for tips on how to make your local vacation even greener.

CHAPTER 14

Conclusion

As I finish writing this book in the spring of 2008, I can't help but notice that a remarkable thing is happening—the American consciousness is beginning to shift. For the first time since the 1970s, mass media is successfully tackling complicated environmental issues, and Americans are listening. The demand for organic food has never been higher, and you can now find clothing made from sustainable fibers like bamboo and tencel in major chain stores across the country. Eco-conscious living is finally coming into vogue.

Time magazine recently listed "Have a Green Wedding" as number 28 in its article "51 Things We Can Do to Save the Environment," and it's easy to see why. With 2.5 million weddings a year hosting more than 150 guests each (numbers that, when multiplied out, equal more than the total number of people in the United States), the impact of these events is undeniably significant. In addition to conserving resources and supporting green businesses, having a green wedding is a way to infuse one of the most important days of your life with meaning and purpose beyond your union. The process of planning a green wedding may also inspire you to incorporate eco-friendly elements into your daily routine and can influence the choices your guests make in the future as well.

I hope this book has demonstrated that you do not have to sacrifice style, comfort, or your budget to be eco-friendly and has given you the tools you need to create the green wedding that is right for you. Congratulations again on your engagement, and best wishes for a happy and green future!

Sustainability Worksheets

Sustainability Worksheet: Questions to Ask a Jeweler

Name of Jeweler _____

Location _____

Contact Person _____

Contact Number _____

Email Address _____

1. Can you supply certified conflict-free
   diamonds?   Y   N

2. Can you supply synthetic or cultured
   diamonds?   Y   N

   If yes:

   a. What kind? _____

   b. At what price? _____

3. Can you supply certified fair trade gemstones?   Y   N

4. Can you use recycled metals?   Y   N

   If yes:

   a. What kind? _____

   b. At what price? _____

   c. Can I supply my own?   Y   N

Sustainability Worksheet: Choosing a Location

Site Name _____

Location _____

Contact Person _____

Contact Number _____

Email Address _____

1. How many guests do I expect? _____
2. How far will they have to travel on average?_____
3. Total number of travel miles
   (Answer 1 x Answer 2) = _____
   (The smaller this number, the better.)
4. Can I have both the ceremony and reception at
   this location?   Y   N
5. Can I supply my own food?   Y   N
   If yes, see Questions to Ask a Caterer Worksheet.
6. Do you have chairs and linens on site?   Y   N
7. Do you offer dinnerware and glassware
   on site?   Y   N
   If yes, do you use non-disposable china?   Y   N
   If yes, do you use biodegradable detergent?   Y   N
   If no:
   a. Are the dishes recyclable?   Y   N
   b. Are they biodegradable?   Y   N
8. Do you have vases on site?   Y   N
9. What other items do you have for me use? _____
   _____

10. Do you recycle on site?   Y   N

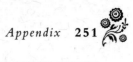

11. Do you compost on site?   Y   N

12. Do you donate or reuse leftover flowers
    or food?   Y   N

13. Does any percent of the site fee support
    a cause?   Y   N

    If yes:

    a. What percent? _____

    b. What cause? _____

14. Do you have toilets on site?   Y   N

15. Does the site have a place to set up in case
    of rain?   Y   N

16. What other eco-friendly practices do you use? _____

    _____

    _____

    _____

Sustainability Worksheet: Questions to Ask a Hotel

Name of Hotel _____

Location _____

Contact Person _____

Contact Number _____

Email Address _____

1. Is the hotel LEED certified?   Y   N
   If yes, at what level? _____

2. Is the hotel Green Seal Certified?   Y   N

3. Is the hotel a member of the Green Hotel
   Association?   Y   N

4. Is the hotel a member of any other green
   group or association?   Y   N

5. Does the hotel have any green practices
   including recycling, energy-efficient lighting,
   sheet and towel reuse options, green laundry
   service, etc.?   Y   N
   If yes, what? _____

   _____

   _____

Sustainability Worksheet: Questions to Ask a Florist

Name of Florist _____

Location _____

Contact Person _____

Contact Number _____

Email Address _____

1. Where do you usually source your flowers from?_____

2. Do you add any chemicals to the flowers when they are in your shop?_____

3. Can you get locally grown/organic flowers?

   Organic   Y   N

   Locally grown   Y   N

   If yes to either of the above, is there an additional cost?   Y   N

   If no, can we provide you with the floral material?   Y   N

   If yes:

   a. What is the cost of labor? _____

   b. When do you need the material? _____

4. Can you provide flowers that are in season?   Y   N

   If yes, which flowers will be in season? _____

   _____

   _____

5. Can you supply pesticide-free petals?   Y   N

6. Will you agree to only use materials that can be composted (no floral wire, no green florists' foam, etc.)?   Y   N

7. Can you pick up the leftover flowers and
   donate them to charity?   Y   N

   If yes:

   a. To which charity? _____

   b. Is there an additional cost? _____

8. Can you provide baskets, vases, and other
   non-disposable containers?   Y   N

9. Do you have other rentable decor items like
   topiaries, wreaths, live plants, aisle runners,
   Christmas lights, or tiki torches?   Y   N

Sustainability Worksheet: Questions to Ask a Caterer

Name of Caterer _____

Location _____

Contact Person _____

Contact Number _____

Email Address _____

1. Is your produce:

   a. Locally sourced?   Y   N

   If yes, from where? _____

   _____

   _____

   If no, is it possible to get local ingredients?   Y   N

   If yes, is there an additional cost?   Y   N

   b. Organic?   Y   N

   c. Biodynamic?   Y   N

2. Do you have vegetarian or vegan options?   Y   N

3. Can you serve only fish in the green zone on
   the Seafood Watch list for this region?   Y   N

4. Can you serve sustainable meat (organic,
   free-range, etc.)?   Y   N

   If yes, what kinds?_____

   _____

5. Do you have kosher options?   Y   N

6. Can you serve only fair trade organic teas
   and coffees?   Y   N

7. Can you provide organic sugar and stevia?   Y   N

8. If you cannot provide any of the above, can we provide you with some of the key ingredients?   Y   N

If yes, which may we supply? _____

_____

By what date? _____

Can I have them shipped to you directly?   Y   N

Can you give me a reduced price quote?   Y   N

9. Will you donate uneaten food to a shelter?   Y   N

If yes, which one? _____

10. Do you compost?   Y   N

11. Do you recycle?   Y   N

12. Do you supply the dishes, linen, etc.?   Y   N

If yes, are you planning on using real china?   Y   N

If no:

a. Are they recyclable?   Y   N

b. Are they biodegradable?   Y   N

c. May we supply these items?   Y   N

(If yes, ask for revised quote.)

If yes:

a. Do you do the washing?   Y   N

b. Will you use biodegradable detergent?   Y   N

13. Do you supply the bar?   Y   N

If yes:

a. Can all drinks, including soda, be served in glasses?   Y   N

b. Will the bar use fountain soda rather than individually packaged soda?   Y   N

c. Can the water come from the tap?   Y   N

d. Can you use organic/local wines, beers, juices, etc.?   Y   N

If yes, which items? _____

_____

_____

Is there an additional cost?_____

May we supply these items?   Y   N

(If yes, ask for revised quote.)

Can you provide recycled paper napkins?   Y   N

Can you recycle all cans and bottles?   Y   N

14. What other eco-friendly practices do you use? _____

_____

_____

_____

Sustainability Worksheet: Questions for Setting Up a Registry

Name of Registry

Website

Contact Number

Email Address

1. Do you accept credit cards (allowing guests to get miles, etc.)?   Y   N

2. Do you ship?   Y   N

3. Can you wait and combine shipping?   Y   N

4. Do you allow for refunds and exchanges?   Y   N

5. How long will you keep our registry list up? _____

6. Do you have environmentally sound goods?   Y   N
   (e.g., sustainable wood, recycled glass, organic cotton)

7. Do you sell fair trade products?   Y   N

8. Do you have lifetime warranties?   Y   N

9. Do you donate a percentage to charity?   Y   N
   If yes, what percentage and to which charity?_____

10. Do you have any other sustainable practices?   Y   N
    Other questions:

    _____

    _____

    _____

Sustainability Worksheet: Questions to Ask a Travel Company

Name of Company _____

Trip Location _____

Contact Person _____

Contact Number _____

Email Address _____

Website _____

1. Do you have a written policy on your environmental practices? (Most reputable ecotourism operations will.)　　　　　　　　　　　Y　N

2. What are the largest environmental problems your company faces, and how do you deal with them?

   _____

   _____

   _____

3. Do you employ local guides and drivers?　　Y　N

4. Do you provide special training for your guides to ensure they are using environmentally sound techniques (e.g., wildlife-approach etiquette)?　Y　N

5. Do you use locally owned and operated venues?　　　　　　　　　　　　　　　　Y　N

6. What proportion of the revenue goes to the local communities? _____

7. How do you avoid overcrowding? _____

   _____

8. Are you or any of the companies you partner
   with in the destination country using
   alternative energy sources (e.g., solar camp
   lights, biodiesel buses)?　　　　　　　　　Y　N

9. Do you work with any local charities?　　　Y　N

10. Do you carbon offset your tours?　　　　　Y　N

11. Can you provide recycling or minimize waste
    in other ways?　　　　　　　　　　　　　Y　N

12. What other eco-friendly practices do you use?_____

_____

_____

_____

13. What part of your program are you most proud of?
    (True ecotour operators will be eager to share their
    hardships and successes in trying to be "green.")

_____

_____

_____

Recommended Reading

CHILDREN

Barnes, Lisa. *The Petit Appetit Cookbook: Easy, Organic Recipes to Nurture Your Baby and Toddler.* HP Trade, 2005.

Greene, Alan. *Raising Baby Green: The Earth-Friendly Guide to Pregnancy, Childbirth, and Baby Care.* Jossey-Bass, 2007.

CLIMATE CHANGE

Gore, Al. *An Inconvenient Truth: The Crisis of Global Warming.* Viking Juvenile, 2007.

Speth, James Gustave. *Red Sky at Morning: America and the Crisis of the Global Environment.* Yale University Press, 2005.

FOOD AND AGRICULTURE

Bittman, Mark. *How to Cook Everything Vegetarian: Simple Meatless Recipes for Great Food.* Wiley, 2007.

Burke, Cindy. *To Buy or Not to Buy Organic: What You Need to Know to Choose the Healthiest, Safest, Most Earth-Friendly Food.* Da Capo Press, 2007.

Fromartz, Samuel. *Organic, Inc.: Natural Foods and How They Grew.* Harvest Books, 2007.

Pollan, Michael. *The Omnivore's Dilemma: A Natural History of Four Meals.* Penguin, 2007.

Schlosser, Eric. *Fast Food Nation.* Harper Perennial, 2005.

HEALTH AND BEAUTY

Loux, Renee. *Easy Green Living: The Ultimate Guide to Simple, Eco-Friendly Choices for You and Your Home.* Rodale Books, 2008.

Malkan, Stacy. *Not Just a Pretty Face: The Ugly Side of the Beauty Industry.* New Society Publishers, 2007.

Uliano, Sophie. *Gorgeously Green: 8 Simple Steps to an Earth-Friendly Life.* Collins, 2008.

HOME AND GARDEN

Cutler, Karan Davis, Barbara W. Ellis, and David Cavagnaro. *Burpee: The Complete Vegetable & Herb Gardener: A Guide to Growing Your Garden Organically.* Wiley, 1997.

Dadd, Debra Lynn. *Nontoxic, Natural & Earthwise.* Putnam's Sons, 1990.

Elkington, John, and Julia Hailes. *The Green Consumer.* Golancz, 1988.

Ellis, Barbara W., and Fern Marshall Bradley, eds. *The Organic Gardener's Handbook of Natural Insect and Disease Control: A Complete Problem-Solving Guide to Keeping Your Garden and Yard Healthy Without Chemicals.* Rodale Books, 1996.

Javna, John, Sophie Javna, and Jesse Javna. *50 Simple Things You Can Do to Save the Earth: Completely New and Updated for the 21st Century.* Hyperion, 2008.

Matheson, Christie. *Green Chic: Saving the Earth in Style.* Sourcebooks, 2008.

Schildgren, Bob. *Hey Mr. Green: Sierra Magazine's Answer Guy Tackles Your Toughest Green Living Questions.* Sierra Club/ Counterpoint, 2008.

INVESTING

Domini, Amy. *Socially Responsible Investing: Making a Difference and Making Money.* Kaplan Business, 2000.

Uldrich, Jack. *Green Investing: A Guide to Making Money through Environment Friendly Stocks.* Adams Media, 2008.

PARTY PLANNING

Cochran, Khris. *The DIY Bride: 40 Fun Projects for Your Ultimate One-of-a-Kind Wedding.* The Taunton Press, 2007.

Collins, Danny Seo. *Simply Green Parties: Simple and Resourceful Ideas for Throwing the Perfect Celebration, Event, or Get-Together.* Collins, 2006.

Editors of *Real Simple* Magazine. *Real Simple Celebrations.* Real Simple, 2006.

Naylor, Sharon. *The Busy Bride's Essential Wedding Checklists.* Sourcebooks Casablanca, 2005.

TRAVEL

Fodor's. *Green Travel: The World's Best Eco-Lodges and Earth-Friendly Hotels.* Fodor's, 2008.

Foehr, Stephen. *Eco-Journeys: The World Guide to Ecologically Aware Travel and Adventure.* The Noble Press, 1993.

Lorimer, Kerry. *Lonely Planet Code Green: Experiences of a Lifetime.* Lonely Planet, 2006.

McMillon, Bill, Doug Cutchins, Anne Geissinger, and Ed Asner. *Volunteer Vacations: Short-Term Adventures That Will Benefit You and Others.* Chicago Review Press, 2006.

Zipern, Elizabeth, and Dar Williams. *The Tofu Tollbooth.* Ceres Press, October, 1998.

Key Resources

The Green Bride Guide offers so many resources that, when compiled, the list is almost forty pages long. In order to save paper I have posted the complete list, including up-to-date hyperlinks, in the About the Book section of thegreenbrideguide.com. The following is a small sample of the many companies, organizations, and non-profits highlighted throughout this book.

ACCESSORIES

Designs by Kristen (designsbykristen.com)
Head Piece Heaven (headpieceheaven.com)
Hemp Elegance (hempelegance.com)
Pamela's Parasols (pamelasparasols.com)

BEAUTY PRODUCTS

Acquarella (acquarellapolish.com)
Aftelier (aftelier.com)
Avalon Organics (avalonorganics.com)
Badger (badgerbalm.com)
Dr. Hauschka (drhauschka.com)
Juice Beauty (juicebeauty.com)

BEVERAGES

Blue Sky (drinkbluesky.com)–soda
Bonterra (bonterra.com)–wine
Elite Naturel (organicjuiceusa.com)–juice
Green Mountain (greenmountaincoffee.com)–coffee
The Republic of Tea (republicoftea.com)–tea
Wolaver's Organic Ales (wolavers.com)–beer

BRIDESMAIDS DRESSES

Aria Dress (ariadress.com)
Earth Speaks (earthspeaks.com)
Olivia Luca (olivialuca.com)

CANDLES AND LIGHTING

American Rental Association (ararental.org)–solar lights
Aura Cacia (auracacia.com)–candles
Bee Natural (beenatural.com)–candles
Pacifica (pacificacandles.com)
USA Soy Candles (http://usasoycandles.com)–candles
Way Out Wax (wayoutwax.com)–candles

CARBON OFFSETTING

Carbonfund.org
Co2balance (co2balance.com)
Native Energy (nativeenergy.com)
TerraPass (terrapass.com)

CAR RENTAL

Evo Limo (evolimo.com)
EvRental (evrental.com)

TripHub (triphub.com)
Zipcar (zipcar.com)

CHILDREN'S GIFTS AND TOYS
National Geographic Kids (nationalgeographic.com)
Our Green House (ourgreenhouse.com)
Peaceful Company (peacefulcompany.com)

CLEANING SUPPLIES
Kokopelli's Green Market (kokogm.com)
Seventh Generation (seventhgeneration.com)

DONATION AND RECYCLING SITES
America's Second Harvest (Secondharvest.org)–food
Brides Against Breast Cancer (makingmemories.org)–gowns
Locks of Love (locksoflove.org)–hair
The Cinderella Project (cinderellaproject.net)–bridesmaids dresses

FAVORS
Beautiful Sweets (beautifulsweets.com)–cookies
Botanical Paperworks (botanicalpaperworks.com)–seed paper objects
Equal Exchange (equalexchange.com)–chocolate
Pamela's Parasols (pamelasparasols.com)–fans
Print Globe (printglobe.com)–personalized items
Seeds of Change (Seedsofchange.com)–seeds
The Arbor Day Foundation (Arborday.org)–saplings
Uncommon Goods (uncommongoods.com)–recycled products

FLOWERS

California Organic Flowers (Californiaorganicflowers.com)
Dried Flowers Direct (Driedflowersdirect.com)
Local Harvest (localharvest.org)
Mountain Rose Herbs (mountainroseherbs.com)
Organic Style (organicstyle.com)

FOOD

Heritage Foods USA (heritagefoodsusa.com)
Local Harvest (localharvest.org)
Organic Trade Association (ota.com)
The Green Restaurant Association (dinegreen.com)
Vegetarian Resource Group (vrg.org)
Wise Organic Pastures (wiseorganicpastures.com)

GIFTS

Cloud 9 Living (cloud9living.com)—experiences
Fair Trade Sports (fairtradesports.com)—sports equipment
Gaiam (gaiam.com)—organic gifts
Taraluna (taraluna.com)—nature gifts
Ten Thousand Villages (tenthousandvillages.com)—fair trade
    gifts
Uncommon Goods (uncommongoods.com)—recycled gifts

GOWNS

Bridal Garden in New York (bridalgarden.org)
Conscious Clothing (getconscious.com)
Deborah Lindquist (deborahlindquist.com)
Save the Dress (savethedress.com)
Thread Head Creations (Threadheadcreations.com)
Wholly-Jo (Wholly-jo.co.uk)

HONEYMOON

Blue Flag website (blueflag.org)–beaches

Cross Cultural Solutions (volunteervacation.org)–volunteer
vacation

Green Globe 21 (ec3global.com)–resorts

International Kitchen (theinternationalkitchen.com)–food
tourism

National Geographic (nationalgeographicexpeditions.com)–
cruises

The International Ecotourism Society (IES) (ecotourism.org)–
eco-tourism

Veg Voyages (vegvoyages.com)–vegetarian tourism

HOTELS AND OTHER VENUES

B & B Scape (bnbscape.com)

Celtic Castles (celticcastles.com/weddings.asp)

Green Seal (greenseal.org)

The Green Hotels Association (greenhotels.com)

INVITATIONS AND
ANNOUNCEMENTS

Blue Mountain (Bluemountain.com)

Creative Papers Online (handmade-paper.us)

Green Field Paper (Greenfieldpaper.com)

Oblation Papers & Press (oblationpapers.com)

Of the Earth (custompaper.com)

Treecycle (treecycle.com)

Twisted Limb Paper (twistedlimbpaper.com)

MENSWEAR

Dress That Man (dressthatman.com)

Hemp Clothing (hempclothing.com)

My Own Tuxedo (myowntuxedo.com)

Rawganique (rawganique.com)

Rusty Zipper (rustyzipper.com)

RECEPTION DECOR AND SUPPLIES

Bambu (bambuhome.com)–bamboo dishes

Classic Party Rentals (classicpartyrentals.com)–chairs, tables, etc.

EarthShell (earthshellnow.com)–biodegradable dishes

Recycline (recycline.com)–recycled plastic dishes

Viva Terra (vivaterra.com)–linens

World of Good (originalgood.com)–linens

REGISTRY

Be the Change (bethechange.org)–charity

Honeyluna.com–honeymoon registry

I Do Foundation (Idofoundation.org)–portal site

Just Give (justgive.org)–charity

Thebigday.com–honeymoon registry

RINGS AND JEWELRY

Cred Jewellery (credjewellery.com)–fair trade gold and silver

Doyle & Doyle in New York City (doyledoyle.com)–rental

Earthwise Jewelry (leberjeweler.com)–conflict-free diamonds

Gemesis (Gemesis.com)–cultured diamonds

GreenKarat (greenkarat.com)–recycled

The Antique Jewelry Mall (Antiquejewelrymall.com)–antiques
Touch Wood Rings (touchwoodrings.com)–wood rings
Wood-Rings (wood-rings.com)–wood and metal rings

SHOES
Allen Edmonds (allenedmonds.com)
Johnston & Murphy (johnstonmurphy.com)
Shoes USA (shoesusa.com)
The Natural Store (thenaturalstore.co.uk)

WEDDING WEBSITES
Wedding Window (weddingwindow.com)

WELCOME BASKETS
Eco Express (ecoexpress.com)
Fresh Fruit Bouquet Company (ffbc.com)
Gourmet Gift Baskets (gourmetgiftbaskets.com)

Index

F

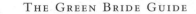

About the Author

$\mathcal{K}$ate L. Harrison grew up in Connecticut and received her first environmental education exploring the beaches of Long Island Sound as a child. After high school she spent a year tending dairy cows and picking strawberries for an experimental desert agriculture project in Israel. There she developed a love of farming and gardening, and an avid interest in the politics of food. In college at Vassar, she majored in Environmental Conservation and Sustainable Development. She wrote her thesis on the economics of organic farming in the Mid-Hudson Valley and graduated with general and departmental honors.

After college, Kate moved to California, where she worked in environmental education and outreach for the East Bay Regional Park District and the Jane Goodall Institute. During that time, Kate wrote original curriculum and delivered slide-show presentations to schoolchildren and community groups in the Bay Area on a wide variety of environmental topics. In 2003, she moved back to Connecticut and began working in environmental politics, first for the legislative Environment Committee in Hartford and later for the Senate Committee on Agriculture, Nutrition, and Forestry in Washington, DC.

In 2004, Kate entered a joint degree program in Environmental Policy and Law at the Yale School of Forestry and Environmental Studies and Pace Law School. On her first day of school, she met Barry Muchnick, a PhD candidate in Environmental History, and two years later they were engaged. Kate and Barry had their own green wedding on October 7, 2007, in New York's Hudson Valley. While they were planning, Kate began writing a column entitled "The Environmentalist" for *Real Estate Valuation Magazine Online*. In the spring of 2007, her article "Organic Plus: Regulating Beyond the Current Organic Standards" was accepted for publication in the *Pace Environmental Law Review*. It was at that point that she decided to collect all of the material she had gathered for their wedding and turn it into a comprehensive how-to book—*The Green Bride Guide*.

In December 2008, Kate finished the joint program, graduating magna cum laude from Pace Law School. She, Barry, and their dog Reuben live in New Haven, one mile from her childhood home, where Kate still spends her summers by the ocean.